Praise for Gri

"Leaning on his t _____,
[Sadler] examines the 1960 investigation into the
death of Frances Lacey through a modern-day lens,
reigniting hope that Mackinac Island's only unsolved
murder might be solvable yet. This one's a must-read!"
—**JENN CARPENTER**, author of *The Cereal Killer
Chronicles of Battle Creek* and *Haunted Lansing*

"Rod Sadler, seasoned retired police officer and now
best-selling author, has applied his thirty years of law
enforcement experience to the unsolved murder of Frances
Lacey to try and discover the truth. GRIM PARADISE
creates a suspenseful, page-turning account of this
63-year-old mystery, including some of Mackinac Island's
deepest secrets. Sadler brings the reader hope for solving
this brutal murder with the possibility that the same
advanced DNA technology that recently solved the Golden
State Killer case might now solve the Lacey murder."
—**ALAN R. WARREN**, NBC News Radio,
Los Angeles, and Best-selling Author

"Things like this aren't supposed to happen on Mackinac
Island. Rod Sadler's access to the actual police file
regarding the murder of Frances Lacey adds much
to this sad story, and as a retired police officer, his
methodological 'investigation of the investigation'
and reporting of this crime are second to none."
—**DEB MALEWSKI**, Historian and Researcher,
Contributing Writer, Community News

"Rod Sadler has done a very good job of researching the materials, providing references and explaining the events in this years-old cold case [and] an exceptional job explaining what the family members have gone through in addition to the feelings and fears of the community."
—**EDWIN MOORE**, Livingston County Sheriff's Office, Cold Case Investigator

"[A]n unyielding quest to bring a killer to justice and closure to the victim's family... a must read for true crime enthusiasts, and anyone familiar with Mackinac Island who enjoys modern Michigan history."
—**DAVID OSTREM**, Michigan Police Officer

"[Sadler] humanizes Frances Lacey and focuses the investigation on those suspects who may have been responsible for her death. Throughout, the cast of witnesses and investigators are prominently featured, weaving an intricate web of mystery, and illustrating the impact of Lacey's death on so many... Grim Paradise is a compelling story and a tribute to the life of Frances Lacey... Though there is no shortage of suspects, some are more likely than others, Sadler is careful to maintain the objectivity of an investigator.
—**KAREN HOLT, Ph.D.**, Assistant Professor, School of Criminal Justice, Michigan State University

"GRIM PARADISE is a concise narrative and draws the reader in the investigative arena. It's well written and spellbinding while providing the true anatomy of a cold case homicide investigation. A terrific read."
—**WM. LENAGHAN**, Mackinac Island Chief of Police (ret.), Cold Case Investigator

GRIM PARADISE

THE COLD CASE SEARCH FOR THE MACKINAC ISLAND KILLER

ROD SADLER

WILDBLUE
PRESS

WildBluePress.com

GRIM PARADISE published by:
WILDBLUE PRESS
P.O. Box 102440
Denver, Colorado 80250

ISBN 978-1-960332-22-6 Trade Paperback
ISBN 978-1-960332-24-0 eBook
ISBN 978-1-960332-23-3 Hardback

Interior Formatting and Cover Design by Elijah Toten
www.totencreative.com

GRIM PARADISE

This book is dedicated to the memory of Frances Lacey.

"Here on this magic Isle, strange things happen casually."
— *Mackinac Island Town Crier, July 24, 1937*

NOTE

Some names have been changed and denoted as such by an asterisk (*).

Quoted material was taken from printed sources and appears as is. Any mistakes are the original author's.

TABLE OF CONTENTS

ACKNOWLEDGMENTS

First and foremost, I'd like to thank my wife for her unending support.

I'd also like to thank the team at WildBlue Press including Steve Jackson, Michael Cordova, Stephanie Johnson Lawson, Jazzminn Morecraft, and Jenn Waterman. They have been a pleasure to work with.

When I began this book, the first thing I needed was the police reports from 1960. Using the Freedom of Information Act, I submitted my request to the Michigan State Police and was excited when I received a telephone call and was told they had the documents I had requested. I was excited to know they had them, and pleasantly surprised to find out the person who was processing my request was a fan of my books. Thank you, Missy S. and the Michigan State Police.

There are very few people left who had direct knowledge of the investigation, and that meant there were few people to interview. I did a book presentation at St. Luke's Lutheran Church in Haslett, Michigan, and by chance, I had the pleasure of meeting retired MSP Laboratory Specialist Walter Holz. Walter worked for MSP in the early sixties when the crime lab was part of the Michigan Department of Public Health, and he worked closely with Dr. Edgar Kivela, the scientist directly involved in analyzing the trace evidence in this case. Walter Holz was instrumental in describing how the crime lab was set up at the time and how evidence was stored.

Part of my research for this book was a two-day visit to Mackinac Island. After checking in at the same hotel where Frances Lacey stayed, I walked to the murder scene along Lake Shore Road for photos and measurements, and I ended the day at the library. I'd like to thank Shepler's Ferry, the Mackinac Island Tourism Bureau, the Mackinac Island Public Library, Horn's Bar, the Great Turtle Brewery, the Island Bookstore, the Pink Pony, and the Murray Hotel.

I was lucky enough to have had the pleasure of speaking with a few Island residents who recalled those frightening days following the murder, and I'd like to thank them while at the same time protecting their privacy by not listing their names here.

In a book titled *Mackinac Island: Inside, Up Close, and Personal,* author Dennis O. Cawthorne describes life on Mackinac Island from the time he arrived in 1960 and beyond. I reached out to Dennis, and he graciously returned my call. I was poised to bombard him with a list of questions, and he suggested I read his book first. He said it would probably answer the majority of the questions I was going to ask, and it did. I truly enjoyed the historical information he offered in both the book and in a follow-up phone call.

Inspector Phil Shertzing (MSP, retired), an MSP historian, was a great help in providing me with information about where to find both crime scene photos and personnel photos of the original investigators.

Finally, to Ryan Wilkinson, Ken Ouellette, Chuck Loader, Vince Green, Greg Michaud, and Elizabeth Walby, thank you for the ideas, suggestions, and tidbits of information that pointed me in the right direction.

PREFACE

Perhaps author Dennis Cawthorne was right. Cawthorne, a former Michigan state legislator who also served as the former director of the Mackinac Island State Park Commission, authored the book titled *Mackinac Island: Inside, Up Close, and Personal.* It's a fascinating look at the history of the Island and her people. Cawthorne arrived on the Island for the first time just one month before the murder of Frances Lacey. In the book, he writes briefly of her murder saying, "[It] had almost every element of high drama."[1]

With automobiles banned in 1898 and transportation limited to foot travel, bicycle, or horse and carriage, Victorian charm is ubiquitous on Mackinac Island, and in 1960, that charm stood in stark contrast to an ongoing murder investigation while modern freighters on Lake Huron passed casually in the distance.

Almost immediately after Frances Lacey was reported missing on July 24, 1960, her mysterious disappearance was chronicled in countless newspaper articles around the state. When the Dearborn widow's body was found four days later, the story became front-page news across the nation. As the initial tips given to the Michigan State Police quickly faded, in time, so did her name, and some visitors to the Island have come to believe the story of her murder is nothing more than local folklore.

---

1. Cawthorne, Dennis O. *Mackinac Island: Inside, Up Close, and Personal.* Arbutus Press, 2014

Along with Dennis Cawthorne's brief description of the murder, two other books have briefly mentioned her death, and in the hope of generating new clues, a magazine article featured the story in 1962. Beyond that, it has become nothing more than a sliver of Island history.

With a three-man local police force and three Michigan State Police troopers assigned to the Island during the summer of 1960, law enforcement quietly began their investigation when Mrs. Lacey was first reported missing by her daughter on that quiet Sunday morning in July.

After the discovery of her body, the police were overwhelmed by the sheer number of tourists, seasonal island employees, and local residents who had to be interviewed. Many of them had left the Island before Mrs. Lacey was ever found. The police presence on the Island quickly grew from six to over twenty-five, and as interviews began, possible suspects started to emerge. Over time, each name was cleared, one by one, and eventually, the case was consigned to the Michigan State Police cold case files.

It's easy to look back at a police report that's over sixty years old and second-guess the detectives. It's easy to say, "They should have done *this,*" or "They should have done *that.*" In reality, given the era, they did exactly what any other detectives would have done. They interviewed a lot of people, and they relied on the specific scientific techniques and analyses that were available to them.

In the twenty-first century, much of the investigation would have been done in exactly the same way. There would be crime scene photos, measurements, the collection of evidence, interviews, polygraph exams, and scientific analysis of evidence. In the same light, it would also be done much differently.

Autopsy protocols, evidence collection and preservation, and forensic analysis have all changed over the last sixty-plus years. More importantly, though not an exact science, the understanding of the criminal mind is far more in-depth today than it was back then.

With the evidence collected in the 1960 murder of Mrs. Lacey, the potential for DNA analysis would certainly be possible today. It's a powerful tool used in solving crimes.

Touch DNA is a forensic analysis requiring only a very small amount as a sample; such as skin cells left on an item after it's been handled. As an example, in an unrelated cold case from 1969, investigators were able to solve the case in 2004 with DNA left by a suspect on a pair of pantyhose found knotted around a victim's neck. With the knowledge that analysis can be done today for touch DNA, investigators are often bypassing serological testing and instead do extraction and quantification.[2] With serological testing, they could identify bodily fluids like semen and saliva, much like the procedures that were done in the Lacey homicide. Today, fewer and fewer of those tests are done in forensic labs. It used to be a standard test to examine a piece of evidence with an alternate light source in hopes of finding fluorescing stains. If staining was found, a presumptive semen test was done with an acid phosphate test and then a microscopic exam for the presence of sperm cells.

Bypassing those initial tests to identify biological fluids, there is significant information missing when a "male DNA screening" is done. Without serological testing, scientists can't determine the number of sperm cells present, whether saliva is present, or whether any tails are present on the sperm cells. The importance of this information is that the quality and quantity of sperm cells can determine the relative time since intercourse. It can be critical information, and it became an issue in Frances Lacey's case.[3]

---

2. Ryan, Suzanna. "How the Lack of Serology Testing Results in a Loss of Information," http://ryanforensicdna.com/serology/
3. Ryan, Suzanna

Ultimately, the key issue isn't centered around whether a DNA analysis could be done today on the evidence collected in the Lacey homicide six decades ago. The issue is whether or not the evidence still exists. In an open murder case that sits in a cold case file, it's reasonable to assume the evidence is still in storage somewhere. In the case of Frances Lacey's murder, the evidence collected in 1960 was transferred to MSP long-term storage in 1976. There is now reason to believe that the evidence has been either misplaced or destroyed. Sadly, if that's the case, her murder will never be solved.

If the person who killed Frances Lacey is a serial killer, the likelihood of that person ever confessing to the crime at this point is slim because he's protecting his own family from accepting his guilt. He won't talk about it or admit that he's killed anyone. He has nothing to gain by confessing to murder, and the one thing he stands to lose if he does is the support of whatever family he has.[4]

Frances Lacey's murder is so much more than a sliver of Mackinac Island's history. In a place that rarely sees violent crime, it's the story of the vicious rape and murder of a quiet and loving woman who was strangled with her own panties along an open stretch of road in a place some people call Michigan's Crown Jewel. Beyond that, Frances Lacey's killer is still at large. This book is the story of her murder and the hunt for her killer, for perhaps he's still alive.

---

4. Hornus, Anthony. *An Ordinary Killer*, 2008

1: THE SCOOP

The tone in his voice gave away his trepidation when he asked, "Will you please see if Pete Marudas is in *The Tribune* press room?"[5] The nervous newsman could hear voices at the other end of the line and realized the phone was in the kitchen of a small diner in Cheboygan called The Hut. The local cafe was a mere fifteen miles from Mackinac Island, across Lake Huron to Michigan's mainland, but at the moment, it seemed a world away.

With a population just shy of six thousand people in 1960, Cheboygan was home to the *Daily Tribune*, a local paper, and the pages for the *Mackinac Island Town Crier* were printed there once each week.

The staffer had tried frantically to call the *Daily Tribune* directly, and he quickly realized the main office had closed at 6:00 p.m. There had to be a way to get in touch with his colleague. He remembered the small restaurant only two doors away from their office, and he desperately dialed the number, hoping to convince someone to run the short distance and check for him.

"Two on one, hold the onions," he heard in the background.[6] Sitting in the *Town Crier* office, he looked at his watch and tapped his fingers on the desk as he waited

5. *Mackinac Island Town Crier*, "Big Story Puts Town Crier Staff in Tizzy, But It Still Scoops State," August 7, 1960

6. *Mackinac Island Town Crier*, "Big Story Puts Town Crier Staff in Tizzy, But It Still Scoops State," August 7, 1960

impatiently. Minutes were ticking away, and he knew time was of the essence.

Five minutes passed, and it seemed like an eternity. Someone picked up the phone. "Yes, he's there," came a voice at the other end of the line.

There was an awkward silence as the newsman waited for the next sentence; the line remained silent. Incredulous, he asked, "Could I speak to him, please?" The man who answered the phone had only checked to see if Marudas was at *The Daily Tribune*. He didn't tell him there was a phone call for him. Frustration set in.

Another five minutes of waitresses barking menu orders and dishes clanking in the kitchen passed. To the newsman, it was as if time had come to a complete standstill. He was hoping they hadn't forgotten him.

Just ninety minutes earlier, he'd become suspicious. While transportation during the tourism season at Michigan's premier resort destination was limited to horse and carriage, bicycle, or foot travel, many tourists didn't know there were seldom-seen emergency vehicles on Mackinac Island. Aside from fire trucks and a police Jeep, there was also an ambulance, and he'd seen both vehicles heading toward Lake Shore Road along the west side of the four-square-mile resort island. Given the week's chaos, he instinctively knew something was up, and the *Town Crier* staff member grabbed a bike. He raced down Market Street to the west until he reached the intersection at Lake Shore Road. Making the turn and leaving the resort city, it became M-185, the only state highway in Michigan where private autos are banned. Pedaling as fast as he could, he was headed toward British Landing along the west side of the Island.

The Michigan State Police had an office at the Mackinac Island Coast Guard Station, and he'd already sent a colleague in that direction to see what he could find out. Now a mile from town, he raced past Devil's Kitchen, a large geologic outcropping and well-known tourist attraction.

There was still no sign of the two emergency vehicles. He followed the gentle curves lined by Lake Huron on the left and steep bluffs with hundreds of cedar trees on the right.

The narrow road made a sharp turn to the right in a northwesterly direction, and he could see a soft curve ahead that turned almost directly to the north. He rounded the curve, and both bicycle tires slid on the pavement as he squeezed the hand brakes.

The police Jeep and the Island's ambulance were stopped in the road, and men dressed in suits were milling around with a couple of uniformed Michigan State Police troopers. On the east side of the road, two small cobblestone fences framed the start of a short path leading to two stone pillars with a large iron gate between them. The small group of men stood in front of it as they quietly talked among themselves.

By 9:00 p.m., his suspicions were confirmed, and he raced back to the *Mackinac Island Town Crier* office to catch Marudas before the pages went to print.

* * *

After an agonizingly long wait listening to clattering dishes and waitresses yelling to short-order cooks, he finally heard Marudas at the other end of the line. His colleague had barely said the word *hello* when the newsman yelled, "Stop the presses!" Without a breath between sentences, he rattled off instructions to Marudas saying, "We've got to make over the entire front page and the banner."[7] After a

---

7. *Mackinac Island Town Crier*, "Big Story Puts Town Crier Staff in Tizzy, But It Still Scoops State," August 7, 1960

quick recap of what he'd found out up to that point, both men knew it was going to be a very long night.

Over the previous three hot July days, with local reporters grasping at every bit of information that came out through the State Police and the Mackinac Island Police Department, the Island's weekly laid-back paper had almost felt as if it had become a daily edition.

The ten-cent paper, published every Friday during the summer, covered all of the previous week's events, and just six days before, the modest weekly featured stories covering the start of the Chicago-to-Mackinac yacht race and the excitement of the visiting guests on the Island to watch the arrival of the winners. Other short articles mentioned the new police chief appointed by city council, the upcoming Christmas in July Bazaar, and picnickers who had enjoyed a visit to Devil's Kitchen on the west lakeshore in 1937. Another short feature mentioned Governor G. Mennen Williams' arrival for a short stay at the governor's mansion just the day before.

Now, on Thursday night, the news spread quickly, and there was a constant barrage of interruptions as the phone continued to ring at the *Town Crier* offices for updates from media outlets around the state. The small staff worked tirelessly past midnight as they added new information and made updates to the story as they learned additional details.

Hours later, the staffer was back on the phone and told Marudas, "Get these papers over here early tomorrow morning, whatever you have to do."[8] It was past midnight, and he'd lost all sense of time. He knew that if the *Town Crier* hit the streets early in the morning, it would be the first paper to report the breaking news.

By 7:30 a.m., Pete Marudas, now near exhaustion, was still in Cheboygan finishing the print. He wouldn't make

---

8. *Mackinac Island Town Crier*, "Big Story Puts Town Crier Staff in Tizzy, But It Still Scoops State," August 7, 1960

it back to the Island until he could catch the first ferry of the day. He loaded the final copy in his car and made the nineteen-minute drive back to Mackinaw City in record time, knowing he had to make it on the first ferry to the Island. Hurrying to the dock, he could see several newsmen from around the state already waiting to be ferried to Mackinac Island. Marudas quietly boarded with them, silently pushing his cart loaded with the *Town Crier*.

By 9:00 a.m., with temperatures already in the mid-seventies and expected to reach the low nineties later in the day, Marudas rolled the pushcart loaded with the special edition across the front porch of the *Mackinac Island Town Crier*, and at 9:03, the first edition hit the streets.

Marudas had done it. This would be the biggest story published by the small newspaper since it first began circulation on the Island just three years earlier.

The original headline was supposed to read "MISSING WIDOW STILL STUMPS POLICE." The revised headline read "WIDOW'S BEATEN BODY FOUND."

2: MICHIGAN'S CROWN JEWEL

Once called the Citadel of the Great Lakes, Mackinac Island was cloaked in legend. Sitting in the Straits of Mackinac, it still reflected a certain beauty and gentle atmosphere from the nineteenth century after having once been part of a struggle between France and England. A landmark to explorers and a fur-trading hub for the Native Americans, the Island was also a battlefield between American and British forces, and at one time, the entire territory was controlled by whoever controlled the fur trade.

It was known to the Ojibwas as "the place of the dancing spirits," and they called it "The Great Turtle," or Michilimackinac.[9] With towering rock formations, the Native Americans worshipped the Island as if it were a shrine, and to them, it appeared as a great turtle resting on the water.

French explorers first visited the Island in the 1600s, but one hundred sixty years later, it was taken by the British after being abandoned by the French. By 1763, the entire Great Lakes region came under the control of the British Crown, and seventeen years later, Fort Mackinac was built on the Island complete with barracks, officers' quarters, a hospital, limestone ramparts, cannons, a blockhouse, and a dungeon.

From a high bluff, the fort faces the southern coast and is visible to anyone approaching from that direction.

---

9. *The Hartford Courant*, "Mackinac Island Mingles History, Charm, Leisure," June 5, 1960, p 44

Fifteen years after the American Revolution, the Island was turned over to the United States but was surrendered to the British during the War of 1812 when a small British force with Native American allies landed on the northwest side of the Island.

When the British were preparing for the invasion, legend says that an Islander named Michael Dousman guided them in. After their arrival, the British were positioned at a point overlooking Fort Mackinac, and they demanded surrender. With only fifty-seven American soldiers at the fort, the Island was turned back over to the British.

As a gift for helping them during the invasion, the British gave Dousman nine hundred acres around the area where they'd come ashore. He eventually sold that acreage to a man named Michael Early, who arrived on the Island shortly after the invasion. Early's son, John, later built a log house on the property in 1912, and John Early's son still owned the log house in 1960. The area was called British Landing.

The Island was regained by the United States in 1815 as part of the Treaty of Ghent. Signed in Ghent, a Sovereign Principality of the United Netherlands (modern-day Belgium), it ended the conflict between the United States and Great Britain. While the treaty was signed on Christmas Eve in 1814, it took a month for word to reach the United States, and it restored the relations between the US and Britain by reinstating the pre-war borders of 1812.

Through the years, writers, celebrities, and Native American legends all contributed to the magical atmosphere and romanticism of Mackinac Island. Forty-four years before surrendering Vicksburg, Mississippi, and over twenty-seven thousand men to General Grant during the Civil War, Confederate General John Pemberton was stationed on Mackinac Island and shared his loneliness when he authored a letter to his wife professing his eternal love as he sat on the porch of the officer's quarters at Fort

Mackinac. During the Civil War, Edward Everett Hale, a minister from Boston and gifted author, wrote his famous short story "The Man Without a Country" while he sat on the porch of the Mission House in 1863. Thirty years later, Mark Twain, on an international tour, garnered a speaking engagement at the Grand Hotel and charged one dollar for admittance, while throughout the years Thomas Edison made frequent demonstrations of his inventions on the Grand Hotel's famous porch.

After the Civil War, Mackinac Island became a favorite summer destination for Victorians, and they traveled by lake excursion boats from all major points across the Great Lakes region to the island destination. For dining, whitefish was often on the menu, and the vacationers walked along the wooden decks enjoying the temperatures of northern Michigan as lake breezes kept the Island cool. After relaxing during the day, they could be found dancing to waltzes during the evening.

For overnight guests, boat and railroad companies began to build hotels on the Island while souvenir shops opened to address the wants of the travelers, and newspapers across the country advertised trips beginning from destinations all across the Great Lakes region.

In 1895, all federal land on Mackinac Island, which was known as Mackinac National Park, was transferred to the state of Michigan and designated as Michigan's first state park, and industrialists who built their own cottages on the bluffs along the east and west sides of the Island were required to maintain a Victorian architecture.

The idea for Mackinac Island's Grand Hotel was originally the idea of Kalamazoo millionaire Francis Stockbridge, and he purchased land on the west end of the Island to build it. When he was elected to the United States Senate, he sold the land to a group of investors that included the Grand Rapids and Indiana Railroad, the Michigan Central Railroad, and the Detroit and Cleveland Steamship Company,[10] and architects soon began designing the five-story structure. With its Queen Anne architecture and Colonial Revival aesthetics, the hotel opened with two hundred eighty-six rooms and unparalleled accommodations in 1887 as a summer retreat for vacationers.

It became a huge attraction to tourists from Chicago, Detroit, Cleveland, and even Montreal, with a three- to five-dollar price tag per night. The huge porch extending across the front of the grand structure soon became the community gathering place. By 1920, a two hundred-twenty-foot serpentine pool was being added in front of the hotel, and over one thousand barrels of cement were shipped to the Island for its construction.

In the late thirties, the hotel faced hard times, and business dropped by ninety percent. In 1939, during one of the hotel's most difficult days, there were four hundred employees to serve eleven paying guests.

After World War II, the Grand Hotel was chosen as a filming location for a Hollywood aqua-musical, and shooting began in 1946. The movie, *This Time for Keeps*, premiered in 1947 and starred Esther Williams, a championship swimmer turned Hollywood actress. Because of the movie's success, the hotel began to rebound. In 1979, the movie *Somewhere in Time* was filmed largely on Mackinac Island and starred Christopher Reeve, Jane Seymour, and Christopher Plummer. Filming took place at the Grand Hotel and at Mission Point Resort, which was originally constructed by the Moral Re-Armament Movement.

By 1957, the Grand Hotel was designated as a State Historic Building, and over the years, it grew to become one of America's favorite destinations. In 1972, it was

---

10. Cawthorne, *Mackinac Island: Inside, Up Close, and Personal*

named to the National Register of Historic Places, and in 1989, it was named as a National Historic Landmark.

As the Island developed from the fur trade to a resort destination, Victorian-era vacationers began to identify it with sweets. The first candy on the Island was developed from maple sugar by the Native Americans, while other treats, including fudge, soon followed, and the idea of enjoying sweets as part of the Island experience quickly became popular.

In 1898, the Mackinac Island City Council outlawed horseless carriages inside the small city. Three years later, the Mackinac Island State Park Commission followed suit.[11] While there were attempts over the years to sideline the automobile ban, it remained in place. For both permanent Island residents and tourists alike, the limited means of transportation was the same.

In the early forties, with no regulations in place, there were several different carriage owners on the Island vying for business, but in 1948, Carriage Tours was formed by the Mackinac Island State Park Commission. Carriage owners were forced to lease their licenses to the newly formed company and, in turn, the owners became shareholders. While a few carriage business owners held out, most of the other companies unified under the new name.

One of the largest summer attractions for the Island was two back-to-back yacht races. The Chicago-to-Mackinac race started in 1886 when the Racine Boat Manufacturing Company began building two fin-keel sloops. The *Siren* measured fifty-nine feet, six inches, and the *Vanenna's* length was sixty-four feet. With constant conversation about which of the two was fastest, a race between the two yachts across the southern tip of Lake Michigan to Michigan City was held in 1896. The *Vanenna* took the prize, but sailors from the *Siren* protested claiming the sails on their boat

---

11. Cawthorne, *Mackinac Island: Inside, Up Close, and Personal*

were insufficient because of their age, and therefore, the race wasn't fair.

Heavy fog contributed to disputes about the second race in 1897 because both ships, racing to Milwaukee, sailed off course, and no one was sure whether or not either yacht had actually finished the race.

The owners of both the *Vanenna* and the *Siren* finally agreed to three races to be held in June 1898, and the owners were both prepared to spend whatever it took to win. Ultimately, the *Vanenna* won all three races.

As a result of the races, the idea of a different and unique race began to emerge the following year, and the Chicago Yacht Club, now at sixty-plus members, created an event that would ultimately attract larger yachts and give new life to the idea of sailing in the Chicago area. The idea of a race to the Island to measure the skills of the sailors began to materialize.

When it began, the race included the *Vanenna* and *Siren,* along with three other schooners. After fifty-two hours, seventeen minutes, and twenty seconds, the *Vanenna* was victorious. The *Siren* took second place, thirty-seven minutes later, beating the schooner *Thorne* by forty-five minutes.

The next Chicago-to-Mackinac race didn't occur until five years later, and it had started to gain momentum with more yachts being added to the race, but hurricane-force winds in 1911 forced the finish to be moved from Mackinac Island to Harbor Springs in 1912 and 1913. The following year, the finish was moved back to the Island.

The annual race was paused for World War I, but in 1921, it had grown to over seventy vessels and has run annually each year since then. Along with the Port Huron-to-Mackinac race, the three hundred thirty-three-mile sailing competition brought several thousand visitors to the Island as the boats began crossing the finish line.

The Mac, as it became known, is the oldest freshwater distance race in the world and is one of the most prominent yacht races in the entire world.

After World War II, other parts of the globe struggled to recover from the ravages of the conflict, but the United States was already prospering far more than previous generations as the economy recovered and began to take hold. Money spent on home ownership and consumer goods helped to boost the economy, and by 1960, the purchasing power of the American family increased by thirty percent over the previous decade. With a recession in 1958 and 1959, President Eisenhower stimulated the American economy by allowing the federal deficit to grow, and by the start of the sixties, there was a budget surplus in the United States. Americans shifted from a society based on production in order to meet basic needs during the War to a society of consumers driven by advertising, and the country's new economic growth relied on that. Low-interest home loans were offered to families through the Federal Housing Administration and the Veterans Administration, and with a bustling economy, a weekend getaway to Mackinac Island was no longer something for just the affluent. With the opening of the Mackinac Bridge in 1957 connecting Michigan's Lower and Upper Peninsulas, a restoration of Fort Mackinac, and a new highway running from Miami, Florida, to Sault Ste. Marie, Michigan, tourism began to boom, and Mackinac Island was once again a destination.

3: FRANCES

Frances Lacey's daughter, Kay, stopped at her mother's home in anticipation of their trip to Mackinac Island. Mrs. Lacey's neighbor was there, and as the three women talked, Frances casually mentioned that she'd been doing laundry and ironing all day in case something happened to her. If someone had to come into her home when she wasn't there, she wanted it to be neat. Only the day before, she'd told Kay that if anything happened to her, she wanted her daughter to have her dishes. The comment about the dishes went unnoticed, but when Frances mentioned cleaning the house all day in case something happened, Kay thought it was odd, but her mother's comment was soon forgotten.

The bronze 1958 Mercury was loaded and ready to go. The overnight drive from Dearborn to Mackinaw City at the northern tip of Michigan's Lower Peninsula would take several hours, but Frances didn't mind. She was looking forward to a weekend away with her daughter, son-in-law, and some of his family, even if the short trip was just for the weekend.

Frances Lacey was a very loving and caring mother, and her short, graying black hair accented her small face while highlighting her infectious smile. At forty-nine years old, her build was slight at only five feet, three inches, and less than one hundred twenty pounds. Growing up near Hastings, Michigan, Frances came from a large farming family with several siblings that included a twin brother. In 1933, after already being divorced twice, she married her husband, Ford, while studying nursing in Kalamazoo. After their marriage, she decided not to finish nursing school, and the two newlyweds decided to start a family.

In 1957, just three years before the trip to Mackinac Island, Ford Lacey passed away at the age of sixty-one. Frances had taken care of him as an invalid for three years before his death, and after he died, she took over his business as a dealer in stocks, bonds, and real estate. Fifteen years separated the two, and she struggled to do the best she could as a widow.

By 1960, she had finally come to terms with his death and seemed content and healthy, although she occasionally struggled with bouts of depression and took medication for it.

At 10:30 p.m. on July 22, 1960, Frances Lacey set off for her trip to what many people referred to as Michigan's Crown Jewel, Mackinac Island. She was excited to go and knew her family wanted her to enjoy a weekend away. She said to one of her neighbors, "It will be my first vacation since my husband's death three years ago."[12] With a few stops along the way, at 6:30 a.m., the small group rolled into Mackinaw City. The Mackinac Bridge, Michigan's still-new connection between the Lower and Upper Peninsulas, was a beautiful morning sight.

It had been a long ride but with a forecast high of seventy-nine degrees, everyone was looking forward to the weekend. Accessible only by boat or plane, it was still too early for the ferries to start shuttling passengers to the Island, so the small group headed to the Post House Restaurant for breakfast.

At eight o'clock, now at the ferry docks, they filed onto the Arnold Transit Line ferry with several other tourists heading to the Island. The eight-mile trip was chilly with

12. *The Detroit News*, "Widow Vanishes; Dogs Join Hunt on Mackinac," July 26, 1960

the winds starting to pick up a little. As the ferry started for the Island, the spectacular Grand Hotel, with its massive white columns and six-hundred-sixty-foot porch, stood perched on a bluff overlooking the Straits of Mackinac while the small city of Mackinac Island came into view.

Kay and her husband, Wesley Sutter, came along on the trip with Wesley's younger nineteen-year-old sister. The four were planning to stay with Wesley's mother, Leona Shermerhorn. She had rented a cabin at British Landing along the west side of the Island and her sixteen-year-old son, Marvin, was with her. Frances was invited to stay at the cabin for the weekend, but she decided she wanted to stay by herself and didn't want to put anyone out. She told Kay and Wesley that she would stay at a hotel.

The ferry began to slow as it neared the docks, and seagulls scattered from dock posts as the boat's engine came to a dull idle and ropes were thrown to dock porters greeting the incoming tourists.

Leaving the ferry, the small group walked leisurely along the dock toward Main Street, and Frances mentioned once again to her daughter and son-in-law that she would get a hotel room for the night. Kay and Wesley were adamant that she should stay with them at British Landing, but Frances had already made up her mind.

At the end of the dock, the four-story Chippewa Hotel stood ready to greet guests. The waterfront hotel was built fifty-eight years earlier to accommodate the growing number of vacationers coming to Mackinac Island.

They stopped at the Chippewa to see if there were any rooms available for Frances. The desk clerk said they wouldn't know until after 11:00 a.m., and Frances didn't want to wait. She took a brochure and tucked it into her purse as they left.

Across the street and slightly to the west of the Chippewa Hotel, the Murray Hotel stood in the morning sunshine. Family-owned since the late 1800s, the three-story hotel still held the Victorian charm that mirrored much of the Island. With her small suitcase in hand, Frances crossed Main Street in front of a passing carriage and walked into the lobby. Even though the tourist population was originally expected to swell, inclement weather had so far slowed the rush, and after a brief inquiry at the front desk, Frances was told there were still some rooms available. Room twenty-six faced the water where the ferries docked, and it was a perfect view from the second floor. She paid five dollars and twenty cents for one night's stay, and after quickly freshening up, she left her luggage in the room. She joined her daughter and son-in-law, along with the others, and the small group of Island tourists flagged down a horse and carriage for the four-mile trip to British Landing to spend the day.

The stress of everyday life seemed to slip away as the horse and carriage made its way west along Main Street while a huge freighter slowly passed through the Straits of Mackinac in the distance. With the antiquated means of transportation on the Island and modern-day shipping passing through the Straits in the background, it was an odd sight.

By the time the Lacey party arrived at British Landing, their carriage driver, Don Smith, had taken notice of Wesley's sister, Merry. Rather than heading quickly back to the city for another fare, Smith decided to stall and see if he could impress her a little, so he stayed for a half hour more to let the horse rest.

The small group of tourists were a long way from town and had no transportation. Smith, wanting to impress the young lady he'd become attracted to, offered them the use of one of his bikes. He worked at Jack's Livery, and he told Merry she could pick it up later. Before he left, he asked her if she'd like to go out on his boat later in the evening when he got off work, but she'd just met him, so she didn't give him a yes or no. She'd have to think about it.

After Smith left British Landing, Wesley suggested the best way to tour the Island was to rent horses. As the group made their way through the small streets and trails on horseback admiring the Island's beauty, they ran into their carriage driver again. He asked Merry if she'd decided whether or not to go boating that night, and she graciously turned him down.

As the late afternoon stretched into early evening, Leona and Merry returned to the cabin in a horse-drawn cab. Frances, Kay, Wesley, and Marvin all stayed in town and went back to the Murray Hotel where Frances freshened up. At 6:15 p.m., the trio decided to have dinner at the Wandrie Restaurant and asked Marvin if he'd like to join them. He decided to head back to the cabin instead, so just the three of them headed for the restaurant. Frances enjoyed the veal, and afterward, they stopped to buy fudge and postcards at May's Candy Shop.

By 7:00, the three had returned to the Murray, and Frances said she'd walk out to British Landing in the morning. Kay, certain that her mom wouldn't change her mind, reminded her that it took about an hour and a half to walk the distance to British Landing from the city and asked her to take a carriage for at least part of the way instead of walking. "We'll see," she said.[13] She knew it was a long walk, but she assured her daughter that if she got tired, she'd hail a carriage for the remainder of her trip. She told Kay she'd be there at around noon on Sunday.

***

While Frances was settling into her room at the Murray Hotel, a small party of tourists were departing from the Chippewa Hotel across the street. At 8:30, the group left

---

13. Craft, George. "Supplemental Report." *Michigan State Police*, July 31, 1960

on their hayride around the west end of the Island. Several hundred feet north of Devil's Kitchen, the horses shied and stopped suddenly. The driver was startled, and his attention was drawn to the figure of a man in the brush holding a bicycle. He stood near a large boulder but never moved. The sun had started to set, and it was too dark for the driver to be able to discern any of the man's features, but he noticed in the quickly fading daylight that the bike had a white stripe around the bar that ran from the crank to the fork. He'd never seen that type of design on any of the bikes on the Island, and he was sure it was an English bike.

After taking note of the man, the horses settled down, and the hayride continued on.

***

The small city was bustling with activity. Expectations were for twice as many Island guests checking into hotels for the finish of the 53rd annual Chicago-to-Mackinac yacht race, but because of the bad weather, there were fewer sightseers than expected. The race began the day before with many of the same boats that had been in the Port Huron-to-Mackinac race just a week prior.

The Port Huron-to-Mackinac race and The Mac, as the Chicago-to-Mackinac race had come to be known, were both covered by Chicago and Detroit papers, *Sports Illustrated* magazine, yachting magazines, and the Midwest metropolitan press. In 1959, over twelve thousand tourists were taken to the Island by just one ferry line for the races. For two back-to-back weekends in July each summer, Mackinac Island became the yachting capital of the world.

While the yacht races attracted thousands of boating fans, the Island's beautiful scenery and spectacular rock formations attracted other tourists as well. Staying on the grounds near the Island's Boy Scout barracks were a group of thirty-seven boys who were encamped for three days. Their adult chaperone had been bringing boys to the Island from Camp Manitou on Douglas Lake near Cheboygan for more than thirty-five years.

In the business district, local deckhands for the Grand Hotel gathered every Sunday morning at around 10:30 to go swimming. An off-duty deckhand was likely part of the small group. Alternating between Round Island and the pool at the Grand Hotel, their usual routine consisted of swimming until late afternoon, and on the morning of July 24, they gathered at the Grand Hotel pool.

While tourists flocked to the Island, local restaurants and hotels were ready to welcome them, and that included the Murray Hotel with their classical pianist returning for his seventh season in the cocktail lounge. The pianist had taught himself piano at the age of four and didn't take his first lesson until age eleven. He truly enjoyed returning each summer to the Island because he loved the slow pace of living, the fresh air and natural beauty, and the quaintness of the entire community.[14]

To tourists over the years, Mackinac Island had become idyllic in every sense of the word, and it seemed it always had been. Past writings by Island visitors described the atmosphere as unequaled, and at night, there was no more beautiful setting to be found. But on July 24, 1960, that peaceful charm was shattered.

---

14. *Mackinac Island Town Crier*, "Murray Pianist Here for Seventh Season," July 24, 1960

4: MISSING

The temperature was already at seventy degrees by 9:00 a.m. when Kay, Wesley, and the other members of the Sutter family were relaxing on a dock along the Lake Huron shoreline waiting for Frances to arrive. It was July 24, and they were supposed to head back to Dearborn. By 11:00, she still hadn't arrived. Maybe she was waiting at the cottage. The small group walked back to the cabin to see if she might have taken a different route than the one planned. Wesley's half-brother, Marvin, called the Murray Hotel and was told she'd already checked out. Two hours later, there was still no sign of Frances.

Too much time had passed, and Kay's concern was growing. She wanted to head into town to look for her mom, and though she knew Frances had said she was going to walk along Lake Shore Road to get to British Landing, Kay and Wesley decided they'd take a different way toward the city in case she'd changed her route. They walked along British Landing Road to Garrison Road. Along the way, there was no sign of Frances. They walked to the Murray Hotel to check for her, but Frances was nowhere to be found. Beyond simple concern now, both started to worry. Kay and Wesley headed back to the cottage, taking Lake Shore Road and hoping she'd be there when they got back. Genuine fear overtook Kay, and she made a call to the state police.

Trooper Herbert Grosse was assigned to Mackinac Island for the day, and he headed directly for British Landing on a bike. Grosse had taken missing persons reports before, and they were always resolved quickly, yet he still took each call with dedicated determination.

As Grosse spoke with Kay and Wesley at British Landing, he wrote down a description of Frances and noted where she'd been staying. He knew it was possible she could have taken some other route other than Lake Shore Road, but he also knew it was the most direct route from the city to British Landing. The first thing he wanted to do was to have her room at the Murray Hotel checked, so he called the city police.

The Mackinac Island Police Department, responsible for law enforcement inside the small one-square-mile downtown area, was a three-man department with an office in City Hall. During the summer months, law enforcement on the Island was supplemented by three troopers from the MSP post in St. Ignace.

Forty-three-year-old Myron Bloomfield, who lived on the Island, was the new city police chief. With just two weeks on the job as the Island's top cop, he headed for the hotel where Frances Lacey was staying. Just two weeks before, Bernard Gough had resigned his position as the chief of police for the city. Mackinac Island's mayor, Robert Hughey, told the city council that he wanted to keep Gough on in some sort of a lesser capacity, so the former chief continued working for the city as a patrolman. He kept his same hours of work and rate of pay, but simply had less responsibility now. The city council had to choose a new chief, and their pool of candidates had consisted of the two officers left in the department. Bloomfield was chosen, and he would be paid $105 per week.[15]

The chief checked with the desk clerk, Jack Donaldson, at the Murray Hotel, and Donaldson thought Frances had

---

15. *Mackinac Island Town Crier*, "Gough Resigns as Chief of Police," July 17, 1960

checked out around 10:30 a.m. A checkout slip was found but there was no time on it. He told the chief that he found the key to room twenty-six on the desk, and since she had paid for one night in advance, it only made sense that she must have checked out. Her brown luggage was found in the luggage area of the hotel too, so he figured that she'd be returning for it later in the day. Bloomfield checked the baggage. It was fully packed, and there were three pounds of fudge from May's Candy Shop in the luggage. The chief checked room twenty-six, and nothing appeared out of place. As he glanced under the bed, he found an empty six-pack carton of Carling Black Label beer. Leaving the Murray, Bloomfield began to check with the taxi carriage drivers and other hotels along Main Street to see if anyone recalled seeing Frances, but no one did.

When Trooper Grosse heard that Frances had likely checked out, he wondered if her car was still parked in Mackinaw City. He called the Mackinaw City Police on the mainland to see if her 1958 Mercury was still parked at the ferry dock; it was.

Whether he was on foot or pedaling a bike, Grosse knew it would take time to check all the roads on the Island, so the police Jeep and the ambulance were both used to begin a search. While the local police were on foot checking around the city, other volunteers began searching the Island's roads and trails.

The officers spoke a second time with the desk clerk at the Murray Hotel, and he couldn't remember anything else other than that the lobby had been crowded during the late morning with several people checking in and out. The ferries were checked to see if anyone recalled Mrs. Lacey, and the employees said that so many people ride to and from the Island, unless something unusual happened on one of the boats, they likely wouldn't recall her.

The late afternoon slowly turned to evening. Even with daylight lasting well past 9:00 p.m., there was still no hint of where the missing Dearborn widow might be and Trooper Grosse, the sole officer in charge of the missing person investigation at that point, knew he had to contact the MSP post commander to let him know what was going on.

***

The sound of the phone ringing at 11:00 p.m. startled Sergeant George Burnette at his St. Ignace home. Located on the southeast corner of Michigan's Upper Peninsula, the small town was just five miles from Mackinac Island. A late-night phone call was never good news.

The young trooper gave the post commander a rundown in an anxious voice. "The feeling here is that she must have got lost on some remote backwoods trail along the way and hasn't been able to find her way back to the main road," he said. Burnette knew Grosse was too optimistic. It had been eleven hours since Frances Lacey's expected arrival at British Landing, and the first thing that crossed Burnette's mind was the possibility of a homicide.[16]

Burnette knew it was too late to organize a search party, so the veteran MSP sergeant told Grosse that he would send some men over to the Island in the morning to help check all the trails leading through the woods to British Landing.

On Monday, July 25, as he boarded a ferry with three other troopers for the quick ride across the open five-mile span of Lake Huron, Sergeant Burnette briefed the officers. It was unlikely for a person to simply get lost on the Island. It was interlaced with so many trails that a person was never more than a few hundred yards from one of them, and every trail eventually led to a main road.

---

16. Remsburg, Charles. "Michigan's Number One Murder Mystery." *True Detective Magazine*, 1962

One of the young troopers suggested that Mrs. Lacey might have amnesia, or maybe she'd hurt herself. Going a step further, he suggested that maybe she'd met with foul play.

Burnette knew that any of those might be a possibility, but since she was still missing, he was willing to bet that Frances Lacey wasn't just lost.[17]

George Burnette hadn't been the post commander at the fifteen-man St. Ignace detachment for very long. The Detroit native had joined MSP in 1941 and was originally assigned to the Mt. Pleasant Post before being transferred first to East Lansing and then to East Tawas. After a shootout with a burglary suspect in the early part of his career, he was promoted to corporal in April 1955. With the promotion, he was reassigned to the Ypsilanti Post near Ann Arbor, and four years later, he was promoted to sergeant and transferred to his position in St. Ignace. He had a reputation as being a very calm and collected Post commander.

Word of the missing tourist had already spread across the Island. As Burnette arrived with his small contingent of MSP troopers, sixty-five more volunteers met the officers for a full-scale search of Mackinac Island. Their goal was to systematically check the wooded areas across the island, both on foot and on horseback. The group of searchers included the three troopers who had come along with Burnette, members of the US Coast Guard, Mackinac Island State Park Police Chief Ron LaCourture, Mackinac County Sheriff Charles Garries, Deputy Max Foss, and the small group of Boy Scouts from Troop #66, who were staying on the Island and serving as tour guides at Fort Mackinac.

---

17. Remsburg, Charles. "Michigan's Number One Murder Mystery." *True Detective Magazine*, 1962

Violent crime on Mackinac Island was a rarity, but even so, the immediate feeling among the general public was that Frances Lacey had met with foul play.

Wesley Sutter felt the same way, and he wasn't going to sit around while his mother-in-law was missing. He joined the search. He and Kay took the opportunity to rent horses from a livery on the Island at 9:00 a.m. It was odd, but to some of the volunteers involved in the search, Kay appeared to be the only family member who seemed concerned. Trooper Grosse took the opportunity to interview Wesley again about his mother-in-law's disappearance before he and Kay headed out on horses. Sutter told Grosse that Frances was in good health, and it wasn't like her to flirt with men. He was certain she must have met with foul play, or she would have called someone by that point. Sutter wanted to do more, and he insisted that MSP bring in bloodhounds. He didn't care what the cost was, adding that his family didn't have to worry about money.[18]

As the foot search got underway, the Mackinac Island Police continued to check with more local businesses in the city. With no sign of her mother and more people joining the search, a nagging thought kept bothering Kay. Her mother had once shared a very private secret with her; she had no ability to scream. She realized her condition years earlier when her hair got caught between the rollers on an old washing machine, and she couldn't reach the power switch. As her hair was being torn from her scalp, frozen in fear, she realized she couldn't scream for help.

Kay had a picture of her mom, and copies were made to pass out to the volunteers who were searching. They began showing it around town in the hope that someone might recall seeing her. All the ferry lines were checked again, but

---

18. Grosse, Herbert. "Supplemental Report." *Michigan State Police,* July 25, 1960

after almost twenty-four hours, there was still no sign of the missing Dearborn widow.

The search dragged on throughout the day and continued into the evening on Monday. By 10:00 p.m., bloodhounds from the Wisconsin-Michigan Search and Rescue Service arrived on the Island. Their dogs were owned jointly by six counties along the Michigan-Wisconsin border on the west end of the Upper Peninsula, and the organization was formed because of the extensive wooded terrain that was often encountered in areas where hikers get lost. They'd just completed a search in Iron Mountain, three hours away, for a lost boy who was found dead.

The dog handlers wore heavy leather belts, and the dogs were chained to each handler. To start their search, the handlers used some of Frances Lacey's clothing from her luggage, and the dogs picked up her scent on Main Street and followed it to the west lake shore. They tracked halfway along the dilapidated boardwalk that curved around the southwest corner of the Island for a short distance.[19] The scent was lost at the end of the boardwalk.

After losing the original trail, the dogs were driven in the police Jeep to the north end of the Island, and they picked up on another scent that led to Wesley and Kay's cabin. It was no surprise since she'd been there on Saturday. By 2:00 a.m., the dogs had lost the trail. Nothing was found, and the handlers suggested having some other personal items sent to the Island from the Lacey home on Lafayette Street in Dearborn. The handlers feared that some of the clothing they were using from her luggage had been handled by relatives prior to the dogs' arrival.

A neighbor of Mrs. Lacey was contacted by MSP troopers in Dearborn, and she had a key to the Lacey home. She allowed the troopers access so they could gather a few

19. *The Detroit News*, "Trail Lost: Fear Widow is Drowned," July 27, 1960

items. She could hardly believe that her quiet neighbor was missing, and it was the least she could do to help in the search for her friend. A bed sheet and bed pad were taken from the bedroom, and troopers from several MSP posts across the state spent the entire night relaying the items from car to car so the search could continue the next morning.

Frances Lacey's concerns that someone would be in her home when she wasn't there had materialized.

5: THE SEARCH BEGINS

By now the investigators were becoming increasingly concerned and were convinced there was more to Frances Lacey's disappearance than simply being lost. Burnette knew there were a lot of people to interview, and he needed more help. With thousands of tourists on the Island each day and foul play now suspected, several MSP detectives from various posts around the state were dispatched to the Island.

Year-round residents were filled with apprehension and fear. No one could remember a time when someone simply disappeared from the Island, and the only murder anyone knew of had occurred fifty years earlier when an employee of the Grand Hotel was killed. That case was never solved.

When the media picked up on the story, reporters headed to the Island for any fragment of information they could gather. As newsmen swarmed the Island and interviewed locals, one resident said, "Every path, every road leads around in a circle, so anyone getting on a road should end up back in town. If the woman is actually lost, there must be something amiss."

Gladys LaPoint*, another Island resident said, "I've lived here twenty-three years, and I've never heard of anything like this. It's hard to understand how anyone could get lost on the paths, or even meet with foul play."

Mackinac Island is two-and-a-half miles long and one-and-three-quarter miles wide. It's covered in a series of horse trails and footpaths, and Sergeant Burnette told the press, "All we know is that the woman is missing. We have little to work with besides that."[20] No one knew for certain if she had taken Garrison Road across the middle of the Island to British Landing Road, or if she had taken Lake Shore Road around the west end of the Island, but police were confident that her route was likely Lake Shore Road, based on the tracking done by the bloodhounds. She'd been along Garrison Road at least once, and that was the shorter route. Burnette continued, "At this point, we don't know whether she decided to walk along the shore to British Landing, which would have been about three-and-a-half miles, or walk across the center of the Island."[21]

On Tuesday morning, Detective LeRoy McCluer, assigned at the East Tawas Post, was told he'd be heading to Mackinac Island to help in the investigation. McCluer arrived at the St. Ignace Post at 5:00 p.m., and when he finally got to the Island, he teamed up with Burnette and another detective. The three men took bikes and followed Main Street around the west side of the Island from the Murray Hotel to the cabins at British Landing. Along the way, they checked along the west beach shore and the abandoned buildings but found nothing.

Even with Frances Lacey's bedding relayed to the Island overnight by MSP cars across the state, the bloodhounds still weren't able to pick up her scent on Tuesday. "I don't think she's on the Island," said one of the handlers.[22]

While police and volunteers continued searching for the Dearborn woman, Kay spoke briefly with the press. "We were supposed to meet Mother at about eleven o'clock Sunday morning, spend the afternoon together, and then

20. *The Detroit News*, "Widow Vanishes; Dogs Join Hunt on Mackinac," July 26, 1960

21. *The Detroit News*, "Widow Vanishes; Dogs Join Hunt on Mackinac," July 26, 1960

22. *The Detroit News*, "Trail Lost: Fear Widow is Drowned," July 27, 1960

leave for the trip back to Dearborn," she said. She continued, "I'm going to stay on this Island as long as it takes to find her. I'll do it even if it takes two years to find her and I have to become a beachcomber in the process."[23]

***

Lieutenant Bob Bilgen was a familiar face to the public, and with his promotion from sergeant to lieutenant in 1958 came the responsibility as the Post commander in Battle Creek. Two years later, a transfer came, and the twenty-year veteran of the MSP was reassigned to the Marquette Post in Michigan's Upper Peninsula along the Lake Superior shoreline. Bilgen hadn't even had time to sell his house in Battle Creek before leaving. He was scheduled to report on Monday morning, July 25, and he left his wife, Adeline, and their fourteen-year-old son, Paul, an Eagle Scout, in Battle Creek as he headed to northern Michigan for his new assignment. His plan was to get settled in his new position, and his family would move north later.

Initiating the state's first police roadblock system during his time at the Battle Creek Post, Bilgen was one of the first troopers to successfully capture two men wanted in the armed robbery and homicide of a local pharmacist. Supervising a shift of twenty-two men, he and his men averaged fifty-five hours in a six-day workweek during the investigation.

At six feet tall and one hundred eighty pounds, Bilgen, with his graying hair, had a lot of experience in his years with MSP. Early in his career, the veteran officer had been shot in the head and shoulder with buckshot when he was mistaken for a suspect while investigating the theft of some melons from a local farmer. As his career began to

---

23. *The Detroit News*, "Trail Lost: Fear Widow is Drowned," July 27, 1960

progress, he became so well known, it seemed that everyone recognized his familiar face. While in Battle Creek, he was part of the Calhoun County Safety Commission and had received a safety award from the Calhoun County PTA.

On his way to the new post, Bilgen drove through the northern Michigan countryside, and as he crossed the five-mile span of the Mackinac Bridge, he heard a news report on the radio about a missing tourist on Mackinac Island. He knew St. Ignace and Michigan's entire Upper Peninsula were in his new district, and he also knew if she wasn't found, he'd be briefed about the missing woman when he reported for work. Surely, she'd be located.

As the new lieutenant walked through the front door at the MSP Post in Marquette, he was quickly told not to unpack. He was being sent back to Mackinac Island to supervise the search for the missing woman. The forty-six-year-old Bilgen had no idea how the case would consume his life for the next few years.

Like Burnette and Bilgen, Detective Anthony Spratto had also served at the Battle Creek Post. Joining MSP in 1934, Spratto served at the St. Clair Post before being transferred to Battle Creek in 1940. He worked in plainclothes with the military on un-American activities and sabotage investigations, but when those investigations began to dwindle, he spent more of his time on criminal investigations and background checks of people hired by the military.

Spratto was well-liked by his colleagues, and in 1947, he was transferred to the detective division at the Redford Post near Detroit. While serving at Redford, Spratto gained the distinction as the only MSP detective to ever obtain a confession in the air. While on a six-hour flight from Tulsa, Oklahoma, to Detroit with the suspect in a 1948 Flat Rock, Michigan, murder, the suspect calmly confessed to Spratto about the killing.

Detective Spratto also gained some notoriety as one of the lead detectives in a 1952 murder investigation of thirty-eight-year-old army veteran Coleman Peterson. Peterson shot and killed former MSP Trooper Mike Chenoweth, the owner of the Lumberjack Tavern in Big Bay, Michigan, located along the southern shore of Lake Superior. A book written about the killing was made into a Hollywood movie called *Anatomy of a Murder* starring Jimmy Stewart. Spratto's part was played by actor Ken Lynch, and the movie had premiered the year prior.

The decorated detective had been assigned to the Marquette Post for some time, and he was retiring in a few years, but as a seasoned detective, he was sent to the Island. The press knew that if anyone could solve the mystery surrounding the disappearance of Frances Lacey, it would be Detective Sergeant Anthony Spratto.

6: PAUL STRANTZ

The man walked into the medical center on the Island, and it was quickly evident that he didn't belong there. Dr. Joseph Solomon, the Island's only doctor, took notice as the man said he was a lock inspector. He began to look at all the doors to the office. Two nurses were watching intently, and they knew something wasn't right, so they asked him to leave.

Later that same afternoon, he returned, and the two nurses were set on edge. He asked how much a shot of penicillin would cost him. After getting his answer, he left again.

Later, he showed up again to see the dentist, but he didn't want to wait and left again before seeing anyone.

Solomon had watched him closely and thought he might be a drug user, so he made mental note of the man.

***

The Mackinac Island Coast Guard Station was built in 1915 after the merger of the United States Revenue Cutter Service, a maritime customs enforcement agency, and the United States Life-Saving Service. Together, they were called the United States Coast Guard. The building had three launching ramps on the lake shore for three small boats, and the second floor had living quarters and a kitchen for the crew. Twelve members of the USCG stationed on the Island served under the leadership of Chief Bosun's Mate

Robert Pollins. A large sign identified the building as the Mackinac Island Coast Guard Station, but the building was shared with the summer detachment of three MSP troopers. Under the Coast Guard sign was a smaller one pointing to two small doors at the northeast corner of the building. It read "STATE POLICE."

On Tuesday morning, heavy rain moved through the northern Michigan region, and the search on the Island was delayed until there was a break in the weather.

As more officers began arriving to help in the search, Spratto's first order of business was to talk to Wesley and Kay Sutter. Every good investigator knew the family was always suspect, and the veteran detective wanted more background information about Frances. The investigation was being run out of the state police office at the Coast Guard Station, and rather than interview the Sutters at British Landing, the detective wanted to interview Kay on his own turf.

Meeting him at the MSP office, Kay began the interview by telling Detective Spratto about her mom. Her mom was a quiet woman who didn't make friends easily but was a very loving person. She was independent and very punctual. After Kay's father died in 1957, she and her brother, William, had each received nineteen thousand dollars in cash, in addition to some stocks and bonds. The remainder of his assets went directly to her mom. Ford Lacey had owned two apartment buildings in Detroit. One was located on Grand River, and the second was in Leicester. When he died, the apartments were left under the control of Frances. According to Ford's will, when Kay and her brother reached the age of twenty-five, they would each receive half of the income from the real estate. If her mother died, both she and William would receive all the income from the two buildings.

Spratto took notes as Kay told him that her mother used both the Manufacturers Bank in Detroit and the Federal Savings and Loan in Dearborn. The detective asked how much Kay felt her mom was worth, and she thought it was around one hundred twenty-five thousand dollars.

The detective was curious about Kay's brother, William. He and his wife had been living with her mom, but over the past few months, he'd been taking care of his uncle, who was extremely ill. On Sunday evening, when the search was ramping up for her mom, Kay placed two long-distance calls to William in Detroit. He and his twenty-four-year-old wife, Valory, quickly left for the Island and left their seven-month-old son, Steven, with Valory's mother, Gina Cook.

Spratto needed to cover all the possibilities in the disappearance, including Frances Lacey's mental state. He asked Kay if her mom suffered from depression. Frances had had an operation the previous year and took medication that she referred to as her "happy pills," but Kay insisted her mom didn't have any emotional problems.

Spratto quietly studied Kay's responses to his questions. She said her mother should be carrying a distinctive purse. It was black with a cream-colored leather interior and bamboo handles. It was about sixteen-by-ten inches, and it should have her checkbook, passport, Social Security card, her pills, and her wallet. She thought her mom had about forty-five dollars in her wallet. She mentioned that her mom wore glasses, and she would have a diamond ring on, in addition to a wristwatch.

While Spratto was speaking with Kay, Trooper Ken Yuill was asking questions at the Murray Hotel. At thirty-six-years-old, the trooper had been born and raised in Vanderbilt, Michigan, and graduated at the age of twenty-eight from the MSP Recruit School six years prior. After serving in the navy as a medical corpsman, he married and drove trucks for a time before joining MSP.

Trooper Yuill was able to get a list of the guests who stayed on the second floor near room twenty-six. None of them were interviewed because they'd already left the Island, but he was able to interview the hotel chambermaids.

Marvel Cruzan and Mary Pearson were assigned to room twenty-six and thought there must have been someone still staying in the room when they went in to clean. There was either baggage still in there or there were still clothes in the room, so rather than make the bed with clean linen, they simply straightened the bedding. A friend of theirs operated one of the city carriage cabs, and he mentioned to them that he had taken a woman up to British Landing. The cab driver was off the Island when the investigators were interviewing the maids, so they'd have to interview him later.

Trooper Yuill also spoke with the desk clerks who were working on Saturday, July 23. The morning clerk, Jack Donaldson, remembered checking Mrs. Lacey in, and the afternoon clerk, Thomas Murray, the hotel owner's son, said that during the evening, after she returned to the hotel, she left at least three times prior to 10:00 p.m. Mrs. Lacey left her room key at the desk each time she left and picked it up when she came back to the hotel. After the third time, she told Murray she probably wouldn't be bothering him anymore. The lobby was closed at 1:00 a.m., and the dayshift clerk found the key to room twenty-six lying on the desk. He found Mrs. Lacey's baggage in the lobby sometime after 10:30 a.m.

As Yuill was gathering information, Kay's interview with Detective Spratto ended, and she left the Coast Guard Station. Spratto was still curious about Mrs. Lacey's mental state and asked Sergeant Burnette to follow up with her doctor to see if she suffered from depression. Maybe she had taken her own life. When his suspicions were confirmed by the doctor about her depression, Spratto called Kay and asked her about it. Kay became upset, yelling at Spratto over the phone and telling him it wasn't true. The detective, known for his calm demeanor, was able to convince Kay to stop back at the MSP office for some more questions about her mom's background.

The second interview with Spratto was much more emotional for Kay. Tears streamed down her cheeks as she admitted to him that after her father's death, her mom suffered from long bouts of depression, and she took medication for it. She said her mother had to take the medication at least once a day to keep her spirits up, and she smoked one-and-a-half packs of L&M cigarettes each day. Her mom would also take an occasional alcoholic drink, but it only depressed her more. When Spratto asked about the possibility of her mom harming herself, Kay insisted that her mother would never do that because of what other people would think of her.

When Spratto finished his second interview, he wasn't completely convinced that Frances had met with foul play, and he wasn't convinced that depression had anything to do with her disappearance either. He was keeping all of the possibilities open.

As Kay left, Chief Bloomfield poked his head in and said there was a dishwasher from the Island House Hotel in the lobby. His name was Paul Strantz, and on occasion, he'd been suspected as a window peeper on the Island. Bloomfield mentioned that Strantz had a habit of seeming to be around the downtown area at all times of the day and night. Spratto definitely wanted to talk to him.

Bloomfield escorted the man into the office where the detective was waiting. As he sat down, Spratto lit a cigarette. The detective studied Strantz closely and couldn't help but wonder if he was the man responsible for the disappearance of Mrs. Lacey.

The thirty-one-year-old, just three days away from his birthday, was an army veteran who served during the Korean War. From South Bend, Indiana, he gave the officers his address at the YMCA.

Detective Spratto started his interview by asking the dishwasher where he was staying. Strantz was working at the Island House Hotel and staying there too. He started out from South Bend two weeks prior with about one hundred dollars in his pocket, and he ended up in the town of Petoskey, where he tried to get a job at the Little Traverse Hospital. After that fell through, he headed to Mackinac Island, and he arrived at about 5:00 p.m. on Saturday, July 23. The detective asked if he'd been to the Murray Hotel, and Strantz admitted he was at the hotel on both Saturday night and Sunday night for drinks. He came to the Island to work different jobs during the summer, and his plan was to wash dishes, work in the kitchens at various restaurants, or even wash windows around the city. On Sunday morning, he got up around 9:00 a.m., had breakfast, and went to the 10:30 church service. When the service was over, he went back to the Island House Hotel, had lunch, and he went to his second job at the National Photo Shop until 7:00. When he left work, he headed back to his room.

Detective Spratto wanted to see his reaction when he asked Strantz if he knew anything about the disappearance of Frances Lacey. Strantz's demeanor abruptly changed, and he became belligerent and defensive about being suspected in the widow's disappearance.

The detective watched him closely. If he was being truthful and didn't know anything about the missing woman, maybe he'd allow the detectives to check his room. Spratto asked casually, and much to his surprise, Strantz agreed. Chief Bloomfield went along, and the three men walked the short distance west along Main Street from the MSP office to the Island House Hotel.

Strantz unlocked the door and let the detective and chief in. The two officers looked around the room. There were several books and newspaper clippings about women's anatomy and some of Strantz's own sketches of women. A few had his original poetry written under them. In his suitcase, along with a twelve-foot piece of thin rope, there were a couple of women's pocketbook mirrors. Spratto's suspicions about Paul Strantz began to grow.

Looking through Strantz's clothes, the detective noted a lightweight gray pinstriped suit and a green short-sleeved shirt. Spratto asked about the suit. Strantz said he'd left the suit at the cleaners when he left the Island the previous year and just got it back on Saturday night when he returned for the summer season. Spratto looked over the clothing very closely. The green shirt, suit, and a pair of socks were damp. Looking closer, he could see pine needles and small stones in the cuff of the pants. The detective asked Strantz about the condition of the suit, and he said he wore it on Saturday night. It had gotten wet in the rain.

The MSP detective continued to check through the clothing, and he noticed a tan and red plaid shirt with four small red stains on the right sleeve. It piqued his interest. The stains were midway between the elbow and the shoulder, and they looked like blood drops. Before Spratto could ask anything, Strantz quickly offered an explanation; it was paint.

Spratto couldn't be sure, and he needed more than just suspicion. He turned to Bloomfield and asked if there was a doctor on the Island who might be able to determine if the four spots were blood. The police chief suggested Dr. Solomon. Spratto dialed the phone, and when the doctor answered, he asked Solomon if he could do a salt and water test on the stains. They needed to know if the spots on the sleeve were blood. The doctor agreed and told Spratto to bring the shirt to his office.

At the doctor's office, Solomon ran two tests, and afterward, he was confident the stains were nothing more than paint.

While the detective and police chief were meeting with the doctor, other officers were already checking Strantz's story downtown. They confirmed what he'd told Spratto, and they had no choice but to release him.

Spratto was quiet about his observations of Strantz and kept his suspicions to himself. That's what made him a good detective. In a report about the interview with Strantz, Bloomfield wrote, "In officer's opinions, this man appears to be mentally retarded, and there is a possibility this is a good suspect in case Frances Stacey is later found harmed or dead by violence."[24]

***

The morning rain had passed, and the search for Frances Lacey resumed across the Island while a pilot from MSP flew the state police plane along the Island's shoreline searching for any sign of the Dearborn widow.

After the interviews, Spratto met with the Coast Guard and joined them in a search of the waters and shoreline around the Island on a Coast Guard boat while a second team of investigators used a second boat to check the coastline in the opposite direction. There was still no trace of the missing tourist.

While Detective Spratto was working the case on the Island, detectives from the Dearborn Police were asked to go to the Lacey home and check for fingerprints. All the dishes in the home were dusted with fingerprint powder, and any latent prints that were found were carefully lifted and sent to the State Health Department in Lansing.

Checking the house thoroughly, the detectives discovered a life insurance policy through Metropolitan Life. It had been written in March 1958, and the most recent payment was due in March 1960, though it hadn't been paid. The policy stated that if Frances Lacey passed away, the beneficiary would receive fifteen thousand dollars, but the policy didn't indicate who that person was. A representative of the Metropolitan Life Company was asked to contact the

---

24. Yuill, Kenneth. "Supplemental Report." *Michigan State Police*, July 27, 1960

corporate office in New York to see who was named as the beneficiary.

The detectives also confirmed that Frances had a hysterectomy a year before, and when they spoke with the doctor about the possibility of her beginning menopause, he told them that some women immediately begin after the surgery, and some of them develop "emotional disturbances."

The investigators took a few minutes and spoke with Mrs. Lacey's neighbor. She and Frances had spoken shortly before she left for the Island with her daughter and son-in-law. They had been planning the trip to Mackinac for about three weeks, and Frances seemed very happy when they spoke. She was looking forward to the trip. The two women only spoke occasionally, but the neighbor mentioned that Frances was sometimes distant, and it seemed as if she was difficult to get to know.

Frances Lacey's bank records at First Federal Savings and Loan in Dearborn were checked, and she'd opened an account in 1958 by depositing one hundred fifty-seven dollars. Her last deposit was five days before she left for Mackinac, and she deposited fifteen hundred dollars. When she made the last deposit in her account, her balance was $6,088.

At the Manufacturers National Bank, Mrs. Lacey had two commercial checking accounts. Both accounts were registered to her, and the first account, opened in July 1958, had $1,096, while the second account had a balance of $4,218.

The mortgage for the Lacey home at 805 Lafayette was held by the Detroit Bank and Trust. With a monthly payment of $106, the mortgage balance was $7,324.

Digging a little deeper into Ford Lacey's background, the detectives contacted the Wayne County Probate Court. Mrs. Lacey's husband had a will that was registered with the county, and it specified that upon his death, Frances would receive twenty-nine thousand dollars after taxes, and both Kay and William were to receive nineteen thousand dollars. Before taxes, the estate was valued at $91,732. Ford Lacey's will also identified two daughters from a previous marriage, and each was to receive one dollar upon his death. In his will, he wrote, "I have not seen or heard from either in many years and I don't know their present married names or whereabouts."[25]

***

For Mackinac Island's tourist industry, a record number of tourists had visited the Island over the previous week to watch the yacht *Freebooter* win the Chicago-to-Mackinac race in the Class A category, with a time of forty-seven hours, fourteen minutes, and thirteen seconds. The sheer number of Island visitors broke all previous records, and at Fort Mackinac, the number of visitors recorded was almost four thousand. Police faced a daunting task.

On Wednesday, July 27, three days after Frances was reported missing, Sergeant Burnette was being hounded by the press. "We've combed that Island over and over again, and we haven't found a trace of her," he said. "It's very unlikely for a person to get lost on the Island. We've combed this Island, especially its forty-six miles of major trails and its few rocky cliffs and other natural hazards." He added, "It is so interlaced with trails, you're never more than a few hundred yards from one of them."[26]

Violent crime on Mackinac Island was virtually unheard of, so it was surprising to the press that the local population almost immediately assumed the worst: Mrs. Lacey had

---

25. *The Detroit News*, "Mrs. Lacey Got $109,000 From Estate," August 1, 1960

26. *Ironwood Daily Globe,* "No Trace of Woman Found," July 27, 1960

been murdered.[27] Others were more confident that she was still alive somewhere on the Island. Frances's daughter-in-law, Valory, said, "We think that maybe she has amnesia or something, because Bill says it isn't like her to wander off like this." She continued, "We got a postcard from her Sunday, and the things she said weren't like her, nor was her writing." Valory never mentioned what was written on the postcard. She only said that she and her husband were praying for the best. "I hope and pray they find her in good health soon," she said.[28]

27. Cawthorne, *Mackinac Island: Inside, Up Close, and Personal*
28. *The Detroit News*, "Trail Lost: Fear Widow is Drowned," July 27, 1960

7: FIRST CLUES

William and Valory left the Island for their return to Dearborn on Wednesday, July 27. Ford Lacey's brother, Claude, had passed away in a nursing home the day before, and now, with his mother still missing, William was forced to return to Dearborn and plan the funeral, leaving Kay and Wesley on the Island.

On Thursday, a dive team from the Marquette MSP Post was searching the deep and turbulent waters around the Island.[29] Swift, dangerous currents in the Straits made recovering a body very difficult. The deep water begins close to the shore around the Island, except for the west side, where there's a more gradual drop-off.

Other searches were done in various locations by discouraged volunteers, and police were beginning to believe that Frances Lacey could have fallen into Lake Huron and drowned. Burnette told the press, "We've gone just about as far as we can go. We've covered all we can." With that, he said the search would still continue.[30]

***

29. *The Detroit News*, "Skin Divers Search for Missing Widow," July 28, 1960

30. *Lansing State Journal,* "Mackinac Mystery Unsolved," July 28, 1960

The couple's trip to northern Michigan the previous week was supposed to be a quiet affair. No one was supposed to know they were there because the man was married.

The pair left Detroit on Friday, July 22, around 11:00 p.m. It was late, and when they reached the Flint area, they stopped to sleep for a few hours in the car. Their brief nap was enough for them to continue when they woke up, and on the morning of July 23, they crossed the Mackinac Bridge and stopped at a motel in St. Ignace. They spent the day relaxing, and the next day, their plan was to take the ferry across to Mackinac Island.

On Sunday morning, the two secret lovers headed toward the docks to catch the first boat. Missing it by only minutes, they waited for the second, and it didn't take long to arrive. They had the whole day ahead of them.

Arriving on the Island, the two strolled up the dock and stopped at the Schwinn bicycle shop to rent a tandem bike for their adventure. The clerk wrote the time on the rental ticket; it was 9:30 a.m. They had no specific plan for the day other than to ride around the Island and enjoy the sights.

As they passed through downtown, there weren't a lot of tourists yet, but as the day went on, more would be shuttled from the mainland, and the streets would be filled. As the pair passed the police department and the hospital, they discovered the paved street they were on turned to gravel, and rather than continue biking on gravel, they decided to follow the Lake Huron shoreline and head up Lake Shore Road toward British Landing.

The weather was beautiful, and they stopped at Devil's Kitchen. Legend said that the geologic attraction once housed evil spirits. As the two enjoyed their brief break, the woman waded into Lake Huron while the man snapped some photos of her.

The pair continued their ride along the coast on the tandem bike as their route made gentle bends paralleling the lake. As the road turned toward the north, the man could see two cobblestone pillars ahead framing a large iron gate. With pillars well over six feet tall, it was posted with a PRIVATE PROPERTY sign. The two tourists on the tandem bike paid no attention to the gate as they passed, and twenty feet or so beyond the gated trail, the man noticed a purse lying off the pavement to their right and mentioned it to his passenger.

"Stop. There might be something in it," the woman said.[31]

They slowed and stopped, and the man walked back toward the purse. Picking it up, a noise in the wooded area caught his attention. He heard rustling in the brush and near the gated trail they had just passed. It sounded like a large animal lumbering through the dense woods. Ignoring the sounds, he looked at the purse and could see it was snapped shut. It was black with bamboo handles that were folded down, and it was lying with the top of the purse pointing north toward British Landing. He thought maybe somebody had thrown out an old purse along the road. Looking inside, he saw some papers with a name on them.

Neither of them noticed anyone walking along Lake Shore Road. They put the purse in the basket mounted on the handlebars and continued toward British Landing for the day. Maybe they'd find the owner of the purse later in town.

At British Landing, the twenty-cent bottles of Orange Nesbitt and Hire's Root Beer quenched their thirst from the ride as they walked around and read about the local Island's history. They decided they'd take British Landing Road back to town and ended up walking much of the way because it seemed as if it was mostly uphill.

Back in town, the pair checked the Chippewa Hotel because there was a brochure from the hotel inside the

---

31. Whaley, Howard. "Supplemental Report." *Michigan State Police,* July 28, 1960

purse, and the papers had the name of Frances Lacey with an address in Dearborn. It only seemed logical that she'd probably be staying there. A quick check at the front desk, and they discovered there was no one registered by that name, nor had there been. Neither the couple nor the desk clerk at the Chippewa Hotel recognized Mrs. Lacey's name because she hadn't been reported missing yet. They decided they weren't going to spend the rest of their day searching for the owner of the purse, so they took it with them back to Detroit, and the woman planned to simply contact Mrs. Lacey at her home to let her know they had found it. They could make arrangements to somehow get it to her.

After checking the Chippewa, they turned the bike in at the Schwinn bike rental and continued shopping throughout the late afternoon. The woman became anxious as she carried Mrs. Lacey's purse throughout the day. She thought that at any moment, Mrs. Lacey might tap her on the shoulder and ask her what she was doing with it.

It was a one-day trip to the Island, and late in the afternoon, they headed back to St. Ignace on the ferry. In hindsight, they knew they should have turned the purse over to the police on the Island as a lost-and-found item, but it might have resulted in their tryst being discovered. They agreed it was better to just call the owner of the pocketbook when they returned home.

After their return to Detroit, the woman took the purse back to the apartment she shared with her roommate and had every intention of contacting Frances Lacey to let her know her purse had been found on Mackinac Island. By Thursday, July 28, it had slipped the woman's mind, and she still hadn't tried to contact Mrs. Lacey.

News about a missing Dearborn widow on Mackinac Island began circulating through the media. All the television stations and newspapers carried stories about the missing tourist as the police continued their search for her. In Detroit, when the anonymous couple realized they had found the purse of the missing Dearborn widow on the day she had disappeared, and then left the Island, the woman called the Detroit Police Department. The man was nervous. He was married, and no one knew he had been on the Island with his mistress for the weekend. He had to be able to remain anonymous. His friend from DPD called another colleague at the MSP Metro Post.

Howard Whaley was a detective lieutenant with MSP, and as he took the information from his DPD colleague, he assured him that the two could remain anonymous as informants, but if it became absolutely necessary down the road, the two agreed to come forward. Whaley arranged a meeting with both of them later that day. They were interviewed separately, and they both described the discovery of the purse in exacting detail.

The MSP detective called MSP Operations in East Lansing, and Operations called Detective Spratto in Marquette. He'd already returned to the Marquette Post with Bilgen, and when he heard about the discovery of the purse, he knew he needed to speak with the two people who had found it. Spratto called each one directly.

It was their first break.

8: GRIM PARADISE

Spratto was certain Frances was dead. If he could pinpoint the exact spot where Frances Lacey's purse was found, maybe her body would be close by. He, Bilgen, and Trooper Albright headed back toward St. Ignace from Marquette by plane, and by 5:30 p.m., they were met by Corporal Conard. The four officers boarded a Coast Guard boat heading back to the Island. When the bloodhounds had picked up Frances Lacey's scent earlier in the week, they had followed the crumbling boardwalk around the southwest corner of the Island, but no one was absolutely sure if that was the route she'd taken.

Bilgen knew exactly where the area was that the informants had described. He'd seen the cobblestone pillared gate with the PRIVATE PROPERTY signs as the searches continued throughout the week. The location certainly suggested that she had actually taken Lake Shore Road and not some other route on the morning of her disappearance.

Arriving on the Island, they grabbed the police Jeep and headed toward the gate on Lake Shore Road. Parking along the inside edge of the roadway, the men began slowly looking around along the side of the roadway where the informants said they first saw the purse, then began a slow and methodical look around the area for anything that might be of interest in Mrs. Lacey's disappearance. A putrid odor permeated the entire area.

Spratto walked along the roadway's edge. A short distance to the northwest of the cobblestone pillars, he noticed several small pieces of something on the blacktop roadway. Looking closer, he saw broken pieces of a denture plate. The denture had likely been run over by a carriage because it was shattered into small pieces. Unusual to say the least, and he was even more confident they were in the right area to begin a more thorough search.

Sergeant Burnette joined the officers, and when Spratto found the shattered denture plate, the five men knew they had to check the wooded area on the other side of the fence that stretched north from the gate. The gate was locked. The officers climbed over the fence and onto the gated property owned by the Moral Re-Armament Movement to look around the heavily wooded area.

From the stone columns at the gate, a two-strand wire fence, five feet high, ran parallel to the roadway and had two rows of barbed wire at the top. Inside the gate, an old trail ran somewhat parallel to Lake Shore Road on an uphill grade for a short distance before turning to the east and continuing up the hill. At the point where the old road turned, a small footpath of sorts continued on through the forested property and parallel to Lake Shore Road.

Looking down the trail, Burnette noticed an old, overturned, rotting rowboat about thirty feet away. It was the perfect place to hide a body, and he moved slowly toward it while looking down as he watched his every step so he didn't disturb anything of significance or miss any evidence. With a small amount of hesitation, he picked up the edge of the small watercraft to look under the bow. He noticed a pair of women's dress shoes. The size 6B black patent leather shoes had an open toe. One of the shoes was inside a plastic bag, while the other was lying on the ground about twelve inches away. Burnette picked up the shoe on the ground and carefully looked at it. It was a Naturalizer brand, and the shoes had been made in Scotland by William

Elliot and Sons. He told the others of the discovery, and the investigators had no doubt they were in the right area now and fanned out to begin a wider search.

It was a beautiful, clear evening, and there wasn't a breeze to be had. Trooper Albright moved north of the trail into the brush and fallen trees as he scanned the ground in front of and around him. Ahead, he noticed two small trees that had been blown over by the wind at some point in the past. On the ground next to the fallen trees, he could see something dark. It looked out of place, and as he neared the trees, he could see branches had been broken off the downed trees and were propped up against them. It looked as if they were being used to conceal something on the ground, and as he neared, it became evident what he was looking at; it was human hair. Four days after her disappearance, the missing tourist had been found.

Frances Lacey's body was lying on a slope with her head pointed downward to the west. She was on her stomach with her head turned to the right, and her right arm was pulled up behind her back with the palm of her hand open while her left arm lay alongside her body. Her knees were slightly bent. The short-sleeve white blouse she was wearing was pulled up above her shoulder blades. She wore a white bra, and her dark green wool skirt was pulled up to her hipline along with the slip she was wearing. She was wearing a girdle, and her garter was still attached to her stockings. Very little of her feet were showing as there was tall grass around the lower portion of her body. The rest of her body was covered with the broken branches from the fallen trees. Her plastic-rimmed eyeglasses were lying two inches from her upper left arm.

Any suspicion that Frances Lacey might have become depressed and harmed herself was now discounted. Her disappearance was no longer a missing persons case. The Dearborn widow had been murdered. At 7:35, Bilgen told Conard to head back to the city and find a photographer and the coroner. He wanted pictures before the sun set and anything was moved.

After Conard left, Spratto and the others carefully looked around the area to see if there was any more obvious evidence in the immediate area. The experienced detectives all knew that specialists trained in evidence collection would be sent to the Island to comb over the entire area, and they didn't want to disturb any more of the crime scene than they had to.

By 8:05, Conard returned with Chief Bloomfield and George Rose, the resident photographer from the Grand Hotel. Thrust into his new role as a crime scene photographer in the midst of a vicious homicide investigation, Rose used his three-inch-by-four-inch press camera to take pictures of the murder scene at the direction of MSP while trying to overcome the foul odor of decaying flesh. Fifteen minutes later, Rose had snapped twenty-four photographs. They included overall pictures of the area, closeups of Mrs. Lacey's body, and photographs of the boat with the shoes under it. Rose turned his film over to Spratto.

After Conard took the photographer back to the Grand Hotel, he was told to pick up four men—a funeral director from St. Ignace, the acting coroner, a state park police officer, and Detective Sergeant Clarence Bloomquist.

***

Ronald Beeck, the justice of the peace in St. Ignace, was surprised to find Corporal Conard knocking on his door late on Thursday night. Beeck was accustomed to having locals stop by his house to pay traffic tickets, and on occasion, he'd even performed a wedding ceremony in his parlor, but he was surprised when the corporal explained that the local coroner couldn't be located and asked if Beeck could stand in. It was out of the norm for something like that to happen, but Beeck knew he didn't have a choice. He joined the funeral director and the officers for a trip to the Island.

After returning to Mackinac Island and dropping the men off, Conard was assigned the difficult task of locating Wesley and Kay Sutter at Little Bob's Restaurant and letting them know a body had been found, and it was likely Kay's mother. Bilgen wanted them notified before word leaked out about a body being found.

**

At 8:30, Detective Sergeant Dan Myre's phone rang at his home in Lansing. Myre was assigned to the latent print unit at the crime laboratory, and he was sent to Mackinac Island to help process the crime scene. He'd be going with three others.

Dr. Edgar Kivela's phone rang at 8:40 p.m. Kivela was a forensic scientist and worked for MSP. He headed for the Crime Detection Laboratory at the Michigan Department of Public Health to meet with the others who'd be making the overnight drive to Mackinaw City before heading to the crime scene on the Island. Two detectives from the Metro Detroit Post were also dispatched to the Island to help get the murder investigation underway.

Back on the Island, Beeck viewed the remains, noted the position and condition of Frances Lacey, and gave authorization for MSP to remove the body whenever the crime lab specialists were done processing the crime scene. He'd followed the news articles about the missing widow but never imagined he'd be called on to act as the coroner.

Bilgen knew the lab specialists wouldn't arrive until very early morning, and after some discussion with Spratto and Burnette, they decided to secure the crime scene by leaving the Jeep and two troopers overnight without moving Mrs. Lacey's body or any evidence. The lab specialists from

Lansing would process the crime scene when they arrived early in the morning, and then the body could be removed. It would be easier to search the crime scene in the daylight.

The Jeep was positioned so the headlights illuminated the body, and the officers stationed at the murder scene for the night had instructions to not let anyone near the scene and to question anyone who might be approaching. Both troopers knew it would be a long night.

***

William Lacey's mother-in-law, Gina Cook, heard on the news late Thursday night about a body being found on Mackinac Island. She called William to let him know what she'd heard. He called MSP, and they confirmed the tragic news to him. Both he and Valory had just returned from the funeral home where they were preparing for his uncle's funeral the following day.

With the stress of his uncle's death and the news that his mother's body had been found, it was almost too much for him to bear. After the service for his uncle, William spoke briefly with the press and said, "I feel like giving up."[32]

***

The wheels were set in motion when the widow's body was finally discovered. After a series of phone calls, two more detectives, another trooper, and two lab specialists from the State Health Department left Lansing at 9:45 p.m.

Rolling into Mackinaw City around 2:00 a.m. on Friday, July 29, they were met by another team of detectives who had just arrived. It was Friday morning, and the seven men waited briefly for a Coast Guard picket boat. The boat

32. *The Detroit News,* "Find Widow Strangled in Mackinac Myst," July 29, 1960

docked at the Coast Guard Station on the Island after the chilly ride from Mackinaw City.

After a briefing on what had been found thus far and what to expect at the murder scene, the seven investigators headed for the west side of the Island where Mrs. Lacey's body still lay undisturbed.

It was 4:40 a.m., and dawn was just beginning to break for the clear day. Spratto had had a short night's rest before meeting the lab specialists. The investigators were shown the crime scene area when they arrived and where the obvious evidence was located. After a discussion about how they would process the scene, the investigators began a detailed search of the area as the first signs of daylight began to appear.

Beginning with the obvious and working from the outside of the crime scene in, the small bits of the broken dentures ground into the blacktop were recovered. The men searched the entire area outside the gate for several hundred feet in both directions and on both sides of the road, then moved inside the gate to begin a methodical search toward the old rowboat. The size 6B women's shoes were photographed again and collected as evidence. By 6:00 a.m., they had slowly moved beyond the boat and in the direction of the body. They found a pink Scripto pen between Lake Shore Road and Mrs. Lacey's body. The location of the pen was photographed before being taken as evidence.

They moved to the body. There was a bluish color to her head and neck, much more than the rest of her body, and most of it was in her face. The marked lividity was consistent with the way her body was positioned on the downward slope. Looking closer, it became clear to the laboratory scientist how Mrs. Lacey's life had been so viciously taken—her white panties were knotted around her throat. A small branch was stuck between the knot and her neck. Dr. Ed Kivela could tell by looking at it that it had been placed there after the panties had been knotted around her neck. He counted fifteen to twenty sticks and cedar boughs that covered her. The soft-spoken forensic scientist was meticulous in everything he did. He examined the ends of each one of the sticks hiding Mrs. Lacey's corpse to see if there were any hairs or fibers on the ends of them. He also checked the trees and shrubs around the body for any evidence.

Looking closer at Mrs. Lacey's body, Kivela removed a hair from the front of her slip near her breasts.

The scientist could see that while her blouse and skirt were pulled up, none of the clothing was torn, but there were several runs in her nylons. Kivela didn't think her body had been dragged there, but rather, she'd been carried to where her body was found.

Her light blue bifocal glasses were hanging in some brush near her left shoulder and were removed and taken as evidence along with the other items.

While some of the investigators were searching for obvious clues on Mrs. Lacey's body, others were checking outward from that point. Detective Myre found one small fiber at the end of a broken branch near the base of the cobblestone wall. It was a light tan-colored piece of nylon material. The fiber was photographed and measured, then retrieved and turned over to Kivela. The forensic scientist was certain it had come from Mrs. Lacey's nylons.

Each investigator knew the importance of even the smallest piece of evidence. The proper collection and preservation of each piece was crucial to the investigation.

The heavy matting of pine needles on the ground in the area prevented the investigators from locating any footprints.

Lieutenant Wallace VanStratt was searching in the area of the small fence that extended from the stone pillars when he discovered two hairs at the base of one of the pillars. One of the hairs was white, while the other was brown.

The Scripto pen and the eyeglasses were both processed at the scene for fingerprints without success.

Five hours after beginning the grim task of processing the Lacey murder scene, Frances Lacey's body was carefully and quietly removed and taken by a Coast Guard boat to St. Ignace. Sergeant Burnette contacted Mackinaw County Prosecutor James Brown, and Brown contacted Dr. Gene Webster in Petoskey. Brown asked that Webster perform the autopsy on Mrs. Lacey.

The detectives from the Eighth District left the murder scene at 8:00 a.m. when the ferry docks opened. Their assignment was to obtain a list of all outgoing Island employees from the two primary ferries servicing Mackinac Island—the Arnold Transit Company and the Straits Transit Company. The men also went to each business on the Island to begin finding out the names of each owner and the names of all the employees.

Bilgen assigned a trooper to ride a bicycle from the point where the anonymous couple had rented theirs and take the same route they took to the point where the purse was found. The trooper was told to leave at 9:30 a.m., the same time the couple had departed. He arrived at about 10:30. It was about the same time the couple discovered Mrs. Lacey's purse. "This means that the couple could have been only a few yards away when Mrs. Lacey's murderer concealed her body under a blanket of brush," Bilgen said.[33]

Now that Frances Lacey's body had been found, Spratto knew exactly who he wanted to talk to. He wanted another interview with Paul Strantz, and he wasn't going to give him a chance to leave the Island. He wanted him held on suspicion of murder.

On Spratto's orders, Trooper Grosse and the Mackinac Island Police were checking the downtown area for Strantz

---

33. *The Detroit News*, "Mackinac Slaying Search Shifts to Wayne County," July 31, 1960

and found him coming out of the lobby of the Island House. Grosse arrested him on the spot and took him to the Mackinac Island Police Department in City Hall.

Mackinac Island's City Hall and police department were part of the old Michilimackinac County Courthouse that was built in 1839 on Market Street. Michilimackinac County covered the Upper Peninsula and parts of northern lower Michigan until 1849 when the name was changed and the county was legally organized as Mackinac County. Inside the police department were two small jail cells.

During the interview with Spratto at the jail, Strantz gave the detectives permission to search his room again in an effort to prove he had nothing to do with the murder. Kivela, along with two other investigators, headed to the Island House where Strantz was staying. The manager was contacted and she allowed them into the room.

Kivela had taken hair from Mrs. Lacey's body, and he told the detectives to look for a brush or comb as they searched so they could check for hair strands from their suspect. Inside room thirty-six, detectives removed some hair from a brush and comb, and the hair was turned over to Kivela. When Detective Myre looked in the wastebasket, he found a crumpled-up newspaper article from the *Chicago Sun Times,* dated June 12, 1960. The title read "EVANSTON WOMEN TOLD HOW TO PROTECT SELVES." The newspaper clipping was taken and turned over to Bilgen.

There was a reticent sigh of relief. With the discovery of the body and the arrest of Strantz, a quick resolution to the murder of Frances Lacey was starting to take shape. No one could have ever imagined how wrong they were.

9: POSTMORTEM

Spratto and Bilgen met with a reporter from the *Detroit News* at the crime scene the day after the discovery of Frances Lacey's body. Lieutenant Bilgen told the reporter that her body was found in a thickly wooded area under a tangle of cedar and balsam trees, and he allowed a photographer from the *Detroit News* to walk through the crime scene and photograph the area where the widow's body was found, in addition to the boat the shoes were found under. "She was hauled beneath these trees as if to hide her,"[34] Bilgen said. Asked about the immediate arrest of a suspect in the killing, he mentioned they were questioning two men. Spratto was asked how they were able to locate the body, and he told them that the finding of the purse led indirectly to finding the missing woman.

The media, covering developments on the Island, was also interviewing Mrs. Lacey's family, friends, and neighbors back in Dearborn. On the tree-lined shady street near Lafayette and Michigan where Frances Lacey called home, her neighbors were stunned. "She was such a quiet person. She seems out of place in a murder," one neighbor said. They described their murdered neighbor as a woman who mowed her lawn regularly and did small repairs around

---

34. *The Detroit News*, "Mackinac Slaying Search Shifts to Wayne County," July 31, 1960

her neatly kept brick home. One woman said, "You can't not like her. She was that kind of person."[35]

William, dealing with the death of his uncle, and now the murder of his mother, told the *Detroit News*, "While I was on the Island, everyone kept telling me no violence ever occurred there. That can't be said anymore."[36]

***

Word quickly spread of the arrest, and local residents were shocked to hear that Strantz was the number-one suspect. He'd been in several of their homes doing menial jobs just before the disappearance.

After the detectives left the Island House, they headed for the George Davis Funeral Home in St. Ignace.

Less than twenty-four hours after her body was found, the autopsy of Frances Lacey began at 3:00 p.m. on Friday, July 29. The investigators from Lansing were there along with Coroner George Davis.

Before beginning, Detective Myre rolled ink onto Frances Lacey's hands so he could take both her fingerprints and her palm prints. He knew they would have to be used to positively identify her.

Kivela and Webster began by examining the clothing worn by Mrs. Lacey before it was removed. They were looking for trace evidence that could be collected before the clothing was preserved. After the examination and the removal of her clothes, Kivela packaged them as evidence to take back to the laboratory in Lansing.

Performing the autopsy, Dr. Webster carefully looked over the body from head to toe. He noted the body was

---

35. *The Detroit News*, "Killing Hard to Believe, Victim's Neighbors Say," July 29, 1960

36. *The Detroit News*, "Killing Hard to Believe, Victim's Neighbors Say," July 29, 1960

"in a state of moderate post-mortem decomposition."[37] There was a four-day period from the time she was reported missing to the discovery of her body, and her skin had already started to deteriorate around her facial features and ears. There was bruising evident on the left side of her chin, and a small laceration on the right side of her chin that measured 1.3 centimeters. It was just below the angle of her lip. There was a deep, jagged laceration on the upper left side of her head behind the temple region that measured 1.2 centimeters. The doctor noticed the distortion of her lips and tongue, and a heavy infestation of fly larvae in the pharynx.

Some of Mrs. Lacey's head hair was removed quite easily because of the infestation of maggots on her scalp.

Her right shin was scraped from her ankle to her knee with moderate hemorrhaging, and Webster opined they were caused before her death.

She still wore a diamond ring on her left hand, but the investigators noted the absence of a watch on either of her wrists.

Her face was swollen and distorted, and her tongue protruded from her mouth toward the right side. There was a large amount of fly larvae on the body, and the infestation of maggots gave Webster a general idea of the timeline involved in her death; he estimated it was at least thirty-six hours prior to the autopsy and no more than fifty hours.

Frances Lacey's height was measured at sixty-four-and-a-half inches. Her weight was one hundred fifteen pounds.

Looking closer at her neck, Dr. Webster could see obvious bruising. Describing it, he said, "Ecchymosis on the lower anterior of the neck, lateral to the midline, suggests digital application."[38] The bruising was at fingertip intervals, and two of the bruises were in the left clavicle area. One was

37. Webster, J.H. "Autopsy Report of Frances Lacey," July 29, 1960
38. Webster, J.H. "Autopsy Report of Frances Lacey," July 29, 1960

below and the second was above. Whoever killed Frances Lacey had strangled her. "There is a knotted garment about the neck which appears to be of woven synthetic fiber and fastened with a granny knot tightly about the neck."[39] The knot was just to the left of Frances Lacey's trachea, and most of the lividity in the head and neck was above the ligature. The bruising on her neck from the strangulation extended completely from the back of her neck to the front of her trachea and matched the width of the ligature. It became clear that the killer had first used his hands and finished strangling Frances with her own panties.

Dr. Webster took vaginal swabs, and those were sent to Little Traverse Hospital in Traverse City. Continuing with the autopsy protocol, the doctor went step by step. He examined the contents of Frances Lacey's stomach, and he found pieces of cantaloupe and small amounts of pancakes and pieces of bacon. It was the last meal she'd eaten, and he estimated that the time of death occurred less than two hours after the cantaloupe was eaten. This could be crucial evidence in determining where she'd eaten breakfast and at what time.

At the hospital, after an analysis of the vaginal smears, the presence of sperm was detected using the King-Armstrong method. In his autopsy report, Webster wrote, "The high acid phosphatase of this fluid and the fact that ninety-five-percent gave a test specific for prostatic acid phosphatase allows the conclusion that this is seminal fluid. We can make no statement as to the probability of criminal attack."[40]

With obvious evidence of sperm in the laboratory examination, the question was when it was deposited. If motile, or mobile, specimens could be found, it would indicate they were deposited more recently, but in order

39. Webster, J.H. "Autopsy Report of Frances Lacey," July 29, 1960
40. Webster, J.H. "Autopsy Report of Frances Lacey," July 29, 1960

to identify those absolutely, they had to be found with both the head and tail complete. That wasn't the case in Frances Lacey's autopsy. The doctor couldn't conclusively determine if Mrs. Lacey had been raped, or if the evidence was the result of a previous consensual relationship.

In his final analysis, Dr. Webster was able to say that Frances Lacey was strangled, and there was evidence of a head injury prior to death, in addition to having detected sperm in the vaginal smears taken at the autopsy.

Afterward, Detective Myre compared the inked fingerprints he took from the body and the fingerprints taken from Mrs. Lacey's home in Dearborn. He matched the fingerprint from the left thumb of the body with a fingerprint from Mrs. Lacey's home. The body found on Mackinac Island was indeed Frances Lacey.

10: THE HUNT

When the *Mackinac Island Town Crier* broke the story, under the headline "WIDOW'S BEATEN BODY FOUND," a second headline read "BODY AT STONECLIFF; POLICE MAKE ARREST."

Specific details about the arrest of Paul Strantz were withheld from the media in addition to the details about the murder. Corporal Conard explained to the reporters why the bloodhounds weren't of more use, saying, "The reason the bloodhounds called in didn't find the body was because of the rain which washed away the scent and confused the dogs."[41] By that time, word had already spread across the Island like wildfire. Curious onlookers made their way to the murder site along Lake Shore Road after the state police had left the scene. For some, it was out of sadness, while others were satisfying their morbid curiosity.

By late in the day on July 29, just a day after the discovery of the body, Detective Spratto already knew he didn't have enough evidence to hold Paul Strantz for the murder of Frances Lacey. The only suspect in her murder was released.

Tips started to come in as soon as word got out that the Dearborn widow had been murdered, and each one was documented and assigned a number.

One of the first tips reported on July 29 to the Mackinac Island Park Police was that a local carriage driver was

---

41. *Mackinac Island Town Crier*, "Widow's Beaten Body Found," July 31, 1960, p 1

spotted near the location where the body had been found, and the tipster knew the driver had a criminal record. Several detectives from MSP were either on their way to the Island or had already arrived, and it didn't take long for two of them to find the carriage driver. The driver said he'd given a *Detroit Free Press* reporter a ride to the spot where the body was found. The detectives would have to verify his story, and he remembered the reporter had given him a business card. He showed it to the detectives, and a quick check with the reporter confirmed the driver's story.

After checking on the carriage driver's story, the two detectives received word that a glove had been found near the murder scene. They met with a maintenance worker who was assigned to clean up along the Island roadways. On the day after Mrs. Lacey went missing, he was cleaning the side of Lake Shore Road near the pillared gate when he discovered a glove on the east side of the road. The detectives wanted to know the exact location, or as close as the worker could remember. They showed him where pieces of the dentures were found, and he thought it was probably in that area. He'd already picked up the glove and turned it in to the Mackinac Island Police.

After interviewing the worker, the detectives went to the local police and looked at the glove. It looked like a driving glove and gave the appearance that it might have fallen from someone's pocket because it was wrinkled, and they were confident that it wasn't associated with the murder. Islanders and tourists riding along Lake Shore Road were unaware they were being watched by detectives staked out in the area where the body had been found to watch for suspicious activity. There was no information in the police report that any additional follow-up was done to determine where the glove came from.

With the murder investigation just getting started, police focused on employees from local businesses who left the Island suddenly. A dishwasher at the Murray Hotel had quit his job the morning Frances Lacey checked out of the hotel and disappeared. The dishwasher lived in Royal Oak, and detectives called the Detroit MSP Post to have him interviewed.

Bill Rankin* was no stranger to the criminal justice system. His first brush with the law was when he was charged with a break-in at the age of eight. At thirteen, he was charged with arson and sent to the Starr Commonwealth facility near Albion in the hope of rehabilitation before he reached adulthood. When he turned seventeen, he was released, and it didn't take long before he was charged with larceny after stealing thirty dollars from the home of a girlfriend.

Rankin was picked up by Detective Whaley for an interview and taken back to the Detroit Post at Seven Mile Road and Grand River.

On Saturday night, July 23, Rankin worked his dishwashing job at the Murray Hotel from 6:00 p.m. until 10:30. After he left work, he went to his room and changed into some khaki pants, white shirt, and a sweater before walking to Little Bob's Restaurant. After he drank a nonalcoholic punch, he went back to his room around midnight and went to bed.

Whaley knew more about him than Rankin realized. The detective could tell that Rankin was lying when it benefited him. During the five-hour interview, when Whaley pressed him about his lying, Rankin began to cry. At other times, he tried to intimidate the detective by staring at him, but Whaley had years of experience interviewing suspects. He was unimpressed by Rankin's attempts at intimidation. He pressed his suspect more, and Rankin eventually admitted to the lies in his story.

The suspect continued his half-truths. He said he woke up when his roommate came back to the room drunk and vomited. He said he cleaned up the vomit and decided to go back to Little Bob's Restaurant. He drank three chocolate shakes and ate three hamburgers before purchasing a fourth burger to take with him. When he got back to the room, he went back to bed and got up at around 9:00 a.m.

When confronted about leaving the Island to attend his grandfather's funeral, he admitted to Whaley it was a lie, and he only told his boss that story because he wanted to head back home for a couple of days. He took the 10:00 a.m. ferry back to St. Ignace, and there was a waitress he recognized from Little Bob's on the same trip, so they chatted until the ferry docked.

When the interview with Rankin was over, Whaley called Lieutenant Bilgen. Whaley felt there was a possibility that Rankin could be considered a suspect in the Lacey homicide because of his constant lying. Rankin would be returning for a polygraph test. Bilgen assigned a detective to check with the waitress from Little Bob's, and she described Rankin on the ride over to St. Ignace. The last time she saw him, he was hitchhiking outside the resort town.

Just two weeks after Rankin's interrogation about the Lacey murder, he was arrested for breaking into a cottage on Clark Lake near Brighton. The cottage was owned by a friend of Rankin's mother, and on August 12, he was picked up by the Livingston County Sheriff's Office shortly after the break-in. Five days later, Whaley heard about the arrest and asked detectives to interview him a second time about the murder on the Island.

Deputies Winberg and Bensinger sat down in a quiet interview room at the Livingston County Jail in Howell for a second interview with Rankin about Mrs. Lacey's death.

In his second interview, Rankin said he left his home in Royal Oak on June 20 to hitchhike to Mackinac Island to find work. It was around June 25 when he arrived, and he found work washing dishes at both the Murray Hotel and the Island House. He also found work as a caddy on the golf course. He confirmed that he left the Island on the morning of July 24.

As Rankin told his story a second time, he mentioned to the Livingston County deputies that he spoke with the waitress from Little Bob's Restaurant when he recognized her during the ferry ride away from the Island, in addition to a man whose parents owned the Murray Hotel.

By August 2, Rankin returned to the Island. He picked up a paycheck that was owed to him and left the Island for Rudyard, near St. Ignace, to visit a friend he met while working as a caddy. After a quick visit, he hitchhiked to Traverse City and visited his aunt. Later, as he hitchhiked back to Royal Oak on August 12, he was arrested for the break-in at Clark Lake.

The morning after Rankin's interview, deputies contacted Whaley and told him about the interrogation. Rankin had taken a polygraph exam the day after his first interview with investigators and had passed the lie detector test. His alibis were also checked out, and he was cleared as a suspect in the murder.

***

While detectives in Detroit had been interviewing Rankin the first time, Bilgen received a call from the owner of the cottage at British Landing that Leona Shermerhorn was renting. The anonymous caller suspected Mrs. Shermerhorn's younger son, Marvin Fineman, might somehow be involved in the murder. He was a half-brother to Wesley and was staying at the cottage with the family. On the morning of Mrs. Lacey's disappearance, Marvin left British Landing on a bike to ride into the city. He was supposed to be going for some milk, and he called the Murray Hotel before he left to see if Frances had checked out. After making the call, he told everyone at the cottage that she had already checked out of the hotel so he would meet her along Lake Shore Road as he rode into town, but he didn't return until 3:00 p.m. Since the Shermerhorn family had left the Island by the time the tip was received, the follow-up was assigned to detectives in Detroit.

When detectives interviewed Marvin, he said he had called the Murray Hotel on Sunday, July 24, and asked for Mrs. Lacey. He was hoping to catch her before she left, and when he was told she had already checked out, he mentioned that he'd meet her along Lake Shore Road but never found her. He first saw Mrs. Lacey when she arrived at the cabin on Saturday with Kay and Wesley at around 10:00 a.m. They visited at the cabin until around 3:00, and he went back into town with Mrs. Lacey, Kay, and Wesley. They rented horses and rode around for an hour or so, and they stopped on Market Street near the bend by the Grand Hotel and sat on a stone fence. When dinner was discussed, the small group asked him if he'd like to join them, but he declined. He headed back for British Landing, and it was the last time he saw Mrs. Lacey alive.

The next morning, Kay, Wesley, and the others waited on the dock at British Landing for Frances to show up. He thought the time was around 9:00 a.m., and by 11:00, when she hadn't arrived, Kay began to get worried, so they all went back to the cabin to see if she had taken a route other than Lake Shore Road. He said they were all together on the dock and at the cabin, and they didn't notice anything unusual that might have had any bearing on Mrs. Lacey's disappearance. Marvin reiterated the fact that he'd called the Murray Hotel at around 1:00 p.m. and was told by the desk clerk that Mrs. Lacey had checked out at about 10:30 a.m.

There was nothing in Marvin's interview to even remotely connect him to the murder. Afterward, the detectives were left with the feeling that the young high school student was being completely honest in detailing what he'd done on the weekend of the murder and wasn't involved.

***

John Thorne*, a native of Mackinac Island, was an alcoholic, and to many on the Island, he seemed a little odd. He was arrested by the FBI on Mackinac Island on May 17, just two months before the murder, and taken to the Mackinac County Jail in Sault Ste. Marie. On June 2, he was transferred downstate to the Bay County Jail, and on June 26, he was arraigned in federal court on charges of forgery and stealing from the US Mail. After his arraignment, Thorne was released on a five-hundred-dollar personal bond and headed back to the Island. Thorne was also the second person considered a suspect in the Lacey homicide.

When Thorne returned to the Island after his arraignment, he bunked with a friend. He was promised a job by the police chief as a dishwasher at the Lighthouse Restaurant. After starting his job in the kitchen, he moved into room thirty-four at the Lighthouse Inn. He didn't like being cooped up in a restaurant kitchen washing dishes, and he wanted to be out in the fresh air. On July 22, Chief Bloomfield told him about a job with the city, so he quit his job as a dishwasher. He was certain he'd get the one-dollar-and-fifty-cent per hour job working for the local government. On Saturday morning, he reported for the new job, but he was told the man he was supposed to replace had returned so the job wasn't available anymore.

Thorne took it all in stride. He knew he had an appointment at the Federal Prison on July 26 anyway, so he decided to hang around the city streets and chat with the carriage drivers for the day. Later that evening, he and his cousin took a boat over to Round Island, a small island just to the south. They were looking for some friends but didn't find them, and when they returned to Mackinac Island, Thorne was thirsty. He borrowed three dollars from a cab driver he knew, and he headed for the Palms Café for a beer. It was after midnight by the time he got back to the Lighthouse Inn and fell asleep.

Thorne was awake on Sunday, July 24, by 8:30 a.m. A half hour later, he was eating breakfast at the Chuckwagon Café and chatting with the waitress. When he left the café, he stood around the street talking with the carriage drivers before grabbing another cup of coffee from the Chuckwagon at about 10:00. Thorne seemed to know a lot of the carriage drivers. There were even a couple of retired cops from Detroit who drove carriages on the Island and knew him. While he seemed to know everybody, he never had any money, and he wasn't afraid to ask a friend or acquaintance for a couple of dollars to grab a meal.

At around 4:30 p.m., he borrowed three dollars from another friend and headed to Ty's Restaurant for dinner. After hanging around the streets for the rest of the evening, he ran into Chief Bloomfield. Bloomfield asked him if he wanted to help in the search for a missing tourist on the Island that was going to start in the morning and Thorne agreed. He told the chief he'd report at 7:00 a.m.

The next morning, Chief Bloomfield was meeting with the rest of the volunteers to begin searching for Frances Lacey, but Thorne never showed.

As the search for the missing widow continued all day and into the evening, Thorne was seen hanging around the streets again, and at around 8:00 p.m., he borrowed a dollar from a friend so he could take the ferry to Mackinaw City. Another friend picked him up and drove him to Bay City so he could make his court appearance on Tuesday morning.

It was 3:00 a.m. when the two arrived. They slept in the car until around 6:00, and at 9:00, Thorne showed up at the Federal Building. Later that day, he was sentenced to federal prison in Milan, Michigan.

***

By July 30, two days after the body was found, police were still no closer to identifying a specific suspect.

Police learned from Kay that there was a matching jacket to Mrs. Lacey's skirt, and it hadn't been found with the body. They considered it missing, and in the hope of finding it, Bilgen made an appeal to the public. "If we can find the jacket, it might give us the lead that we've been looking for," he said. He was hoping for even the smallest bit of information that could help. "Any information, no matter how insignificant it may seem." He was hopeful that whoever murdered Mrs. Lacey was still on the Island. "We're looking for something that may indicate the killer is still on the Island," he added.[42]

Everyone on the Island was hesitant and fearful. Women were startled at the slightest sounds, and the murder was already starting to haunt the Island. The islanders knew about the 1910 murder that was still unsolved.

At the docks, detectives watched outgoing passengers for any behavior that looked suspicious by either Island residents or employees who were working on the Island for the summer.

***

That same Saturday morning, the Operations Division of MSP in East Lansing called the Mackinac Island Post to pass on information about another person who they felt should be checked out. According to the information they had, the person either had mental problems or was an alcoholic; maybe he was both.

Philip Goethal, an employee at the Lansing television station WJIM, had either been fired or quit his job; Operations didn't know specifically. He was staying on

---

42. *The Detroit News*, "Woman's Trip to Tragedy is Retraced on Mackinac," July 30, 1960

Mackinac Island at the time of the murder, and as troopers started to check his background, they found a couple of aliases that he used. They also learned he was staying in a cottage behind Sainte Anne's Catholic Church.

When police found the cottage, the owner told them she didn't have anyone by that name staying there. The only way he might be staying there was if the two boys renting the cottage would have allowed him to bunk there. She let the officers look around inside, and they found a suitcase with the name Philip Goethal on it. She said the boys who were renting the cottage worked at the Astore Café on Main Street.

Both boys were found at the restaurant and interviewed about their guest. The teens were juniors at Gaylord High School and had several days off from the restaurant, beginning on Sunday, July 24. They decided to grab a ferry to the mainland, and they hitchhiked the sixty-five miles home for their time off. The two boys made it about ten miles south of Mackinaw City when they were picked up by Philip Goethal. He drove them the rest of the fifty or so miles to Gaylord.

Goethal was very talkative along the way and said he worked at WJIM-TV in Lansing. He'd been on Mackinac Island since July 22, and he had just left around 5:30 p.m.

The boys were hesitant. They thought he was weird, but the more he talked, the more they began to like him.

Goethal was on the Island for several days and he ran out of money. He decided he was going back to Lansing to quit his job at WJIM because he worked too many hours. As the boys listened intently, he said he'd be back to the Island the following day and asked if they knew of a cheap place he could rent for several weeks. The boys had to be back to work on Monday evening, and they offered their cabin to Goethal. He accepted, and since he was heading back north, he offered to pick them up in Gaylord and give them a ride back.

On Monday, holding true to his word, Goethal picked up the teens around 4:15 p.m., and the three headed back to Mackinac Island. As the investigators pressed the boys for any small bit of information their driver might have offered, they remembered that during the ride, Goethal said he had tried to stay at the Iroquois Hotel when he originally got to the Island on July 22, but there wasn't a room available. Instead, he stayed at the Windemere, but he ended up spending at least some of his time at the Iroquois. The two teens said that after they settled back into the cabin, they didn't see their chauffeur very much but had played some golf with him at one point.

The officers knew Mrs. Lacey's watch was missing, so they asked if the boys had seen any jewelry of any sort that Goethal might have had, but they hadn't.

After interviewing the two teens, detectives headed to the Iroquois Hotel. The owner, Sam McIntyre, remembered Goethal but didn't know him by name. He couldn't remember which day he'd been to the hotel asking about a room, but he did recall that Goethal had eaten at the Iroquois several times. McIntyre had seen him several times at the bar.

The Windemere Hotel was the next stop for the police. The Doud family had owned the Windemere since 1904 and were prominent citizens on Mackinac Island. Robert Doud was happy to help and checked the registry. He found that Goethal had rented a room on the evening of July 22, but he checked out on July 23. The officers mentioned that Goethal worked for WJIM in Lansing, and Mr. Doud quickly remembered the guest. He said Goethal checked out at noon, but he left his bag at the hotel while he went swimming at the Grand Hotel pool. To Mr. Doud, Goethal seemed a bit odd.

The investigators also spoke with another person who met Goethal while they swam in Lake Huron on July 26. He also thought Goethal seemed a bit odd, and he was always talking about his job at WJIM. The officers asked if there was any discussion about the missing woman on the Island, and he said it was mentioned, but nothing much was said after that.

That was as far as the officers could track Goethal. Like so many of the other tips that had started pouring in, the information was documented, and it would be assigned for more investigation later.

It was later that afternoon when Goethal heard that the police wanted to question him, so he stopped by the MSP office at the Coast Guard Station. It was a prime opportunity to interview him about his activities a week prior, and the detectives already knew he'd been on the Island for eight days or so.

Now a person of interest, Philip Goethal said he came to Mackinac Island on July 22. He was under a lot of pressure at the television station, so he quit his job and came to the Island for some rest and relaxation. With twenty-seven dollars to his name, he took a room at the Windemere Hotel. That night, he started drinking. In fact, he drank to excess.

The next day, he decided to leave. His brother-in-law lived in Wisconsin, and he was going to make the drive there to see him. After he took the ferry to St. Ignace, he drove for about a half hour before changing his mind. In his own mind, he thought one more night on the Island would be good for him since he was still under a lot of stress.

Short on money, he called his dad in Lansing to see if he would wire him some cash. His dad wired twenty-five dollars so he could stay one more night.

Goethal met a girl that evening on the Island. They went dancing at the Grand Hotel, spent the night together on the beach west of the city, and at around 4:00 a.m., she left and headed back to her hotel while he slept until around 6:00.

Walking back into town, he ended up on the coal dock, then headed to Little Bob's Restaurant for some breakfast. He was going to go to mass at Ste. Anne's church but it was still early. He walked to the Grand Hotel and back just in time for the service. It was 9:15 when the mass ended, and he headed back to the Iroquois to get a towel so he could go swimming at the Grand Hotel. After his swim, he drank two or three cups of coffee, and he ended up on the lawn of the luxurious hotel where he fell asleep for a couple of hours. He said when he woke, he ended up back at the bar but only had twenty-eight cents in his pocket so he drank ice water and ate peanuts. He was hoping to find the woman he'd spent the night with so he could borrow some money and head back to Lansing to close his bank accounts.

Goethal waited as he chatted with a waitress. He finally saw his female companion from the previous night, and he borrowed five dollars so he could get back to Lansing. It was the evening of July 24.

Back in Lansing by the following morning, he closed his accounts. He was still owed money from a former employer, and he picked up the twenty-five dollars he was owed before he headed back to the Island later that day. Goethal said he wasn't one to pass up an opportunity, and on Thursday, he left Mackinac Island again to head to Detroit for a job prospect. By Saturday, July 30, he was back on Mackinac Island again.

Goethal was completely cooperative with the detectives, and after the interview, he agreed to have the detectives come with him as he left the Island and headed to his car in St. Ignace so they could search it. They found nothing of significance.

***

Fear blanketed Mackinac Island.

The cabin where Kay and Wesley were staying was owned by Helen Worley*. On Saturday night, just two days after Frances Lacey's body was found, Mrs. Worley changed her usual routine. For the first time ever, rather than walk back to her home from town, she took a carriage taxi instead. "It's the first time in our lives we ever did that. It never occurred to us to be afraid before," she said.[43]

Islanders and tourists alike were on edge. The police had questioned one man and had even detained Paul Strantz, but he'd been released and was back on the streets. Everyone was suspect.

Given the four days between the disappearance and the discovery of the body, police theorized that if the killer was a transient, he likely had time to escape the Island before Mrs. Lacey's body was found.

While Islanders and tourists watched over their shoulders and took extra precautions, reporters began to wonder if there was a connection to another gruesome triple murder at a state park in Illinois.

***

The first mention of a connection to the Starved Rock murders was during a briefing between the detectives working the Lacey homicide on July 30. The triple murder at an Illinois state park had been front-page headlines across the country four months earlier, and whoever had committed the murders in Illinois was still at large. Investigators began to wonder if the killer responsible for the Starved Rock murders could have struck again, this time in a Michigan state park?

On March 14, three socially prominent women from Riverside, Illinois, decided to take a few days away and go hiking at the year-round Starved Rock State Park in Ottawa, Illinois. The park was set along the Illinois River about one

---

43. *The Detroit News*, "Slain Woman's Relatives First Tenants in Cottage," July 31, 1960

hundred miles southwest of Chicago and consisted of over fourteen hundred acres of trails and canyons.

All three women had been well thought of in their community. They were married to prominent businessmen and were devoted to their church and other community activities. Two of the three were already grandmothers, and together, they all attended the Presbyterian Church in Riverside. Through their shared friendship, they had several things in common, but their most common interest was a love of the outdoors. They all loved hiking. After checking in at the park lodge, even before unpacking their luggage, the three set out on the trails for an early spring hike.

By mid-week, no one had heard from the three women, and police theorized they might have fallen from one of the cliffs in the park.

One of several search teams sent out to look for the women found their badly beaten bodies lying close together just inside the mouth of a cave in French Canyon, and heavy snow had drifted around the entrance to the sandstone cave. Two of the women were nude from the waist down, and the third still wore a girdle. Their skulls were crushed and bruises covered their bodies from being beaten. Two of the friends were lying side by side, while the third was lying four feet away. All three were lying face up.

Because of the knee-deep snow around the mouth of the cave, police used a flame thrower to melt it in an attempt to find any evidence that might help identify a killer.[44] Blood drops were found leading to the cave, and inside, investigators found streaks of blood. They were almost certain the women had been raped, and they couldn't rule out the possibility there could have been more than one attacker.[45]

---

44. *Galesburg Register*, "Police Search for Murder Clues, Use Flame Thrower," March 17, 1960, p 1

45. *Mt. Vernon Register*, "Melt Snow for Murder," March 17, 1960, p 1

As the area was searched for clues, a four-inch-diameter, blood-stained tree limb was found six feet from the entrance to the sandstone cave. Police also found lengths of red cord tied around two of the victims' wrists.[46]

With the investigation into the Starved Rock murders just beginning, police received a tip about two possible suspects, and they were immediately picked up for questioning but quickly released. By Wednesday night, police had questioned at least six different men, some with scratches on their faces who were stopped at roadblocks in the area of the park as police continued to check with homeowners who lived nearby.

With the limited information that police had, one theory was that the three women had been cornered by their killer or killers in an area of the park where there was only one way out. As fear spread in the area, homeowners imposed their own curfews for their own safety.

As the first few days of the investigation into the Starved Rock murders passed, authorities planned to conduct the largest mass fingerprinting of men in the state's history in an effort to find the killer. They planned to fingerprint five hundred or more people who were employed by the state or as concessionaires in the park and included the road gangs that worked in the area.

By Friday, word had leaked to the media that bloody fingerprints were found on the clothing of the victims, and the fingerprinting would include all the men who'd been questioned up to that point.[47]

As Michigan investigators poured over the meager clues they had thus far in the Lacey murder, they had to consider the possibility that there could be a connection between the Starved Rock murders and the murder of Frances Lacey.

---

46. *Moline Daily Dispatch*, "Blood-Stained Limb and Cord Are Only Clues," March 17, 1960, p 1

47. *Chicago Tribune,* "Mass Finger Printing May Find Triple Killer," March 17, 1960, p 1

It was common knowledge that the police had already interviewed two men for "more than routine questioning" in the Starved Rock murders.[48] The Michigan detectives knew they'd have to wait for more information to arrive from Illinois to compare them with the Island murder.

***

Corporal Fantini was working the desk at the St. Ignace Post on July 31 when the phone rang. He scribbled notes, listening intently to a trooper on the other end of the line. Someone had called the Bridgeport Post and reported to Captain Ralph Kasten that he was on the Island with his family on July 26, just two days after Mrs. Lacey's disappearance. He saw a blue woman's shoe in the water near a log, and he also saw a pair of men's tennis shoes that were tucked under a log on the beach. There was a snorkel floating in the water, and he took the snorkel home with him when they left but didn't take the shoes. After reading an article about the discovery of Frances Lacey's body, he realized it was in the same general area where she was found.

When Fantini hung up the phone, he made a call to the Coast Guard Station on the Island and spoke with Corporal Conard to pass on the information.

Trooper Grosse was given the information, and he headed to the area where, only days before, police had made their grim discovery.

Grosse and a volunteer officer checked the shoreline and waters along the beach area, and much to his surprise, there was a woman's grey suede shoe on top of a log in the shallow beach waters. It could easily be mistaken for blue. It was nine-and-a-half inches long and three-and-three-

---

48. *Galesburg Register*, "Two Face Questioning for Triple Slayings at Park," March 19, 1960, p 1

quarters inches wide. A quick check along the beach for the men's tennis shoes proved fruitless.

The only way to know if the women's shoe belonged to the murder victim would be to send it to the Redford Post and have a detective show it to Mrs. Lacey's family, but first, it would have to be sent to the crime laboratory for analysis.

Bilgen told the press that the discovery of the shoe was only a minor phase of the investigation, but the media reported that it could be the key to the murder. Since the men's tennis shoes weren't found, the news report accurately stated there were three shoes of interest and a pair of men's tennis shoes that "may exist only in the colored imaginations of vacationing children."[49] They were referring to the shoes found at the murder scene that were tucked under the bow of an overturned rotting rowboat and the most recent single shoe found on the log in the water near the murder scene.

As Bilgen spoke to the media, he mentioned that they hadn't found any men's shoes. The fact that Frances Lacey was barefoot when her body was found still puzzled MSP. Until the one gray suede woman's shoe was found, the dress shoes found under the boat were the only shoes found that were associated with the murder victim. He wondered if it was possible that the shoes found under the boat might be the shoes the victim was wearing. It was possible that she stopped to take them off, placed them in a bag she had, and continued her walk to British Landing. Bilgen was hoping the family might help solve that small portion of the investigation by identifying the gray suede shoe found on the log as one of Frances Lacey's.

***

49. *Detroit Free Press*, "Shoes May Prove the Key to Mystery on Mackinac," August 2, 1960

The owner of the Grand Hotel was a tall and imposing man who wore tailored suits. He carried a walking stick, and he was certain the killer couldn't be a resident of Mackinac Island. W. Stewart Woodfill was also the chairman of the Mackinac Island State Park Commission. He started his career at the grandiose resort as a desk clerk when he was twenty-three. When the hotel's owner died, he was already in a position as the hotel manager, and with a couple investors, he tried to buy it. That attempt fell through and Woodfill sold out to the other investors. During the Great Depression, the hotel was put up for auction because it was in receivership. W. Stewart Woodfill was the only bidder, and he became the new owner. An article in the *Saturday Evening Post* just one month before the murder of Frances Lacey described him as "a feudal prince whose realm was Mackinac Island."[50]

The *Saturday Evening Post* may have been right in their descriptor. "There is no murderer among my people," he said. "It's ridiculous to hint such a thing."[51]

In an article about the widow's murder, *The Detroit News* wrote: "An angry vibrance is the usual dispassionate voice of Woodfill. It betrays his regret that gallows justice disappeared from Mackinac Island 129 years ago."[52]

W. Stewart Woodfill was passionate about Mackinac Island, and he considered it a Michigan shrine. He made certain that hotel guests weren't disturbed by the ongoing murder investigation. Day-to-day activities continued in spite of the Island murder, and at the end of each day, he left the resort to walk to the house where he lived alone, and the front door remained unlocked.

---

50. Cawthorne, *Mackinac Island: Inside, Up Close, and Personal*

51. *The Detroit News*, "Murder-Stunned Mackinac Clings to Storied Ways," July 31, 1960

52. *Detroit Free Press*, "Shoes May Prove the Key to Mystery on Mackinac," August 2, 1960

"This was done by some animal from either shore. My people may be rough in horseplay and adept with their bare knuckles in a dispute, but their courtesy to outsiders is a tradition," he said.[53]

The chairman of the Mackinac Island State Park Commission believed that whoever had murdered Mrs. Lacey had invaded the sanctity of Michigan's Victorian treasure and "struck among the gentle and the innocent."[54]

***

The colored photo of Arch Rock was beautiful, and the postmark showed it was mailed from Mackinac Island on July 26, 1960. The handwritten postcard was brief. "Hi. Just a line to say hello. A friend always."

Two days later, the card arrived at the Ionia State Reformatory and was addressed to an inmate, but there was no signature. The inmate quickly recognized the handwriting and knew immediately it was from another inmate with the last name of Austin.

Eight months before the murder of Frances Lacey, Austin had been released from the Ionia State Hospital on an extended visiting leave. He was originally committed to the Reformatory as a criminal sexual psychopath, and when he first arrived, electric shock therapy was used in an effort to tranquilize him. Some of the doctors at the state hospital felt that Austin was still psychotic and capable of committing any type of sexual attack, including murder in some sort of sadistic way because he was a homosexual. Their assumptions were merely a product of the times. Whenever he had been involved in assaultive behavior

---

53. *Detroit Free Press*, "Shoes May Prove the Key to Mystery on Mackinac," August 2, 1960

54. *The Detroit News*, "Murder-Stunned Mackinac Clings to Storied Ways," July 31, 1960

before, he had always claimed he couldn't remember what he'd done.

While state troopers were talking with the doctor at the State Reformatory, they learned a second postcard had been received by one of the attendants at the Reformatory. He received a postcard on July 28 from Mackinac Island, and it was from Austin, but he wasn't surprised or suspicious about the card. He'd received another one about a week before, and Austin mentioned to him that he was going on vacation. It was obvious he went to Mackinac Island. The troopers explained that their questioning was regarding the murder of Frances Lacey, and the Reformatory attendant said he didn't think Austin was capable of anything like that. Still, he offered the postcard to the troopers to take with them.

When Bilgen was told about the postcard, he contacted the Jackson Post. A detective and two troopers headed to the home of Austin's parents and asked if they would be willing to come to the MSP Post for an interview.

The couple told the troopers they left Jackson around 5:00 a.m. on July 23 and were headed to Mackinaw City. Some friends of the family went along, as did their son. When they arrived at noon, they checked in at the Ottawa Motel and got two rooms. After grabbing lunch, they took the 2:00 p.m. ferry to the Island.

Austin's parents decided to walk around and see the sights while their son took a carriage ride around the Island with the other couple. By 4:30, they returned, and the small group of tourists continued their stroll around the downtown area until 6:30 when they took the ferry to St. Ignace. They took a bus across the still-new Mackinac Bridge back to Mackinaw City where their car was parked. On the morning of July 24, they headed back to Jackson and only stopped once for dinner at the Embers Restaurant near Mt. Pleasant.

The officers interviewed Austin separately. He had been an inmate at Ionia for eleven years. He was due to report back in early August, and his hope was that he might be released at that point. He added that each time he reported back, he had to have a reevaluation.

Austin admitted to mailing the postcards from the Island on July 23. As they were all waiting to board the ferry to St. Ignace, he had handed four postcards to the dock attendant and asked him to mail them for him because he couldn't find a postbox.

The officers knew that at least one of the cards had a postmark from July 26. When asked about it, Austin told them he was back in Jackson by then because he had to work on July 25.

Following up on Austin's story, the officers checked with the construction company he worked with and confirmed he had been at work on July 25. The likely explanation for the postcard dated July 26 was that the dock attendant hadn't mailed them on July 23 when Austin had asked him to.

The couple who had gone on the short trip with the Austins were interviewed too, and they said their son was with them the entire time they were on Mackinac Island.

***

The investigation into the Lacey homicide started to widen and literally spread across the entire state. Interviews were being done in several places by Saturday.

The lead investigators received a phone call from the crime lab in Lansing suggesting they find out which hotels served cantaloupe for breakfast. During Mrs. Lacey's autopsy, the doctor had found remnants of cantaloupe in her stomach along with remnants of pancakes and bacon. It was clear she had dined on that for breakfast. Maybe it would give the detectives a starting point in tracking her movements around the Island on the morning of July 24.

Although there were twenty-two restaurants on the Island, it made sense to start with the Murray since that's where Mrs. Lacey had been staying.

To a tourist walking into the lobby, the old-world charm still resonated in the hotel décor. The front desk sat along the left side in the lobby area, and a large staircase leading to the second floor was to the right. Beyond the front desk and staircase was a small dining area and lounge.

The restaurant opened at 8:00 a.m. on July 24, and a waitress at the Murray checked the breakfast tabs in the dining room for that day. She found one person had ordered cantaloupe, pancakes, bacon, and coffee. Detective Sobolewski, now assigned to the case with another detective from a neighboring post, showed her the picture of Mrs. Lacey. She paused and said the picture resembled a woman who'd eaten breakfast in the restaurant on Sunday morning, but she couldn't be certain. It was possible that she'd eaten there, but the detectives wanted to check the other local restaurants.

The two detectives moved on to the Astor Café only to find cantaloupe wasn't on the menu.

They moved to the Buggy Whip Café. Cantaloupe was served there, but they never kept their breakfast tabs, so the two detectives weren't able to find out if Mrs. Lacey had dined there.

There was a much more pressing follow-up that had to be done, so the two investigators decided they'd continue checking the other restaurants later. Since the Murray Hotel served cantaloupe, it was more likely that she probably did eat breakfast there, but they'd finish checking the other eateries later.

***

The two detectives moved from checking menus at the local restaurants to collecting names and addresses of employees at various hotels, shops, and restaurants around the Island, including the famous Grand Hotel.

During the afternoon of July 31, Lieutenant Bilgen received a phone call from Dr. Webster. His findings from the autopsy were complete, though his report wouldn't be available for a few days. He told Bilgen that after further testing of the vaginal swabs taken from the post-mortem exam, it was clear that Frances Lacey had been raped.

Bilgen also discovered that the missing jacket similar to Mrs. Lacey's skirt never existed, and he clarified it with the press, saying, "Her skirt was aquamarine and had no matching jacket. The bluish suit we thought she had been wearing was found in a closet at her home."[55]

Frances Lacey's son, William, already had a theory about his mother's murder. "I think whoever did this must have come up behind Mom and hit her," he said. "She would have given him money freely if she had been given the chance, because Dad always told her that if she were being robbed, 'Give the money away. You can always replace it.'"[56]

The investigation was just beginning.

***

Three days after the discovery of the body, the media pressed for updates on the investigation and whether or not there were any suspects. On Monday, August 1, Corporal Conard said that "seven or eight" suspects had been questioned and released. "We are open to any information anybody might

55. *The Detroit News*, "Mackinac Slaying Search Shifts to Wayne County," July 31, 1960

56. *The Detroit News*, "Murder-Stunned Mackinac Clings to Storied Ways," July 31, 1960

have, no matter how meager it is," [57] he said. By that time, police were certain Frances Lacey was killed on July 24, the day she was reported missing, and she was raped before being strangled with her own panties.

***

Chief Lloyd Hart didn't think too much of the driver's comment when he made it. The Onaway police chief had stopped the maroon 1949 Chevy for a traffic violation, and as he talked to the driver, he learned the man had been on Mackinac Island but was now heading to Port Huron. As the two men casually talked, their conversation turned to the murder of the wealthy widow on the Island. The driver casually said, "Anybody could choke a woman with underclothes."[58]

When the car drove away, the chief drove back to his office. Maybe the driver's impromptu statement was just a coincidence, or maybe the killer had slipped up and inadvertently implicated himself in the murder. Either way, the chief knew he had to pass the information on to detectives working the case.

The driver was working for a construction company that had contracted with the Grand Hotel. After Detective Sobolewski received the information about the comments made to the Onaway chief, he checked with the hotel, and all of the construction employees working on the Island were staying at the Island House Hotel.

Sobolewski headed there, and he was able to track down the driver who'd made the statement to Chief Hart. He said he left the Island on July 22 at 5:30 p.m. It was a day before

57. *Battle Creek Enquirer*, "No Suspects Left in Widow's Slaying," August 1, 1960

58. Hofmann, L. N. "Supplemental Report." *Michigan State Police*, August 3, 1960

Mrs. Lacey even arrived on the Island. He didn't return to the Island until Monday, July 25, at around 7:00 a.m., and he spent the night before at his parents' house. He went to church on Sunday morning and spent the afternoon picking berries with his parents.

After some checking with the man's parents, his story was confirmed. He was just making an arbitrary comment to the chief while they were talking about the murder. The tip had seemed promising, but it was another dead end.

***

As tips were recorded and handed out for follow-up investigation, Sergeant Burnette still needed Kay Sutter to identify the shoes found under the bow of the rotting boat near Mrs. Lacey's body. They'd already been checked for fingerprints at the crime lab, and none were found. The sergeant packed the shoes up and mailed them to Lieutenant Whaley at the Detroit Post. Whaley would take them directly to the Sutters.

After the identification of the shoes, Whaley returned them to the St. Ignace Post so they could be stored with the other evidence.

The purse that was found on the Island was shown to Kay Sutter too. She knew immediately it belonged to her mom, but the wallet was missing. Her mom had a Lady Buxton wallet the color of a blue jay. The wallet had a detachable picture folder and a change pocket on the inside. A strap around the end of the wallet secured it once it was closed. Kay said the wallet likely had less than forty dollars in it, and her mom had bought it from the Holden Red Stamp Store.

Frances also had two watches, and Kay was trying to remember which one she'd been wearing on the Island. It wasn't found on the body, and they needed a description of it. After finding the second watch at home, Kay was certain the missing watch was a Benrus and would have had a woven yellow gold chain band with a clasp. She thought the watch was about eighteen years old and was certain that at one time it had been repaired by a jeweler. The investigators knew they'd have to track down the store where the repairs were done to get a more detailed description. They were now working under the assumption that the killer must have taken the watch when he murdered the Dearborn widow.

***

Each day new tips were called in, and MSP received a call from police in Indiana about a man coming into a gas station on July 21. He bought four new tires and had them put on his car. The next day, he came in again and bought four more new tires to put on another car. He told the mechanic that he was in a hurry because he was going to an island. On the evening of July 24, he called the gas station and wanted to know if he could cash a one-hundred-dollar check, but the clerk told him he couldn't. He called again the following morning, and he still wanted to cash the one-hundred-dollar check. He was told again that he couldn't, and he asked if the mechanic wanted to buy a good lady's watch. The mechanic didn't think too much of the conversation until he saw the story of Mrs. Lacey's murder on the news. He told investigators that the man left the gas station after being told he couldn't cash the check, and he went to a drug store across the street and cashed a one-hundred-fifty-dollar check. It turned out that check was bad.

The Michigan investigators were intrigued, and a call was made to the Indiana State Police. Since the Michigan case involved a homicide, the ISP would continue the follow-up investigation on their end.

As the media pressed MSP each day for more information, Bilgen told them, "We're digging hard. This case is wide open."[59]

---

59. *Detroit Free Press*, "Find Widow Was Attacked," August 1, 1960

11: MORAL RE-ARMAMENT

Mostly a Protestant movement, the Moral Re-Armament movement was criticized by some Catholics yet praised by others. Originally called the Oxford Group, the name was later changed to the MRA.

Frank Buchman, a former Lutheran pastor from Pennsylvania, was a lecturer in personal evangelism at the Hartford Seminary Foundation in Connecticut. When he left his position in 1922 to begin a non-denominational movement with a goal to strengthen the spiritual lives of others, his new path was based on a person's guidance from moral absolutes.

Moving to Princeton University, he hosted discussions with students who confessed their sexual matters publicly. After word spread about the discussions, he was asked to leave the university. He left Princeton, and his movement took up residence at Oxford University in England. With each conference that was held, the movement began to grow and become more successful. By 1938, the name was changed from the Oxford Group to the Moral Re-Armament movement as conferences were held around the globe.

The movement continued to flourish, and Buchman tried to make it more appealing by including more faiths. He believed that by people experiencing a moral and spiritual awakening, conflict and war could be avoided. After World War II, the MRA was already known worldwide, and to spread its word, the group presented theatrical productions that emphasized cooperation, honesty, and mutual respect between opposing groups.[60]

The MRA mantra was simple. Moral absolutes were the basis of their beliefs and included purity, unselfishness, honesty, and love, while absolutely opposing communism.

Frank Buchman's MRA grew to a point where the group had headquarters in Switzerland, Japan, New York, and on Mackinac Island, Michigan.

In 1942, the first MRA conference was held at the Grand Hotel, but more room was needed, so they rented the vacant and crumbling Island House Hotel. In the years that followed, the conferences became so successful that by 1954, the group purchased several parcels of land at Mission Point on the southeast corner of the Island.

Over the next several years, the MRA began construction at Mission Point. The first building was an eight-hundred-seat theatre that was used for the theatrical productions the group produced. Other structures included the Great Hall, featuring a cylindrical lobby, a large brick dormitory, and a film studio.

Just two weeks after the murder of Frances Lacey, celebrities from Hollywood who were followers of the movement visited the MRA Training Center on the Island. Lloyd Nolan, Victor Jory, Marvin Miller, Patrick McVey, Sheb Wooley, and Beaulah Bondi all flew to the Island airport on a special plane from Hollywood for their stay on the MRA grounds.

It was estimated that by 1960, the MRA had purchased at least twenty percent of the land not owned by the state parks on Mackinac Island, and there was a rumor that they had the Grand Hotel in their sights for a future purchase.[61] Devotees of the MRA became regulars on Mackinac Island

---

60. "Moral Re-Armament (MRA)." Encyclopedia Britannica, https://www.britannica.com/event/Moral-Re-Armament

61. Cawthorne, *Mackinac Island: Inside, Up Close, and Personal*

while suspicion and division among the local Islanders continued to grow. With a member of the MRA on the Mackinac Island City Council, there was fear of a political and economic takeover.[62]

One of the prime pieces of real estate acquired by the MRA sat on a stone bluff along the west side of Mackinac Island with an all-encompassing view of Lake Huron. It was the only stone structure on the Island and retained an opulent appearance with elaborate paintings, furniture, and carpet, and it was called Stonecliff. It included two ballrooms, a private bowling alley, stables, barns, and even some smaller quarters for employees.

Stonecliff was originally owned by Alvin Hert. Hert was from Louisville, Kentucky, and became wealthy through the sale of creosote. Together with his wife, Sallie, the couple often entertained politicians at their vacation estate, and it was so beautiful that at one point in the late '20s, after his death, Stonecliff was offered as the summer White House to President Calvin Coolidge, but he turned it down.

The Michigan State Park Commission tried to purchase Stonecliff in 1942 as a summer residence for Michigan's governor, but Sallie Hert refused to sell. After Mrs. Hert's death three years later, the mansion and grounds were left to the Episcopal Diocese of Washington, DC, and later sold to the MRA as a guest lodge.

Still owned by the MRA in 1960, no one ever imagined that Stonecliff would take center stage in the Lacey homicide investigation.[63]

Within a day of the body being found, police were back at the crime scene searching for more clues and followed a trail up through the woods that led to the sprawling estate. Four gardeners working for the MRA were in the large yard.

---

62. Cawthorne, *Mackinac Island: Inside, Up Close, and Personal*

63. *Mackinac Island Town Crier*, "Stonecliff is Setting for Murder Mystery," August 7, 1960

They were questioned by the detectives about guests at the estate over the previous weekend, and one of the men said a couple had stayed at Stonecliff on the night of July 23.

Police were able to track the couple down, and they said they stayed there on July 23, but they were alone. They didn't see or hear anything the following morning, and they left the property around 10:00 a.m. After the discovery of the victim's body on the property, they said they saw some trespassers, but they turned out to be members of the media who were later seen trying to find out information about the murder.

***

Ten days before the murder, Pete Marudas was riding a bike up Lake Shore Road on his way to British Landing. A woman and her two children were riding along near him as they passed the stone-pillared gate marked PRIVATE PROPERTY that led to Stonecliff, and just after passing the gate, they saw a nude man sitting near one of the beach houses along the shore of Lake Huron. Marudas stopped and confronted him, demanding he either put pants on or leave the area.

The tall man apologized profusely. "He wasn't belligerent and said he didn't realize he was so close to the road," Marudas said. The *Town Crier* reporter detected what he thought was a British accent when he spoke with the man. After the brief confrontation, he slipped on black trousers and continued making his way down the beach.

Now that the body of the missing tourist had been found on the MRA property near the pillared gate, Pete Marudas knew he should report his encounter to the police.

Detective McCluer and an officer from the Mackinac Island Police took Marudas back to the area to see if he could point out the beach house near which he'd seen the nude man. The three men looked around but nothing was found near the one he identified. Checking across the road, they followed the same trail up the hill, moving inland. At the top of the hill, the gate to Stonecliff was open. The investigators walked through, and the trail picked up again, cutting to the right. Continuing on, they discovered the trail came back out on Lake Shore Road near the pillared gates where the body was found, and it looked like the trail had been recently used. Walking back up to Stonecliff, they found an MRA employee. He said the gate they had come through was the same gate where he'd seen a man on a bike just a few days earlier asking for directions. He was looking for the airport, and after he was told which direction to go, the MRA employee asked the man if Mrs. Lacey had been found. The man hesitated before answering, and eventually said he hadn't heard whether she'd been found or not and left on the bike.

It was another small piece to the puzzle, and Detective McCluer knew he had to find the man who'd been on the beach naked.

***

If the detectives working the case weren't checking out specific tips assigned to them, they were in the downtown area trying to find anyone who might have seen Frances Lacey before she was murdered.

Detective Sobolewski stopped to talk with some of the carriage drivers, and he found one of the drivers who had worked on July 23, the same day Mrs. Lacey arrived at the Island. Sobolewski showed him the photo and he recognized her. He said he recalled seeing her on July 23, but the only time he had seen her was when she crossed the street in front of his carriage as she walked from the docks toward the Murray Hotel. He worked on July 24 but didn't make any runs on Lake Shore Road.

There was something odd about the carriage driver but the detective couldn't put his finger on it. As their discussion deepened into talking about the possibility that Mrs. Lacey was raped, he told Sobolewski that he masturbated at least once a day, and on several occasions, he had sex with his horse, Judy. The last time was about ten days before. The detective couldn't help but wonder why anyone would offer that type of information during questioning about an ongoing murder investigation.

Sobolewski found a second carriage driver who worked just as a cab; he wasn't allowed to give tours around the Island. He mentioned to the detective that he had a year-round residence on the Island, and his father was the former city marshal, O.J. Smith.

The detective quickly learned that the younger Smith was the same man who had taken Mrs. Lacey and her party to the British Landing. He recalled Mrs. Lacey, Kay, Wesley, and Merry, Wesley's younger sister.

Smith thought it was around 8 or 9:00 a.m. on July 23 when he'd picked up the party to take them up to British Landing. After they arrived, he hung around for twenty-five minutes or so to let the horses rest, and during that time, there was a discussion among the guests about being so far from the town. He offered to let them use one of his two bikes, and he said that Wesley's nineteen-year-old sister could pick it up at Jack's Livery Stable where he worked. He finally admitted to the detective that the only reason he offered his bike was that he was trying to impress Merry.

Sobolewski asked Smith if he recalled putting Mrs. Lacey's luggage on his carriage, and although he couldn't recall whether he had or hadn't, he remembered there was some discussion that she'd be coming back to town for the night and heading back out to British Landing the next morning. He had seen them later in the day, and he asked Merry if she had decided on the boat ride.

The detective moved his questioning to the next day when Frances Lacey was reported missing. Smith's day had started at 6:00 a.m. on July 24. His first trip had been to the Grand Hotel, where he had to pick up some tourists and take them to Ste. Anne's Church for 6:30 mass. After describing the route, Sobolewski asked if he saw any of the group from the previous day; he had. Smith had seen them later in the afternoon at Little Bob's restaurant, and when he spoke with them, they had mentioned that Mrs. Lacey was missing. He also admitted that he eventually spent some time with Merry on the evening of July 26 and into the morning of July 27.

Sobolewski watched the driver very closely during the interview, and it was clear to the detective that the carriage driver fancied himself quite a ladies' man. Detective Sobolewski had a hunch that Smith was somehow involved in Mrs. Lacey's disappearance. He was certain of it. He told Smith that his story would be checked out and asked if he'd be willing to take a polygraph exam if it became necessary. Smith told him he'd take the test if it was needed.

***

In the week following Frances Lacey's murder, police were still trying to determine where the victim had breakfast on the morning she was murdered. Knowing she had eaten pancakes, bacon, and cantaloupe within a couple hours before her murder, Detective Sobolewski, having just heard about the sexual exploits of one of the carriage drivers, decided to recheck at the Murray Hotel to see if he could find out anything more than what they already knew.

He spoke with one the waitresses he'd already questioned, and the more she thought about it, she remembered that on the morning of July 24, a woman wearing glasses came into the dining room and wanted breakfast. The waitress thought the time was between 8 and 8:30 a.m. She told the woman that breakfast couldn't be served yet because the kitchen staff was having trouble with the gas on the stove, and they couldn't cook anything. The woman had a quick cup of coffee, then left for a short time. She came back around 9, and by then, the problem in the kitchen was resolved. The woman ordered pancakes, bacon, cantaloupe, and coffee. She tried to pay her tab to the waitress but was told she had to pay at the front desk. After she paid, she left, and the waitress thought it might have been around 9:30.

**

While Sobolewski was tracking down leads on the Island, a detective in the Muskegon area was assigned to find another stable hand who worked on the Island but left abruptly the day following Frances Lacey's disappearance.

The detective met with Fremont Police Chief Roy LaCrone to see if he'd heard of the man. LaCrone was very familiar with him, and his last name was Remington*. He described him as a habitual drunk who didn't work any more than he had to, and his wife had kicked him out of the house on several occasions. LaCrone said he picked him up in various states of drunkenness over a period of time but never actually arrested him.

The detective and the chief of police headed to the man's home on Main Street to see if Remington was there, and they were surprised to find his entire family.

The two questioned the man alone. Remington said he was a blacksmith and owned a portable blacksmith shop. He first came to Michigan in 1936 or 1937, but he only stayed about eight months before he left and went to Arizona. While there, he worked as a horse trainer and blacksmith.

The chief didn't believe him. He didn't think Remington had ever shod a horse in the Fremont area while he lived there.

Remington said he ended up back in Michigan, and his most recent job was on Mackinac Island working for Carriage Tours. He heard about the job from a friend who worked for another carriage company. He thought the job was misrepresented when he took it because he ended up working seven days a week in the barns as a barn hand. There were forty horses in the barn, and he only made nine dollars per day while working from 5:00 a.m. until 7:00 p.m.

Remington said he stayed in room eleven at the Lennox Hotel and added that the work in the barn was too much for him because he had heart problems.

It was on July 22 when he told the barn boss that he was tired of the job, and the job was causing him to have breathing problems because of his heart condition. He quit on Friday, but he had to wait until Monday to get his remaining pay. He sat around drinking at Hardy's Bar and the Palms Café throughout the weekend.

The detective zeroed in on July 24 by asking what he did on Sunday. Remington got up around 5:00 a.m. and left his room at the Lennox and walked down Main Street. He said he stopped and talked with one of the Mackinac Island policemen, and by 8:00 a.m., he was back in his room. After returning to his room, he decided to have breakfast and went to Little Bob's, and he ran into the same officer at the restaurant. He had a few beers in the afternoon, but he was back in his room by 9:00 p.m. He added that his usual beer intake was four to six beers.

On Monday, he got up at 5:00 a.m. and called his wife to let her know he was coming home. When Carriage Tours opened, he picked up his remaining pay and went back to Hardy's Bar where he paid a four-dollar bar tab that remained. After paying off the tab, he started drinking several more beers before he left the Island.

The detective asked Remington if he ever struck his wife, and he said he hadn't but there were times when he should have. He passed his statement off by saying every married couple has arguments.

The detective asked if he'd ever been arrested, and he said he hadn't. Chief LaCrone knew he was lying, and pressed him about it. He finally admitted he'd been arrested on at least four different occasions. He was arrested twice in Minnesota and at least twice in Michigan. His last arrest involved a minor boy, but he wouldn't go into details about it, and he only said that he posted bail and never heard anything else about the case.

LaCrone knew of another arrest involving a stolen horse, and at the time of Remington's arrest several years earlier, he was living in Twin Lakes, just north of Muskegon. LaCrone also knew that was the same place where a woman living in Muskegon Heights had been murdered just three months earlier. Remington's son-in-law lived in Muskegon Heights. LaCrone didn't bring up the Muskegon murder because Remington agreed to take a polygraph test about the murder on Mackinac Island. That would give detectives working on the Muskegon murder more time to check into his background. LaCrone recalled that the investigation into the unsolved Muskegon murder was around the same time that Remington left to go to Mackinac Island.

After the interview with Remington, the detective and chief interviewed his wife briefly, and she said there was nothing unusual in her husband's behavior since his return from the Island. He had written her a letter about a week prior to leaving the Island, saying the job was too much for him because of his heart and he'd likely have to quit. She also mentioned they had a lot of debt.

After the interviews, the chief discussed it with the MSP detective. They would get another chance to interview Remington when he came in for the polygraph test. The two officers knew there was at least one similarity between the Mackinac murder and the Muskegon murder: in both cases, the victim's watch and purse were missing.

The report about Remington's interview was sent to Bilgen. Spratto and McCluer were handed the follow-up investigation.

Spratto contacted the Mackinac Island Police to see which officer was working on the morning of July 24. The detective was trying to confirm Remington's story about chatting with an Island police officer that morning. Officer John Brenzie was the officer on duty when Mrs. Lacey went missing. Spratto and McCluer spoke with the patrolman briefly, and Brenzie couldn't say one way or the other if he'd spoken with Remington on July 24. He told the detectives that he could have, but he didn't know Remington by name.

Two employees from the Lennox were questioned too. They saw Remington walking along Main Street around 6:15 a.m., and they saw him again thirty minutes later sitting on the porch of the hotel. He was still there until about 8:00 a.m. They were certain he didn't eat at the restaurant. The employees also told the detectives that on August 5, a phone call came in to the hotel from Tucson, Arizona, for Remington, but since he'd already left the Island, the operator was referred to Fremont.

A colleague from Carriage Tours was questioned about his former coworker, and he said Remington had started working for the company as a barn man on June 13. His last day of work was July 22, but he couldn't get paid until Monday, July 25. On the afternoon of July 23, a couple with a young child came to visit him, and they were from Fremont. Later that evening, Remington was seen coming back to his room and was extremely drunk. He went into the wrong room at the hotel and tried to crawl into bed with someone before he was kicked out of that room and eventually made it to his own room.

On the afternoon of July 24, one of the hotel employees went to Remington's room to check on him sometime between 2:30 to 4:00 p.m. and found him passed out.

When the detectives spoke with the barn boss at the stables where Remington had worked, they discovered that he didn't report for work on July 23 or July 24, but he came to the barn on July 25 to let them know he was quitting. According to his boss, he didn't give a reason and didn't claim to have any medical problems either. He added that Remington was a good worker when he was sober, but he would start drinking as soon as payday arrived.

No one at the barn could vouch for Remington on July 24.

McCluer wrote a supplemental report and forwarded it back to Detective Bruno Guzin. Guzin was assigned to the MSP Sixth District Headquarters in Grand Rapids. He'd have to track Remington down at his home.

12: EXPANDING THE SEARCH

"No one is under arrest," Bilgen told the reporter from the *Detroit Free Press*. "We have a lot of information. We're working to check it all." He added, "We're talking to people employed on the Island."[64] Part of the focus shifted to Island employees who had left their jobs since the date of the widow's disappearance. "Somebody knows. They may be in Detroit, Chicago, or almost anywhere. Somehow, we have to find them if we are going to solve this crime."[65]

While MSP had the mirthless task of tracking down a killer, yachts continued to sail to and from the Island while ferries dropped off an endless stream of tourists every half hour or so. Horse-drawn carriages quietly made their way through the downtown area and island trails while smiling vacationers took in the sights and sounds of their tranquil vacation destination.

The year-round residents of the Island saw things differently. Faced with the murder of a tourist in their own backyard, they became apprehensive. Was the killer still on the Island stalking another victim? Was the murderer of Frances Lacey an Island employee? Worse yet, was the killer one of their own?

At the Coast Guard Station, Lieutenant Bilgen seemed to be constantly answering the phone while Trooper Grosse used two fingers to peck away typing reports. He offered

---

64. *Detroit Free Press*, "Grim Paradise," August 3, 1960

65. *The Detroit News*, "Woman's Shoe is New Clue in Widow's Slaying," August 1, 1960

information to the press by letting them know they had established two facts in the murder investigation: based on the injury pattern, which included the laceration to the left side of Mrs. Lacey's head, the killer was right-handed, and he was strong enough to carry Mrs. Lacey to the spot where her body was found. The police knew she'd been attacked on the roadway because they'd found her denture plate ground into the pavement, but there was no indication she'd been dragged to the point where her body was left.

Since the discovery of Frances Lacey's body, there was a constant stream of tips from the public. Each tip was prioritized and assigned to one of the many detectives helping out on the Island. If the tip was in a different venue, it was given to whoever might be available.

On August 2, five days after the discovery of the body, MSP was contacted by a person offering information about someone they felt was suspicious and should be checked out. On the day Mrs. Lacey was found, a man came into the Oden, Michigan, Post Office, and while he was chatting with the postmaster, he mentioned he'd been on Mackinac Island on the day Frances Lacey was murdered. It seemed odd to the postmaster because it was during the day, and he knew Mrs. Lacey's body wasn't found until 7:30 p.m. The man also mentioned the Starved Rock triple homicide during their conversation.

The postmaster knew the man was living in a trailer with his wife and two kids, and he worked for a drilling company often traveling around the country. The man mentioned that he worked on July 23 and July 25 but couldn't remember what he'd done on July 24.

When an MSP trooper was finally able to speak with him, he said that on July 24, he went for a drive with his wife and kids, and he filled the gas tank in Pellston. They continued on to see the Mackinac Bridge, took a tour through the fort in Mackinaw City, then returned home.

They never went out to the Island. The trooper interviewed his wife separately, and she told the same story.

In a separate tip, a hitchhiker was arrested in St. Ignace for disorderly conduct, and he had a woman's watch with him. When interviewed by the state police, he said he was from Pennsylvania, and each summer, he came north for work. When asked about the watch, he said he picked it up at a carnival he worked at down south. The trooper was suspicious but when he saw the watch, there was no doubt. It was a cheap woman's watch worth no more than ten dollars.

There was even a call made to MSP from an agent with the Clyde Beatty Circus. The circus arrived in Sault Sainte Marie on the morning of July 24 and was scheduled to stay over until the morning of July 25. Having read about the murder, he was sure there would have been enough time for someone who might have been discharged from the circus to travel to Mackinac Island. A quick check showed that all of the employees were accounted for on the day of Mrs. Lacey's disappearance.

The FBI stepped in to help in the murder investigation where they could. On August 3, Special Agent Skip Gibbons forwarded a file to Lieutenant Bilgen about a man staying at the Globe Hotel in Alpena who left without paying his bill. Prior to staying at the Globe, he worked at the Grove Restaurant in Alpena and Downing's Restaurant in Mackinaw City. A background check showed that he was a deserter from the army in 1958 when he was stationed in Fort Ord, California. Coincidentally, his home address was within thirty miles of the Starved Rock murders, and he matched the description of a possible suspect in the triple murder.

Bilgen decided to find a photograph of the man and have it shown around the Island to see if anyone might recognize him. It was another of many catalogued tips.

***

On August 3, MSP Trooper Allen Seyfred was serving a traffic warrant in White Pigeon just north of the Indiana-Michigan border when a woman approached him. She told Seyfred that she and her husband were on Mackinac Island on July 24, and they had some eight-millimeter film they had shot while touring the Island that morning. She offered the film to the state police hoping it might help in finding Frances Lacey's killer.

Trooper Seyfred took the woman's name, and a series of phone calls were initiated around the state. MSP Operations in East Lansing finally contacted Seyfred and asked that he interview the woman to find out what time she and her husband were on the Island, where they went, and what time they left the Island. MSP also accepted the woman's offer to look at the film to see if it might help find the killer.

Seyfred contacted Detective Andre Muth, and Muth went to the woman's home to speak with her.

The woman said there was fifty feet of film reel, and she thought between her and her husband, they had shot about thirty-five feet of it. To help out, she drew a small map of the route they traveled around the Island. She said that she and her husband arrived at around 11:40 a.m., and they left around 6:30 p.m.

Their first stop was at the Grand Hotel where she shot movies of some houseboys and their activities. Her husband was certain that the houseboys must be of some interest in the investigation but had nothing more than mere suspicion. After filming them, the couple headed back through town and on to Arch Rock along the east side of the Island. While there, she was startled by a man who came out from behind a large rock. He was about six feet tall and weighed two hundred pounds. She said he was wearing a white shirt and dark pants, and as he walked away, he was heading south on Main Street, though she hadn't filmed him.

As the couple sat down on a bench near Arch Rock, she noticed a woman's blouse laying on the bench. It was white with blue stripes, and she estimated the size at thirty-six to thirty-eight. The buttons were loosened on it but not torn off. She liked it and thought about keeping it, but it was too large for her, so she put it over the back of the bench. The couple headed toward Fort Mackinac, and while they were there, she shot some movies of a man and woman climbing some steps. She thought the woman in the movie might be Mrs. Lacey, and she felt the man was acting suspiciously, but like her husband's feelings about the houseboys at the Grand Hotel, hers were nothing more than suspicion.

Seyfred took the film from the woman, and it was transferred to the Battle Creek Post and eventually on to the MSP Operations in East Lansing. Their hope was to catch a glimpse of the victim and her killer.

***

The shoes found under the abandoned boat at the crime scene were sent to the Detroit Post along with the lone gray suede woman's shoe that was found near the murder scene. The detectives needed to know if it actually belonged to Frances Lacey.

When Kay saw the gray suede shoe, she knew immediately it didn't belong to her mom. She said there was no way her mom could have worn a shoe without a heel, and she knew she hadn't seen a second pair of shoes in her mom's luggage. The theory that Frances may have stopped briefly as she made her way toward British Landing, then put the shoes she'd been wearing into a plastic bag to finish her trip became even more of a possibility. Kay was able to identify the shoes that were found under the boat as her mom's.

Beyond the shoes, detectives were trying to track down where the bag came from that read MADE IN SCOTLAND, ELLIOT AND SONS.

Now that Kay said the gray suede shoe didn't belong to her mom, detectives were baffled.

***

The investigation into the murder was expanding across the state and the entire country. Tip after tip filtered in, and the latest was from the Ann Arbor Police Department. A man was picked up for using two names and acting suspiciously, and he had a handwritten note in his pocket about the murder on Mackinac Island. The Island investigators asked to have him interviewed by state detectives and the Ann Arbor Police.

The man worked for the Grand Hotel in 1958 and 1959, and he worked for a laundry service on the Island too. The detectives noticed the new shoes he was wearing and asked about them. He said he bought them on the Island, but the detectives were suspicious because they looked brand new.

During the interview, he was asked about living on the Island, and he said he hadn't been on the Island this year but he was arrested there last year. He said the arrest was for "drinking with some college boys."[66]

Detective Roy Tanner asked about the handwritten note that was found in the man's pocket that read: "THURSDAY NIGHT, lying face down, shady slope 200 yards from lake shore road. 31-year-old hand (Indiana) man & Part time scene artist (black & gray hair (trousers) hair), found

---

66. Tanner, Roy. "Supplemental Report." *Michigan State Police*, August 4, 1960

in trousers Sunday 7-24-60 8 & 10 AM Sunday."[67] He admitted he wrote the note after reading newspaper articles about the murder in the hope of being able to help the police.

Tanner wondered why the man used two names. He said it was for religious purposes. He assured the detective that he was in Ann Arbor for the previous three weeks.

While there wasn't enough to hold him for the murder on Mackinac Island, the detective wasn't going to simply take his word at face value. Tanner headed to the man's home and spoke with the landlord. The landlord was able to verify his tenant's story. He got to Ann Arbor on July 21 and he hadn't left town since then.

Unless his landlord was covering for him, it was another dead end.

***

With the investigation ongoing, Detective George Strong continued to contact each business on the Island to get a list of their employees. Some were fired or had quit voluntarily on July 24, and they would all have to be checked.

Six days had elapsed since the discovery of the body. Detective Spratto had been all but certain that Paul Strantz was involved, but he couldn't prove it. Investigators suspected that Remington was lying, but they weren't sure why. They'd questioned Smith, the carriage driver who'd taken the Sutters and Mrs. Lacey to British Landing, and the detective had strong suspicions that he was somehow involved, but like the other potential suspects, had no way of proving it. There were others who'd been cleared, and the mountain of tips was growing each day, suggesting others who would have to be checked out. Each tip could

---

67. Tanner, Roy. "Supplemental Report." *Michigan State Police*, August 4, 1960

take days, weeks, or even longer to investigate. It was frustrating.

Nationally, the murder rate between 1950 and 1960 had risen by over ten percent,[68] but most of the murders across the country were solved. Even though Frances Lacey's body had been found just six days prior, police were still confident they could sort through the growing pile of tips and find her killer.

68. Langberg, Robert. "Homicide in the United States 1950-1964." *National Center for Health Statistics*, October 1967

13: HURRIED GETAWAY

It had been eleven days since the Dearborn widow was reported missing, and exactly one week since the discovery of her body. By August 4, ninety-seven tips had been given to police in hopes that the slightest piece of information might lead to the killer.

The phone rang in Spratto's office. It was the crime lab, and several people at the lab had viewed the tourist's eight-millimeter footage taken on the morning of July 24. Spratto was hopeful but unfortunately, there was nothing on the film that was of any value to the investigation.

Sobolewski was busy taking each tip as it was assigned to him. The latest was based on information that Clarence Ferrell, an employee at the Grand Hotel, was fired on July 20 for drinking. His brother worked at the Grand too, and after Clarence was fired, his brother accompanied him to St. Ignace. That night, Clarence was arrested by the St. Ignace Police Department for being drunk and disorderly. He was released from custody on July 23.

On July 24, he made two collect phone calls to his home in Muncie, Indiana. One call was from Detroit, and the second was from Fort Wayne.

While on his way back to Mackinac Island on August 3, Ferrell was arrested in a car stolen from Indiana, and Sobolewski knew he'd have to enlist some help to have him interviewed.

The detective got another tip the next day when he received a call from Doc Solomon. The doctor detailed a strange visit from a man shortly after the murder. He thought the date was around the time that Mrs. Lacey's body was discovered, and he described how the man had come into the medical center saying he was a lock inspector. Solomon told Sobolewski about all three visits the man had made on that particular afternoon.

Sobolewski began checking around, and he learned from the Grand Hotel's bartender that there was an employee with the same last name as the man had used in Solomon's office, and he'd quit his job on July 28, the same day that Mrs. Lacey's body was found. The man was from Evanston, Illinois, and his last name was Bell. To the bartender, he didn't seem to be the type of person to use drugs, but he was a little peculiar. His biggest fault was that he was always trying to entertain white women. The bartender added that his best trait was that he was always on time to work, and his worst trait was that when he got there, he messed everything up. If he hadn't quit on July 28, the bartender was going to fire him.

Sobolewski found out that on July 24, Bell worked from 8:00 a.m. to 11:30 and from 12:30 p.m. to 2:00. He also worked the evening shift. While the work hours listed would likely clear him from any involvement in the murder, the detective still felt that the Evanston Police should check on Bell in case he was tied to any crimes in Illinois.

***

Parts of the murder investigation were playing out all around the state of Michigan and beyond, but there still weren't any solid leads developed in the week since the gruesome discovery.

The detectives, along with a couple men from the Coast Guard, decided to make another thorough search, starting where the body had been found. Each member of the search team fanned out in a different direction for one-quarter mile in a slow and methodic search, hoping to find another small piece of the puzzle. They were hoping to find Mrs. Lacey's missing watch or another pair of shoes. Lieutenant Bilgen extended the search area to the northwest so it would include the forested terrain leading to Stonecliff, but like so many of the other searches, the searchers came up empty-handed.

When Bilgen returned to the office, a copy of the autopsy report was waiting for him. Reviewing it, the lieutenant found there was nothing in it he hadn't already been told by phone.

***

On August 5, Mr. Remington, the man who had so abruptly left the Island shortly after the murder, showed up at the MSP Post in Rockford. He was scheduled to take a polygraph test.

Before the test, Detective Guzin used the opportunity to interview him a second time.

Remington said that on July 22, he worked at the horse barn until around noon. He had to pick up a money order to mail to his wife, and he got permission to head into town. It was about a mile from the barn. He purchased the money order and put it in the mail, then headed back to the Lennox Hotel, where he relaxed for the rest of the day. That evening, he went downtown for a while before returning to the Lennox.

The next morning, around 6:00 a.m., he saw his boss at the barn, and he told him he was quitting because he couldn't take the long hours anymore. He was owed some money for his work, but his boss told him he'd have to wait until Monday when the Carriage Tours office was open. After he quit, he went back to his hotel and spent the day. When Remington made that statement, the detective remembered the interview only a few days before when he said that after he quit, he went to two bars where he drank before heading back to his room.

On the morning of Mrs. Lacey's disappearance, Remington got up at around 5:00 a.m. and walked around the hotel for a short time before walking downtown where he ran into a state trooper. The two spoke briefly, then Remington headed back to his hotel. It was around eight when he left the Lennox again and walked to Little Bob's Restaurant where he had a cup of coffee. When he left, he ran into the state trooper again, and the two talked before he headed back to the hotel. During the interview, he insisted that the only time he left the hotel was to go downtown to eat or drink beer.

The detectives moved their questioning to Remington's knowledge of the Island. He'd only been there for a few weeks, so he said he didn't really know it that well. He couldn't tell which direction was which—north to south or east to west—and he wasn't really familiar with the layout of buildings on the Island either. In his previous interview, he said he wasn't familiar with the MRA or where their buildings were located on the Island. In the second interview, he contradicted himself and said he was familiar with the MRA.

Guzin asked if he stayed anywhere else on the Island other than the Lennox House. He said he hadn't, but the detective had already checked his background and knew that on July 9, his wife visited the Island, and they rented a rooming house near the Chuckwagon Restaurant.

Remington said there were never any women around the barn where he worked, and the only women he was acquainted with worked in the kitchen at the Lennox Hotel.

When the detective asked if he knew about Mrs. Lacey's disappearance before he left the Island, Remington's answers became vague. He said he may have heard about her disappearance from someone on the Island. He couldn't remember who, but he was pretty sure the first time he heard of it was when his wife had read about it in the Fremont newspaper and mentioned it to him.

Several things in Remington's account of his activities on Mackinac Island didn't add up. He said he left his job because of his heart problems and visited a doctor on the Island. He was taking some pills prescribed by the doctor. During the interview, he admitted he hadn't seen a doctor and wasn't taking any medication.

When Guzin asked about Mrs. Lacey, Remington was even more vague about knowing anything or even having heard about the disappearance, yet during his polygraph, he admitted he knew she'd been strangled with her own panties. He said he'd heard the detail from his wife but wouldn't admit why he was so elusive when asked about her disappearance on the Island. When asked more questions about Mrs. Lacey's disappearance, he said he heard her blue jacket was missing, and it was something his wife had read to him from the paper, but the detectives in Rockford weren't certain if that information had been released to the papers.

At the end of the interview, when asked by the detectives if he knew where the Murray Hotel was, he said he didn't.

Remington's wife was interviewed by Detective Guzin a second time. When her husband returned home from the Island, she asked about a little boy who was injured on the Island and how he was doing. Her husband told her the boy was going to be okay and mentioned there was a woman missing on the Island. When pressed by his wife for details about the missing woman, he said, "I don't even know or have the slightest idea who she was or where she was from, or whether she lived there or was merely visiting on vacation."[69]

Detective Guzin was suspicious of Remington, but he was also limited in what he knew about the murder of Frances Lacey. His hope was to get a summary of the details before speaking with Remington again.

In his report about the polygraph examination done on Remington, Detective Sergeant Bill Menzies, the examiner, wrote:

> The subject stated he did not know what was used to strangle with and a test was set up, and then he stated his wife told him it was an undergarment of the victim. Then he said he did not know what undergarment, and he responded under panties. After this test he stated his wife told him it was under panties. Also, through the oral interrogation period of this examination, he was evasive and would change his story. It was recommended to the investigating officer that further work be done on this subject.[70]

The following day, Detective Guzin interviewed Remington yet again. The detective was certain he was lying about something when he pulled in the drive at Remington's Fremont home around 2:00 p.m.

As the two men talked, Guzin asked Remington if there was anyone who might have seen him on the morning of July 24 after he had coffee at Little Bob's Restaurant. There was a pause before he answered, and like before, he became evasive and vague in his answers. He couldn't name anyone who could vouch for his movements on the morning of the Lacey disappearance. After he thought for a minute, he said

69. Guzin, Bruno. "Supplemental Report." *Michigan State Police*, August 5, 1960

70. Menzies, William. "Supplemental Report." *Michigan State Police*, August 4, 1960

that maybe some carriage drivers who stayed at the Lennox Hotel might have seen him in the morning. He mentioned a couple drivers by first name only and the carriage numbers they drove each day.

He gave Guzin a photo taken on the Island with a couple people in it he knew. In the background of the photo was the Murray Hotel, yet Remington had consistently said he didn't know where the Murray was. Guzin was certain Remington did know where the hotel was, and he was suspicious of why he repeatedly said he didn't when the Murray was only one block from the Lennox. If Frances Lacey were heading toward the Grand Hotel or Stonecliff, she would have passed by the Lennox, and Remington maintained that he spent much of the morning on the porch of the Lennox. Why didn't he recall seeing the lone woman walk by?

Remington denied having ever left the city or going on the trails around the Island, yet as he spoke with the detective, he admitted he'd done a complete circuit of the Carriage Trail on numerous occasions.

The detective knew Remington had a roommate at the Lennox and asked if the roommate might be able to verify his story about being at the Lennox all morning. He said his roommate couldn't because he was working on Sunday morning.

Guzin was determined to find out why Remington was so evasive in his answers, and he knew there was more to the man's story than what he was letting on but all he could do at that point was to provide a supplemental report about his findings and forward it to Lieutenant Bilgen.

***

Two weeks after Mrs. Lacey's disappearance, Detective Sobolewski received some information that the bandleader on a ship called the *North American*, docked at Mackinac Island, might have some information that would be helpful.

Sobolewski met with the man on the ship, and he told the detective about an unusual incident.

On July 24 at about 2:50 p.m., the musician was walking up to the Union Terminal Pier ticket sales office near the docks to pick up the mail because the ticket sales office sells both ferry tickets and Greyhound Bus tickets. At the same time, another man came up to the office, and it was obvious he was in a hurry to get off the Island and get as far away as he could. He asked the sales agent how far away he could get for seven dollars and forty-five cents. The man kept looking over his shoulder and from side to side, and the bandleader asked the man what he would do if the money didn't take him far enough away. He said he'd hitchhike. The bandleader described the hurried man as wearing a blue sport shirt, carrying a sports jacket, clean shaven with medium-length brown hair.

After Sobolewski got a physical description, he went to the ticket sales office, and by sheer luck, the same agent was working who had waited on the man on July 24. The agent only recalled that there was a man in a hurry to get off the Island but not much more than that.

He thought the man only bought a ferry ticket, but the bandleader who spoke with the detective thought he'd bought both a ferry ticket and a Greyhound ticket.

After Sobolewski left the pier, he headed back to the Coast Guard Station and asked that a check be made with the Eastern Greyhound Lines in Cleveland, Ohio, for a list of all fares and destinations that were purchased on Mackinac Island, in Mackinaw City, and in St. Ignace on July 24.

A detective from the St. Ignace Post, Edwin Hill, began to check the bus ticket sales for St. Ignace and Mackinaw City. He was looking specifically for buses that left after 3:00 p.m. on the day of the murder.

Hill discovered the first bus left from St. Ignace to Sault Ste. Marie at 5:30, Detroit at 9:10, and Duluth at 10:45. From Mackinaw City, buses left for Chicago at 4:45, Grand Rapids at 5:15, Sault Ste. Marie at 5:13, Detroit at 9:40, Duluth at 10:25, and a second bus to Sault Ste. Marie at 10:30. Hill also collected the number of tickets sold to various destinations on July 24 and the amount spent on each ticket, though he wasn't able to get information on the tickets sold on Mackinac Island. None of the employees at any of the bus terminals could recall anyone matching the description given of the man seen on the Island.

Sobolewski also checked for bus tickets sold on the Island on July 24, but the records for that particular day couldn't be located.

It was another day without any progress, and the information he gathered would be recorded and stored for further follow-up at a later date.

14: HAROLD ASP

Two weeks after the murder, Kay Sutter sat at home in Detroit feeling helpless. She wanted to do anything she could to help the investigation and find the person responsible for her mother's murder so she took it upon herself to contact a private detective.

Police had already opened Frances Lacey's safety deposit box at the Dearborn Branch of the Manufacturers National Bank on the slim chance that it might aid in somehow identifying her killer. It contained some personal papers along with 951 shares of stock. Investigators found her will, which was dated February 17, 1954. There was also a codicil dated April 24, 1959, and two divorce decrees from 1932 and 1933.

Kay's brother, William, was indignant when the press suggested that there was somehow a connection between his mother's previous marriages and her murder.

On August 6, the phone rang in Lieutenant Bilgen's office at the Coast Guard Station. At the other end of the line was Ralph Beverly. Beverly owned the Beverly Detective Agency in Detroit, and he had been hired by Kay Sutter, along with James McEvoy, another private detective who owned the McEvoy Detective Agency in Bay City. Beverly told Bilgen that he was retained by Kay Sutter, and he took the liberty of contacting McEvoy because of his expertise as a polygraph examiner. Both men were now working on the murder of Frances Lacey.

The private detective wanted to clarify a couple of points with Kay Sutter before he got too far into the investigation, and knowing that a victim's family is always suspect, he arranged to have Kay take a polygraph examination. He invited Bilgen to assign an MSP detective to listen in as Kay's polygraph exam was conducted. He also asked that his and McEvoy's parts in the investigation be kept confidential,[71] and he promised complete cooperation with the state police.

Kay had come back to Mackinaw City with McEvoy and was staying at a separate motel. Beverly's plan was to have a hidden microphone leading to an adjacent motel room so the MSP detective could listen to Kay's polygraph exam.

A mile south of Mackinaw City, Beverly and McEvoy were staying at the Val-U Motel. Bilgen assigned Detective Edwin Hill from the St. Ignace Post to meet with the men and listen to the polygraph exam. Beverly told Hill that he felt the murder case was wide open, and Kay was the starting point.

McEvoy set up his Keeler polygraph machine in the motel room, and to Hill, it looked similar to the machines used by MSP. With the hidden microphone and a speaker in the adjacent room, Kay Sutter had no way of knowing that there were two other people listening to her interview and polygraph exam.

Before starting, McEvoy interviewed Kay for quite some time, and during the subsequent exam, his questions focused on whether she knew anything about her mother's murder or if she knew anyone associated with the murder of her mother.

After looking at the results of Kay Sutter's polygraph exam, McEvoy was confident that Kay knew nothing about the events surrounding the murder.

---

71. Hill, Edwin. "Supplemental Report." *Michigan State Police*, August 6, 1960

Both private detectives told Hill that if they came across any information regarding Frances Lacey's murder, they'd contact the state police.

* * *

The *Mackinac Island Town Crier* continued their weekly coverage of the Island murder on August 7 with the headline reading MANHUNT BLANKETS MACKINAC.[72] The investigation into the murder of the Dearborn widow was described as the greatest manhunt in Mackinac history while detectives made tedious checks of the Island employees. Bilgen told reporters, "We are stymied. We are checking many tips which seem minor on the surface, but anyone could develop into the lead we need to break the case."[73]

For a brief moment on August 7, Detective Sobolewski, who had returned to the Centerline Post by then, thought MSP might just have the small piece of information that Bilgen was hoping for. He received a request to contact the Detroit Police Department's Fourteenth Precinct about a person they were holding regarding the murder of Frances Lacey.

It was around 1:00 a.m. when two Detroit officers were dispatched to a family disturbance call near Grand River and Schaeffer. The man causing the problem was drunk, and during his arrest, he told the two patrolmen that he had killed Mrs. Lacey on Mackinac Island. He was questioned at some point later that morning and retracted the statement he'd made. He didn't kill Mrs. Lacey, but he said he knew something about the murder.

---

72. *Mackinac Island Town Crier*, "Manhunt Blankets Mackinac," August 7, 1960, p 1

73. *Mackinac Island Town Crier*, "Manhunt Blankets Mackinac," August 7, 1960, p 1

Sobolewski interviewed him around 3:00 p.m. He had sobered up, and he didn't deny making the statement to the two officers that arrested him. He was out of work and depressed. He'd read all the news articles about the murder, and in some odd way, he thought if he made some type of admission to the murder, it would lessen his "imagined difficulties."[74] He told Sobolewski he didn't kill Frances Lacey, and he wasn't even on the Island when the murder occurred.

Sobolewski wasn't surprised. He still had to do some quick checking to verify the man's story. He headed over to the house where the man was arrested earlier that morning and spoke with the other parties involved in the disturbance. They were certain he was at the house on July 24 because they had a barbecue in the backyard. He didn't have any transportation, and he was broke.

Sobolewski's report was added to the ever-increasing stack of paperwork related to the murder.

Back on Mackinac Island, three detectives were being released from their homicide assignments and returning to their posts. With no new suspects, the detectives who were on loan from other posts around the state had to return to their regular duties. For the investigation into the murder of Frances Lacey, it meant there would be fewer investigators directly involved on the Island.

***

On August 8, Sergeant Burnette had a meeting with some of the men assigned to the investigation. Actionable leads had started to dwindle, and after their discussion, a decision was made to contact Michigan Bell Telephone Company and have the extra phone lines installed at the Coast Guard

---

74. Sobolewski, A. "Supplemental Report." *Michigan State Police,* August 7, 1960

Station disconnected. The task force of detectives would be reduced there too.

When the investigators began arriving on the Island after the body was found, they were put up at three separate hotels on the Island. Burnette contacted the Island House, the Windemere, and Mrs. Chamber's Rooming House to make sure the bills were taken care of for the detectives and officers who were staying there while assigned to the investigation.

Even though they were scaling back the number of investigators working on the case, there was still work to be done and tips to be followed up on.

The following morning, Detective Hill was at the Grand Hotel asking about a former employee named Harold Asp. Asp was a bartender at the hotel, and he'd started working there on July 8. He was quiet and rarely smiled. His last day of work was on July 25, the day after the murder. Hill had gotten information from the Detroit Post that Asp strolled casually into the New Woodward Hotel in Detroit late in the afternoon on July 27. The desk clerk noticed he didn't have any luggage with him, so he asked the man to pay for his room in advance. Harold Asp shelled out the seven dollars and twenty-five cents for a week's stay. It was the last time the desk clerk ever saw him.

After two days, the clerk hadn't seen or heard from the hotel guest, so he checked the room Asp had rented. The only thing he found was a black sports coat. The clerk checked the pockets and found matchbooks, a Greyhound Bus envelope, and a paycheck stub from the Grand Hotel on Mackinac Island. The last pay period on the check stub ended on July 26. Looking through the other pockets, he found a luggage claim check with the number A4558 from the Grand Hotel.

It seemed suspicious to the clerk, who by now had seen the headlines about the murder of a tourist on the Island. He called the Detroit Police Homicide Division. Detective

George Craft knew of the murder too, and he wasted no time in getting over to the New Woodward Hotel. He picked up the sports coat and the contents found in the pocket and made sure they were taken to the crime laboratory in East Lansing.

Now, as Detective Hill stood at the front desk of the Grand Hotel, he listened intently to see if there was a reason Asp had left so abruptly.

Asp had worked on the evening of July 24 from 6 until 10 p.m. After work, he went out drinking with some other employees from the hotel, and on the following night, when he showed up for work at 6, it was obvious to the other staff that he was still drunk. The head bartender was thinking about letting him go but decided to let him continue working for the rest of the night. Asp finished his shift and left at 10.

After his shift, he already suspected he was going to be fired because of his drinking, so he went in on the morning of July 26, collected his pay, and quit.

When Harold Asp started working at the hotel on July 8, he was broke, but when he quit two weeks later, he picked up fifty dollars owed to him, plus an additional eighteen dollars in tips. He roomed at the Grand Hotel and had two roommates who worked with him. One of those men quit on July 24, and the second quit on July 25.

Hill dug further into Asp's movements after he left the Island. He had the baggage claim number from the ticket found in the pocket of the sports coat in the former bartender's room at the New Woodward Hotel. When Hill started checking the number A4558, he found that an old, tan suitcase with two brown stripes was found in the baggage claim area of the Arnold Ferry Line dock on the Island. The green tag on the suitcase was A4558. When the detective spoke with the supervisor at the ferry dock, the suitcase was turned over to Hill. It had been sitting in the baggage area since the day Asp left the Island.

The detective went a step further and checked with all the dock porters. None of them remembered Harold Asp or which boat he took to leave the Island, but there was a general consensus among them that the suitcase belonged to a former bartender from the Grand Hotel.

Hill headed back to the Grand. A drayman at the hotel remembered that on July 26, he took two people to the dock on his first trip of the day. It was the drayman's job to haul the luggage down to the docks, and he specifically remembered he had passengers that morning. The passengers were two men, and one was very quiet while the other talked continuously and mentioned that his wife was sick, and that's why he was leaving the Island. One of the men was Harold Asp. On the way to the dock, Asp got off at Hardy's Bar and asked the drayman to pick him up on his next trip while the other man continued to the dock. When the drayman got to the dock, he left Asp's suitcase, and on his next trip, he picked up Asp at Hardy's, but he dropped him off at Mary's Restaurant and Bar. He never saw him again.

Hill left the Grand Hotel and headed for Hardy's Bar. No one recalled Asp, so he walked to Mary's Restaurant and Bar to see if anyone there could recall him. One of the employees remembered that Asp had been there several times and said he was in on the morning of July 26, but he hadn't seen Asp since then.

Hill now had the old, tan suitcase with two brown stripes on it. One of the locks was broken, and the suitcase was tied together with white string.[75] When he got it to the Post, Lieutenant Bilgen and Captain VanLandegen were there when the string was cut that was holding it together. When it was opened, the three men looked inside but didn't touch anything. They could see some men's clothing but

75. Hill, Edwin. "Supplemental Report." *Michigan State Police*, August 9, 1960

nothing more, and Bilgen told Hill it should be sent to the crime laboratory. Since Bilgen and VanLandegen were flying to East Lansing the next morning, they agreed to take the evidence directly to the crime lab.

Detectives had started to dig deeper into Harold Asp's background, and they discovered he was from the Indianapolis area. The Indiana State Police were asked if they could come up with photos of Asp. The photos were flown to the Detroit Metropolitan Airport on Delta Airlines Flight 444. It was 1:15 a.m. on August 10 when the flight arrived, and the photos of Asp were turned over to a detective from MSP. He took them to the District Two Post and gave them to Lieutenant Whaley the next morning.

Later that morning, detectives from the MSP Headquarters called the Indiana State Police again, and by then, attempts to track down Harold Asp were already underway.

The investigators received information later that morning from the ISP by phone that his last known address in Indianapolis had been checked, and they were unable to locate him. The ISP suspected that he wouldn't be returning to the address because he'd left owing a considerable amount of money. The ISP did learn that Asp and the other two roommates at the Grand Hotel had been sent to Mackinac Island by the National Employment Service in Indiana, and their bus trip had been prepaid by the employment agency.

***

Back on Mackinac Island, detectives working on the case were checking the names of guests at various hotels, and that included the Murray Hotel where Frances Lacey had been staying. All of the guests had left since the time of the murder, so MSP Posts around the state were contacted to have the former Island visitors interviewed.

One of those guests received a postcard at his home from the Murray Hotel that read, "FOUND. ONE LADY'S OVERNIGHT BAG." It seemed odd to him, but knowing of the murder, he contacted MSP.

In Newago, Trooper John Houchlei was asked to contact J. Donald Murphy. Murphy had served as the Newago County Prosecuting Attorney from 1939 to 1951 and along with his wife and another couple, had stayed at the Murray Hotel on the same night that Frances Lacey had stayed there.

Trooper Houchlei spoke with Murphy at his home, and he told the trooper that he and his wife checked into the Murray Hotel at around 5:30 p.m. on July 23. The second couple was his wife's brother and sister-in-law. The former prosecutor said he was given room thirty-four, and his brother-in-law and wife were given either room twenty-four or twenty-seven. Both rooms were connected by an adjoining bathroom.

Houchlei asked if he saw anyone that looked unusual or out of place, and Murphy said he saw two men who were Mexican. They were staying in a nearby room, but he didn't know the room number. There was a third man with them, and he was given a room by himself. He told Houchlei that those three men were the only people that looked out of place to him while he was on the Island. After the two couples had dinner, they walked to the Grand Hotel and danced until around 11:00 p.m. When they left the Grand, they walked back to the Murray and went to bed. The next morning, after eating breakfast, they rented a carriage and headed on a short sightseeing tour by traveling northwest out of the city, then going between the Grand Hotel and the Murray Hotel and back southeast into town. They didn't see anything unusual on their short carriage ride, and when it ended, they had a cup of coffee at the Buggy Whip Lunch Room, then left the Island by boat at around 12:15. They never saw Mrs. Lacey as they headed out on their tour.

It was a few days after they arrived home when he received the card from the Murray Hotel.

While Houchlei was interviewing Mr. Murphy, Corporal Conard was contacting the Murray Hotel to ask about the postcard Murphy received. The manager told Conard that a brown leather ladies' overnight bag was left in the lobby of the hotel around the time of the murder. The initials on the bag were CKM. After finding the bag, he sent postcards to all guests who stayed on July 23 and had a last name that started with *M*. He never received any replies. (If all of the initials on the luggage were of the same size, it would indicate first, middle, last name. If the center letter was larger, it would indicate first, last, middle name; thus, the manager could have checked guests with last names starting with the letter *K*. The report isn't clear about that, or whether there was any additional follow-up done to attempt to find the owner.)

Conard checked the bag and discovered several ladies' garments inside, but no identification. He was able to get the names of the three men James Murphy had described who looked out of place.

The three men Murphy had seen were teachers in the Ann Arbor area, and they arrived on the Island on Saturday, July 23. Detectives from the Ypsilanti Post were able to interview two of the men. After getting their rooms at the Murray, they went out for the evening and didn't return to their rooms until around 11:00 p.m. Two of them shared a room next to Mrs. Lacey while the third had a room of his own. All three men were together the entire trip, and the only time they were split up was when one of them attended mass on Sunday morning. After mass, the three met up at the Grand Hotel. They all traveled around the Island on bikes taking pictures, and they returned to the Murray at around 1:00 p.m. then caught the 2:00 p.m. ferry back to St. Ignace before returning to Ann Arbor. None of the three men felt that their companions would have had anything to do with the murder. They did see one person traveling on a bike along Lake Shore Road, and they thought he was associated in some way with the Grand Hotel because he was wearing a white jacket.

The detectives were hoping they may have seen something—anything—at the Murray since their rooms were on the second floor and one was next to room twenty-six, but neither of the men interviewed saw anything suspicious or out of the ordinary.

15: THE BILLFOLD

Detective Victor Beck was working at the MSP Post in Kalamazoo when he received a request from the St. Ignace Post to check on a former employee from the hotel who had abruptly quit on the morning of July 24. After working for just sixteen days, the former employee gave no reason when he suddenly quit on the morning Mrs. Lacey came up missing. Maybe it was the break they'd been waiting for.

Lemuel Kemper, a former tool maker, listed his address at a sixteen-unit apartment in Kalamazoo, but when Detective Beck checked, he found that Kemper had moved to Kalamazoo's Burdick Hotel.

The detective checked into Kemper's background and discovered that in December 1958, in a fit of rage, he had punched his fist through a window and tried to kill his wife with a knife. He had also tried turning on the gas jets at their home in another attempt to kill her. After moving to the Burdick Hotel, he had made advances toward one of the maids, and there was a rumor that he tried to rape her. Beck also discovered that Kemper had been arrested in the past for drunk driving in his '57 Ford convertible.

Beck decided to call the Kalamazoo Police and see if they knew of Kemper. If they were familiar with him, maybe they could help locate him so he could be interviewed.

Working with another detective from the KPD, Detective Beck met with a maid from the Burdick Hotel. She didn't know Kemper by name, but she quickly recognized his picture. She said he lived in room 307, and he drank quite a bit. She also said he was the kind of guy who felt all women "fell" for him, but she considered him conceited. She was afraid of him. She had another part-time job babysitting, and on one occasion, she was walking home when he pulled up next to her and tried convincing her to get in the car. She never gave him the chance. "I kept my distance," she said to the detective.

Beck also spoke with Kemper's former wife, and she said she was deathly afraid of him. She didn't want him to know where she lived or have her phone number. "He goes crazy when he's drinking," she told Beck. She had him arrested at one point for assault, but at his trial, a jury found him not guilty.

When the detective spoke with the chef at the Burdick Hotel, he remembered Kemper but said he hadn't seen him around Kalamazoo in quite some time. He mentioned that Kemper's convertible had been repossessed so he likely didn't have a car at that point.

Lem Kemper's girlfriend heard that the police were looking for him, and she contacted Beck on her own. She gave him Kemper's address, and she assured him that if she heard from him, she'd contact him immediately.

After their initial interview, Kemper's girlfriend continually called back to the detective bureau and even showed up one day. She claimed she still had no idea where Kemper was, but said that she'd notify them immediately if she heard from him. She also had some books belonging to him that dealt with sexual fantasies and wanted to get rid of them. They were given to Kalamazoo's chief of detectives.

***

While Beck was checking on Kemper's background in Kalamazoo, Anthony Spratto was meeting with the other detectives on the Island to discuss the status of the murder investigation and see if there were any new developments. Each detective reviewed the various tips that had been given to follow-up on and discuss any new information that had been developed.

As Detective Hill was beginning his investigation into Harold Asp on August 10, just seventeen days after the murder, Lieutenant Bilgen handed a tip sheet to Sergeant Burnette. It read, "At 4:35 p.m., the victim's billfold was turned in by J. R. DeBlecourt, the head gardener of the Grand Hotel."[76]

Burnette wanted two of his best men to interview the gardener so Spratto and L. N. Hofmann were assigned. The seasoned detectives headed right for the stately hotel. They discovered that it was actually the assistant gardener at the Grand Hotel, John McKay, who found the wallet around 1:30 p.m. in a clump of shrubbery. The shrubs ran adjacent to a path from the boulevard leading to the Grand Hotel through the tennis courts. The path and shrubs stopped at the Grand Hotel's swimming pool, and the billfold was found fifteen feet from the edge of the sidewalk.

After finding the billfold, McKay, who had poor eyesight and needed glasses to read, kept it with him until he was done with his daily routine. When he got back to the hotel, he had the owner of the Chuckwagon Restaurant look at it, and it didn't take long to determine it belonged to Frances Lacey. The blue Lady Buxton billfold contained Frances Lacey's driver's license and vehicle registration, in addition to numerous other documents with her name on them. It also had her birth certificate from Hastings, Michigan, in Barry County, but there was no money. The billfold was turned over to DeBlecourt, and he took it directly to the Coast Guard Station.

---

76. Burnette, George. "Supplemental Report." *Michigan State Police.* August 10, 1960

***

Police from all over the state and other parts of the country were interviewing tourists and former employees who'd been on Mackinac Island on the morning of the murder.

Bill and Mary Young* lived in Mt. Pleasant and arrived on the Island on July 22 at around 2:00 p.m. Their nephew was with them, and they were registered at the Grand Hotel. Their entire time was spent at the hotel until the morning of July 24 when they rented a carriage from Jack's Livery for a short tour. The three tourists took the carriage up to British Landing along Lake Shore Road and stopped at a small refreshment stand to have a Coke. They chatted briefly with the woman at the stand, and then headed back along Lake Shore Road toward the city. Along the way, they saw a man and woman riding on a tandem bike, and they saw a man walking along Lake Shore Road.

When they returned to the city, it was around 11:00 a.m., and they had turned in the carriage before shopping for an hour or so. They returned to the Grand Hotel around noon and left the Island on the 2:00 p.m. ferry. At the time, they had no idea Frances Lacey had just been murdered along Lake Shore Road. They never realized the couple they'd seen on the tandem bike was very likely the same couple who found Mrs. Lacey's purse after just missing the murder, and it had never occurred to them that the man they saw walking along Lake Shore Road may have been Frances Lacey's killer.

After Bill Young relayed his story to Trooper Pomeroy from the Mt. Pleasant Post, his wife, Mary, was interviewed, and she told the same story. Their nephew had since returned home to Pennsylvania and wasn't available for an interview. Mary said that she and her husband had thought about their carriage ride after hearing of the murder but couldn't come up with any more details that might help in the investigation.

Trooper Pomeroy asked her to describe the man they'd seen walking along the road at around 10:30 a.m. They described him as about eighteen-years-old with an average height and build. When they saw him, he was wearing slacks, and his shirt was open. They added that he wasn't wearing a hat.

On the same day that Bill and Mary Young were interviewed, Lieutenant Bilgen and Captain VanLandegen took MSP's plane number three for the flight from Marquette to St. Ignace, where they picked up Detective Hill. He had Frances Lacey's dental plate, along with her billfold that had been found at the Grand Hotel. He also had the suitcase left by Harold Asp at the ferry dock when he left the Island. All the evidence was being taken to the crime laboratory at the Michigan Department of Public Health in Lansing. At the crime lab, the billfold and the documents inside—that were dry—were checked for latent prints in the hopes of finding something that might lead to the killer, but nothing was found. Most of the items in the wallet were still damp from being exposed to the weather.

Lieutenant Bilgen also had received a list of possible suspects in the Starved Rock murders from July 30 and left the list with Captain Grant at the crime lab. Grant assigned a detective to go through the list and compare each name and address listed in the Lacey homicide with each name and address listed in the Illinois triple murder. The lists had no names in common.

With the sports coat recovered from the New Woodward Hotel in Detroit now at the crime lab, detectives from MSP Headquarters were trying to track down the store where the coat had been purchased. The label on the inside of the coat led them to a men's clothing store in Flint. It was part of an ensemble that had been in stock four or five years earlier. Harold Asp's name wasn't in the store's card file as a customer, so the clerk was certain that Asp wasn't the person who purchased it originally. The investigator was curious if the company that manufactured the coat was still in business, but they had closed over a year before.

While the command officers were in Lansing at the crime lab, detectives were also back in Detroit at the New Woodward Hotel. Room twenty-three, where Asp had stayed, had already been cleaned since his stay, but the management found a receipt in the room and turned it over to police. It was a sales slip with the number 9860 on it. It was from the J. L. Hudson Company in the amount of two dollars and fifty-one cents.

The manager of the hotel was interviewed again and said Harold Asp had checked in on July 27 at 4:40 p.m. and paid for the room through August 3.

The bellboy said that Asp acted very nervous when he arrived at the hotel. Asp gave the bellboy a one-dollar tip for getting him a pack of Marlboro cigarettes, and when asked about his luggage, Asp said that his car had broken down and he left it in the car.

The hotel porter was interviewed, and he said Asp was dressed in a black sports coat and tie with gray pants. He came into the hotel asking about a room. Asked how much he wanted to pay, Asp said he'd pay around seven dollars. It was clear to the porter that Asp had been drinking, but the porter showed him three different rooms that were available. Asp left for twenty minutes, and when he returned, he paid for the first room that he'd looked at.

Knowing Asp was a bartender, the detectives checked with the Local 705 AFL-CIO Bartender Union in Detroit in the hopes that they might be able to track down Asp that way. He wasn't a member, but the union representative said most of the bartenders who go to Mackinac Island are members of the Local 25 in Chicago.

It seemed as though Asp was a good suspect, and the detectives were resolute in their effort to track him down.

On a whim, they checked the bars along Michigan Avenue in Detroit to see if they might find their new suspect but came up empty-handed. Their determination was fading.

PHOTOS

Frances Lacey
Courtesy of the Michigan State Police

The Murray Hotel
Courtesy of the Michigan State Police

Route Mrs. Lacey walked to British Landing
Courtesy of the Michigan State Police

Trooper Herbert Gross
Courtesy of the Michigan State Police

Sergeant George Burnette
Courtesy of the Michigan State Police

Lieutenant Robert Bilgin
Courtesy of the Michigan State Police

*MSP detective points to location where
Mrs. Lacey's purse was found
Courtesy of the Michigan State Police*

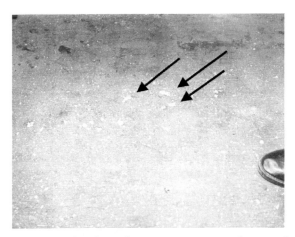

*Mrs. Lacey's broken denture pieces in the roadway
Courtesy of the Michigan State Police*

Gate leading to path where Mrs. Lacey's body was found
Courtesy of the Michigan State Police

Overturned boat that concealed Mrs. Lacey's shoes
Courtesy of the Michigan State Police

Photo from path looking back toward the open gate
Courtesy of the Michigan State Police

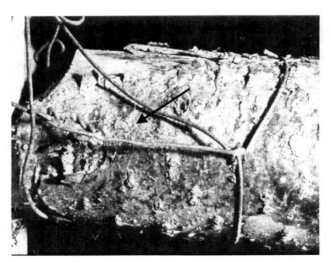

Strand of hair located just inside the gate
Courtesy of the Michigan State Police

An MSP trooper stands next to where
Mrs. Lacey's body was found
Courtesy of the Michigan State Police

View from the body location looking back at gate
Courtesy of the Michigan State Police

A watch similar to Mrs. Lacey's missing watch
Courtesy of the Michigan State Police

Location where Mrs. Lacey's wallet was
found near the Grand Hotel
Courtesy of the Michigan State Police

Detective Anthony Spratto
Courtesy of the Michigan State Police

MSP lab technician Ed Kivela
Courtesy of the Michigan State Police

MSP Mackinac Island Post located
in the Coast Guard Station
Courtesy of the Michigan State Police

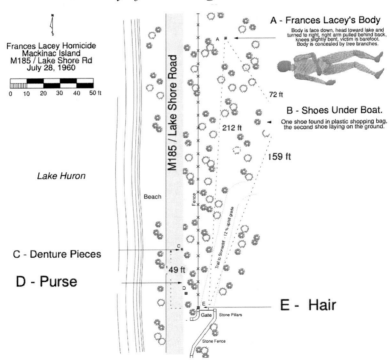

Diagram is based on measurements recorded by Michigan State Police on the morning of July 29, 1960, with additional measurements taken by the Rod Sadler in May, 2021.

16: TRACE EVIDENCE

As an MSP laboratory scientist, Dr. Ed Kivela knew that one of the most common types of evidence encountered at a crime scene was hair evidence because it's so easily transferred from one surface to another during a crime. The theory of human hair transfer was based on the Locard Exchange Principle, which simply states, that if there was any contact between two surfaces, an exchange of material would occur.[77]

By 1960, hair analysis in criminal investigations was commonplace and had been used for at least one hundred years when the first use of human hair comparison was done by Rudolph Virchow in 1861. Virchow wrote:

> The greatest majority of the hairs of the victim represent a thorough and complete accord with the hairs found on the defendant that there exists no technical ground opposite to looking at the hairs found on the defendant as being the hairs of the victim … However, the hairs found on the defendant do not possess any so pronounced peculiarities or individualities that no one with certainty has the right to assert that they must

---

77. FBI. "Review Article - Forensic Hair Comparison: Background Information for Interpretation - April 2009," https://archives.fbi.gov/archives/about-us/lab/forensic-science-communications/fsc/april2009/review/2009_04_review02.htm

have originated from the head of the victim (as cited in Bisbing 1982). [78]

By August 10, Kivela had already finished an early examination of some of the evidence. He found the hair on Frances Lacey's clothing appeared to be much finer than her head hair, and it was light brown to blonde in color. He also removed two more hairs from her skirt, and they appeared to be pubic hairs, but it would take a laboratory examination before he could be sure. He knew the analysis would be vitally important because he might be able to demonstrate an association between a suspect and the crime scene, or a suspect and the victim. Equally important was the ability to show that no evidence existed for an association between a suspect and the crime scene, or a suspect and Mrs. Lacey. The scientist's examination and analysis of the hairs recovered would never result in an identification of one specific individual to the exclusion of all others, but it could certainly provide the basis for an association. To identify one individual based on one human hair had never been successful, and he knew it wouldn't likely ever be.

Kivela's first evaluation was to determine whether the hairs recovered were of human or animal origin, and it was based on morphological characteristics. Once the determination was made that the hairs recovered were human, Kivela began evaluating the other characteristics. By analyzing those characteristics, he could categorize them into smaller groups such as ethnicity, the area of the body where the hairs came from, color, and growth phase. When complete, he would be able to determine whether or not a questioned hair could or couldn't be excluded as coming from a known sample taken from an individual.

---

78. FBI. "Review Article - Forensic Hair Comparison: Background Information for Interpretation - April 2009," https://archives.fbi.gov/archives/about-us/lab/forensic-science-communications/fsc/april2009/review/2009_04_review02.htm

Beginning the analysis, Dr. Kivela used a pattern-recognition process and step-by-step analysis of the unknown hairs taken from the body in comparison to Mrs. Lacey's own hair. He would use the same process for any subsequent known hair samples to be compared in the future. He tried to determine if similar microscopic patterns existed at different points along the shaft of each hair for comparison. The only way for there to be an association between the known and unknown samples was to identify the same characteristics in both.

Dr. Kivela knew the cuticle, which protects the hair from the harsh environment, has flat, scale-like cells that overlap each other. The free ends point toward the tip of the hair and interlock with the inner root, holding the hair in the follicle. With no pattern in the cells, Kivela could tell that the unknown hairs taken from Frances Lacey's body were human hairs because if they were from an animal, there would be a regular and repeating pattern in their scales. He looked closer at the cuticle and could identify other characteristics now; thickness, pigment, and color were all evident in the unknown samples.

The cortex of each strand was made up of elongated and spindle-shaped cells, and they contained pigment granules. The most informative feature he noted was the organization, density, size, and distribution of the granules, as these vary between racial groups and individuals. He also took note that the large, oval-shaped structures that were apparent in the strands were well-defined clumps of undispersed pigment.

At the base of the follicle, Kivela looked at the root, hoping to help identify when the hairs were separated from the body. Some of the other characteristics he looked for that were valuable in his comparison process included the texture, size, shape, and damage to the cortical cells.

The core of the strand, called the medulla, could be continuous, fragmented, or even absent, and the diameter was another characteristic that could be used in the comparison. The MSP scientist knew the cells might appear translucent or opaque, and could vary between each individual strand because air trapped within each strand caused opaque regions.

Kivela also knew the nature of the root is dependent on the growth stage. Because hair grows from the dermal papillae lying at the base of the hair follicle, the older portion is slowly pushed out as new hair is added and is eventually shed from the body.

Looking closer, the presence of an anlagen root would tell Kivela that there was some force used to remove the hair from the body because it would still be growing and attached to the follicle. If it had simply fallen from the body during the normal course of a daily routine, he didn't expect to see it attached. If the hair was removed as a result of force, the scientist wouldn't have any way of knowing how much force was used but there would likely be follicle material that could still be present.

Kivela could identify the growth stages of the strands including the second, or transitional stage, and the dormant stage. At the dormant stage, the strands are characterized by a decrease in the pigment near the root and increased cortical fusi near the root. Fully formed at that point, the root wouldn't be attached anymore and only be anchored because of the interlocking cuticular scales and the inner root sheath of the hair follicle.

Dr. Kivela considered several characteristics in comparing the samples, and those included the color shade, whether that shade was light or dark, and the intensity. Other considerations he was looking for included the tip of each strand. The tip of newly formed hair tapers naturally to a point, and as the hair is groomed or cut, or even subjected to artificial treatments, microscopic characteristics became evident.

Kivela submitted a report about his part in the investigation at the crime scene and his analysis of some evidence he'd recovered after the body was found.

He examined the hair removed from the breast area of Mrs. Lacey, and it appeared to be hers. Beyond that, the two hairs that were found by Lieutenant VanStratt on the base of the cobblestone pillar were similar in appearance to Mrs. Lacey's hair, and he could see that the white hair had a reddish stain on it. It appeared to be blood, and Kivela was certain the hair had been bloodied prior to the victim being carried through the pillared gate.

When he examined the hair taken from Mrs. Lacey's skirt, he could see it was finer than her hair, and it was light brown to blond. It hadn't come from Mrs. Lacey's head.

The two hairs taken from Mrs. Lacey's blouse were the same color as the hair taken from her skirt, and Kivela was also certain they hadn't come from her.

In his report to Michigan State Police Commissioner J.A. Childs, Kivela wrote:

> Of the three head hairs found not similar to the hair from the victim, their length is one and three-quarter inch, three-quarter inch, and five-eighth inch. Two of them taper to a fine tip, indicating that it has been a very long period of time since they were cut. The longest hair has been cut in a diagonal fashion and the tip is quite worn.[79]

It was crucial information that Dr. Kivela could use if future samples were submitted for comparison.

The scientist submitted a second report to the MSP commissioner about the other evidence he examined. His brother, MSP Detective Arthur Kivela, delivered an evidence envelope that had items taken from the suitcoat left by Harold Asp in the Woodward Hotel in Detroit. The

---

79. Kivela, Dr. Edgar. "Report to MSP Commissioner J.A. Childs." *Michigan Department of Public Health*, August 9, 1960

envelope contained two matchbooks, two pay stubs from the Grand Hotel that were made out to Harold Asp, a Greyhound bus envelope, a green baggage check marked A4558 from the Grand Hotel, and an advertising card from the New Woodward Hotel in Detroit. The Kerry Keith-brand suitcoat was also turned over to the scientist in a plastic bag. Dr. Kivela looked closely at the suit. It was black, made of a ribbed material, and was relatively clean.

When Kivela examined everything, he found seven hairs on the suitcoat. Five of those were white, and two of the shorter hairs were blond. He examined the hairs under reflected light and discovered there was a small difference in their color. When he looked at them by transmitted light, they were similar to the hairs taken from Mrs. Lacey's clothing. Based on that alone, Kivela felt the hairs from the suitcoat and the hairs from Frances Lacey's clothing could have come from the head of the same person. If the suitcoat belonged to Asp, the hair lifted by Kivela could still conceivably belong to someone else. Kivela knew he needed a known hair sample taken directly from Harold Asp.

For the detectives at MSP, it was the first promising lead they'd been waiting for.

***

Two days later, the suitcase recovered from Mackinac Island was turned over to the lab in Lansing. Dr. Kivela examined and inventoried the contents. The suitcase contained things like a razor and toothbrush, but also contained an assortment of soiled men's clothing.

Kivela meticulously looked over the clothing, knowing that he had made a possible connection between the hair found on the suitcoat and the hairs found on Mrs. Lacey's body. As he looked over the undershorts and socks in the suitcase, he discovered both head hair and pubic hair. He could see the head hair was similar in all respects to the head hair taken from Frances Lacey's body. He also noted that the pubic hair taken from the clothing in Asp's suitcase was similar in all respects to the pubic hair found on Mrs. Lacey.

Kivela wasn't simply looking for hair. Samples of evergreen needles had been taken from the area where the body was found but he couldn't find any on the clothing, nor could he find any bloodstains or hair on any of the shirts in the suitcase. With the hair comparison being similar, there was still a glimmer of hope.

While Kivela was looking at the evidence to make a connection in the murder, detectives were still trying to track down Asp. They discovered that between 1951 and 1954, Asp had six arrests under his belt but most of those were related to fraud or bad checks.

Employees at the Grand Hotel were questioned about the former employee who suddenly quit. Detectives learned that Harold Asp had had trouble with various people around the hotel. On the morning of the murder, the head bartender saw him around 9:00 a.m. A female cook complained that Asp had become upset about something and had used some profanity toward her while she was cooking eggs for him. She didn't really know why he'd suddenly become angry, but he said, "You can shove those eggs you're cooking for me up your ass." When the supervisor tried to talk to him about it, he said, "You all can go to hell." The bartender saw him again at around 11:30 when they rode in the elevator together. Asp mentioned that he was going to quit and wanted his money. The bartender told him the paymaster wouldn't be around until Monday, so he'd have to wait until then to get paid.

Detectives also interviewed the head chef from the Grand Hotel, and he said he had trouble with Asp when he tried to keep him out of the kitchen. He added that Asp was always surly and was always complaining about different things.

When police spoke with the husband and wife who cooked for the employees at the Hotel, they said they'd both witnessed the egg incident, and Asp was very abusive to everyone he spoke to. They recalled Asp saying, "I'll go anywhere, do anything, and eat any place I damn well please."[80]

Everyone interviewed by the detectives said they recalled Asp, at one time or another, wearing a dark-colored sport coat, so Detective Spratto asked that it be sent back to the Island to see if the employees could identify it as the coat they'd seen Asp wearing.

Spratto also spoke with cashiers from the Grand Hotel, and one of the cashiers said she only saw Asp away from the hotel on one occasion, and it was at the Iroquois Hotel Bar. She was having a beer when Asp approached her and sat down without being invited. When she wouldn't have anything to do with him, he became belligerent, and she finally told him to leave.

A second cashier said she had actually gone out with Asp on one occasion, and they stopped at Mary's Pantry for a beer. She didn't care for him because he was egotistical, and on several occasions after that, he asked if she'd go out with him again. She always made up an excuse to avoid him until he finally quit calling her. On one occasion, she lied to him as a way to avoid him, and then she went to play tennis. During the game, she looked over and noticed Asp was standing near the tennis courts staring at her.

Detective Spratto listened intently. He had a keen sense of observation and noticed something as he interviewed the waitress. Her resemblance to Frances Lacey was remarkable. She had the same build, the same color hair,

---

80. Spratto, Anthony. "Supplemental Report." *Michigan State Police,* August 24, 1960

and the same hairstyle. Even her glasses were the same shape as the murder victim's. Spratto quietly wondered if Asp had spotted Mrs. Lacey on July 24 and mistook her for the waitress. He made a mental note to himself.

***

The investigation was still very active on August 12, now nineteen days after Frances Lacey's disappearance, when the MSP Detroit Post received a phone call from a woman reporting an odd encounter she had on the same day that Frances Lacey's body was found when she and her husband were on the Island.

The small family arrived on Mackinac Island around 10:00 a.m. on Thursday, July 28, for their one-day adventure, and they had their one-year-old baby with them. They were out sightseeing and by early afternoon, they were near the golf course by the Grand Hotel. There was something unusual about a man they saw standing with two others near the boulevard leading to and from the Grand. He was waving his arms around, and as a horse-drawn carriage approached from the hotel heading toward Main Street, he flagged it down and climbed on the rear of it.

Late in the afternoon, the young family was downtown near the Murray Hotel when they saw the same man as they walked along Main Street. He noticed their baby and walked up to them to bend down and admire their child. He'd wanted to buy the baby some candy from a nearby store, and it was obvious to the couple that he'd been drinking. "A woman's been murdered here," he'd said as the three of them spoke.

The couple had already heard about Mrs. Lacey's disappearance. "I thought she was just missing," the woman had replied.

"Oh, she's dead all right," he said as he turned, walked away, and mumbled something about either being from, or having worked in, Farmington.

The woman thought the conversation was odd, yet she got the impression that the man was somehow connected to the investigation or knew some of the officers involved.

The couple continued on their way and approached a man wearing fatigues. They assumed he was a police officer and asked if he might recommend a good place to eat. He mentioned he wasn't from the Island and was only there to help in the search for Mrs. Lacey. When the woman mentioned the conversation she'd just had with the drunk who said she was dead, the man ignored her.

The couple ended up eating at the Murray, and as they were speaking with the hotel owner's mother in the lobby, they noticed the drunk come in the front door, look around quickly, and leave.

Recalling the odd encounter, the woman said she was certain that when he told her that Mrs. Lacey was dead, her body still hadn't been found. There was no further investigation of this person mentioned in the police report.

***

Detectives still hadn't found anyone who had seen Mrs. Lacey on the morning that she was murdered other than the waitress at the Murray Hotel. Police now theorized that it was likely Frances.

On August 13, Sergeant Burnette received a phone call from the editor of the *Mackinac Island Town Crier*. The editor was also a professor in the journalism curriculum at the University of Michigan. He and his family had taken a tour around the Island on bikes with another visiting family from Ann Arbor on July 24. He didn't recall anyone in particular on their bike trip, but he'd recently been back to the University and had dinner with the other family that had been on the Island with him. As they dined, his colleague mentioned that she recalled seeing Mrs. Lacey walking along Lake Shore Road on the morning of their bike ride.

When the group had reached an area where there had been some sort of previous landslide along Lake Shore Road, she noticed a woman walking along the right side of the road toward British Landing. It was around 9:30 a.m. She recalled the woman was wearing a street-length skirt, some sort of a winter-looking outfit that was dark colored, and a sleeveless vest. She described the woman's hair as being pulled up from the neck. The woman was wearing leather shoes, and she was carrying her right arm bent at the elbow as if she was carrying something. After she saw the photo of Frances Lacey in the newspaper, she was certain it was the same woman she'd seen.

Burnette asked the editor to speak with her again and see if she recalled whether the woman was wearing glasses or may have been carrying a purse. It sounded promising to Burnette, and the timeframe fit, but he wanted to be sure. He knew the location the woman was describing. The rockslide she spoke of was directly west of Stonecliff along Lake Shore Road, and it was one-eighth of a mile from the murder site. Frances Lacey would have been minutes away from being raped and murdered when the woman had seen her.

Burnette also set up another search from the point where Frances Lacey's body was discovered to the point where her billfold was found near the Grand Hotel. His hope was to find the missing watch or a pair of walking shoes that she could have been wearing when she was murdered. Burnette was confident the killer likely took Lake Shore Road back to the south from the scene and cut inland near the Grand Hotel swimming pool.

***

Eighteen days after the discovery of the body, the local Island headlines on August 14 read "HUNT SPREADS TO OTHER STATES." Sergeant Burnette told the media that one hundred twenty-nine tips had been checked by that point. "We have nothing definite. The other officers have compiled a vast amount of information, and we are checking it out, although nothing looks like it would have a connection," he said.[81] There were over twenty-five hundred phone calls between St. Ignace and Mackinac Island that had been checked. He also mentioned that polygraph tests had been done at several MSP Posts around the state to check suspects' alibis. Police also checked all the bike liveries to see if Mrs. Lacey might have rented a bike on the morning of her murder but found she hadn't.

By that time, the number of investigators directly involved in the investigation on the Island was reduced to two detectives from St. Ignace, Sergeant Burnette, and the three-member Mackinac Island Police Department, but other detectives and officers from around the state were still following up on leads at other Posts as they were received.

Word spread to the media that the police were looking for a former bartender from the Grand Hotel about the murder on Mackinac Island. On August 16, Detective McCluer was sent back to his Post, but he'd still be working the Lacey homicide while two more detectives arrived on the Island from Lansing.

James Brown, the Mackinac County Prosecuting Attorney, called Burnette at the Coast Guard Station for an update on the investigation. As they talked, Brown told Burnette that there wouldn't be a need for a coroner's inquest.

The investigators tried to keep key details about the homicide and possible suspects confidential. After Burnette

---

81. *Mackinac Island Town Crier*, "Hunt Spreads to Other States," August 14, 1960

spoke with the prosecutor, his phone rang again. It was W. Stewart Woodfill, the owner of the Grand Hotel.

Woodfill mentioned receiving a call from a reporter at the *Detroit Times* wanting information about the former bartender, Harold Asp. The reporter knew the police were looking for Asp, and he even knew about hairs that had been found on the sport coat found at the Woodward Hotel.

Burnette took the information from the Grand Hotel's owner, and he called Lieutenant Whaley at the Detroit Post. Whaley told him that word had already leaked to the media about Asp being a suspect, and since the information was out, he could release it to the other media outlets when they made their daily inquiries about the case.

On August 18, the Indiana State Police received a phone call from a man who identified himself as Harold Asp. He'd heard the Michigan State Police were looking for him. He politely gave his address to the detectives at ISP and told them that he'd make himself available if they wanted to speak with him. Detectives from the ISP headed for the address, but Asp wasn't there so they waited. Thirty minutes later, the suspect arrived at the address, and the detectives accompanied him to the ISP headquarters. Asp went along voluntarily, and the investigators decided not to ask him any questions because they had limited information about the Mackinac Island murder.

Within an hour of Asp being located, Whaley received a phone call from Captain Grant at MSP Headquarters. Grant told him that the Indiana State Police had located Harold Asp, and they were holding him for MSP regarding the Lacey homicide until MSP could get there to interview him. He told Whaley to meet Detective Spratto and a trooper at Lansing's Capitol City Airport. They'd be taking an MSP plane to Indianapolis.

The officers left the airport at 2:00 p.m. and landed in Indianapolis at 4:00 p.m.

Spratto, Whaley, and the trooper headed to ISP headquarters accompanied by two Indiana detectives. They were eager to interview their prime suspect.

Sitting in an interview room at Indiana State Police Headquarters, Harold Asp was cordial when the interview started. He told the detectives that he'd found work at Downey's Diner on Pennsylvania Street since arriving back in Indianapolis.

The skilled detectives quickly learned Asp was being intentionally vague about his activities from July 24 through July 26. He'd eaten breakfast at around 7:30 a.m. on July 24 because the Grand Hotel quit serving employees at 8:30 a.m. Asp said he might have walked around the hotel, or maybe down the boulevard to the path that led to the beach. He mentioned that he could have stayed in his room and read, then later headed to the beach for some sun. As evening neared, he went to work at 6:00 p.m., and at 1:00 a.m., he quit, but the records the detectives had showed that Asp quit work at 10:00 p.m., three hours earlier than he had said.

When the investigators asked about his off time, he said he mostly stayed in his room at the Grand Hotel on the fifth floor or hung out with the carriage drivers behind the hotel.

On Monday, July 25, Asp went through his same daily routine, and on Tuesday, he decided to formally quit, but he knew he couldn't get his pay until Wednesday. He paid two dollars to a carriage driver to deliver his bag to the Mackinaw City Bus Terminal, and he caught the boat for Mackinaw City himself on Wednesday.

After getting to Mackinaw City, Asp took the bus to Bay City, and when he got there, he started drinking and missed the bus to Detroit. Since he was stuck in Bay City, he stayed at a hotel overlooking the river and grabbed another bus for Detroit the following morning. When he arrived, he checked a couple of hotels on Woodward Avenue before deciding where to stay, but he didn't remember the Woodward Hotel by name.

Once he arrived in Detroit, Asp began looking for work along Woodward Avenue and started checking the classified ads for work, but he didn't have any luck. On a whim, he decided to head for Indianapolis. He told Spratto that he thought he arrived there on July 29.

The detectives asked Asp to provide hair samples for comparison purposes and he agreed. He gave the detectives both head and pubic hair, and he turned over the pants he'd been wearing since he left Mackinac Island. The pants hadn't been cleaned since before he left the Island, and it was evident to the detectives because they had stains on them and an accumulation of various small debris in the cuffs.

Harold Asp agreed to take a polygraph exam during the interview. An examiner from the ISP conducted the test, and it was his opinion that if there was any intentional deception, it was slight, and it didn't appear Asp was lying when he answered the questions. His answers to questions about his activities from July 24 through July 26 were still vague, and when confronted with why that would be, he said each day on Mackinac Island was like the other. Asp admitted he was angry with one of the other bartenders because a private party that had been handled by that same bartender should have been given to him. During the test, Asp also said that on occasion, he did take walks on the path that ran between the tennis courts and the pool, and he might even have done that on July 24, but he wasn't sure. When asked about other trails around the Grand Hotel, he said he'd never taken the carriage trail up to British Landing. The detectives were curious if he ever had any type of sexual relations with any women on the Island, and he told them no.

Spratto asked Asp if he would be willing to go back to Mackinac Island to help clear up any other questions they might still have, and he agreed. Whaley got permission from his command officer, and the three MSP officers accompanied Asp to the airport. All four men headed back to the Island, but made a brief stop at the Lansing airport where the items Asp had turned over were taken to the crime lab just four miles from the airport.

Kivela was given a manila envelope with a pair of men's pants inside. The trousers contained forty-six cents, a facial tissue, a handkerchief, and a crumpled piece of paper with a phone number on it. In a second package were two envelopes. One was marked "PUBIC HAIR" while the other was marked "HEAD HAIR."

Kivela sat at the bench in the crime laboratory as he peered through the eyepiece on the microscope. He was comparing the head hair voluntarily given by Asp with evidence taken from Mrs. Lacey's body, and he couldn't find any similarities.

When the scientist compared Asp's pubic hair with the pubic hair taken from Mrs. Lacey's body, there were enough similarities that he couldn't rule out the possibility that they might have come from the same source. He didn't have enough similarities to say beyond a doubt that the hairs matched or that Harold Asp was the killer.

Each time Dr. Kivela made an examination of the microscopic evidence, he kept possession of it at the crime lab so it could be used in further analysis with other samples turned in.

***

By the time the four men arrived back on Mackinac Island late in the afternoon, word had already been relayed about Kivela's findings.

Based on Asp's willingness to return to the Island, the calm demeanor in the way he answered his questions, and the results of his lie detector test, Spratto and Whaley were convinced he wasn't involved in the murder of Frances Lacey. They also felt he had an airtight alibi. "The suspect was very cooperative, and we cleared him in Indianapolis, but he consented to return to Mackinac to further clear himself," Spratto said. "There's no question that this particular individual is cleared."[82]

Now convinced that Harold Asp wasn't involved, he was flown back to Pontiac, where he purchased a ticket back to Indianapolis. Detectives dropped him at the bus station, but before he left, they asked about one of the other bartenders that worked with him.

Asp said that Clark Sutherland, one of the other employees who had roomed with him, used to have light-colored hair, but it had grayed. He also told them he'd seen him in Indianapolis, but beyond that, he wasn't sure where he was.

***

During their interview with Harold Asp about the sport coat that was found at the Woodward Hotel in Detroit, detectives discovered that the coat didn't belong to him after all. He did bring it with him to Detroit from the Island, but it belonged to whoever had used the room prior to him. Whoever that person was had left it. Asp took it with him when he left because no one had returned for it.

The investigation turned to the men who had stayed in that same room before Harold Asp.

Sergeant Burnette called the MSP Flint Post. The sport coat had been purchased from a store in Flint, and with the name of the store, along with the names of the two men

---

82. *Mackinac Island Town Crier*, "Former Island Employee Cleared of Connection with Lacey Case," August 28, 1960

who occupied the room prior to Asp, Burnette was hopeful that they could find out who actually owned the coat.

Frances Angel was one of two men who stayed in the room. In November 1955, Angel and his then wife had purchased a two-piece man's suit at a store in Flint and paid sixty-five dollars for it. A topcoat was also purchased by his wife. The suit was manufactured by Schloss Brothers in Baltimore, but the company had gone out of business since the purchase.

In 1956, Angel purchased a second sport jacket from the same store, but none of the identifying numbers on the clothing from Angel's purchases matched the number on the tag in the sport coat recovered at the Woodward Hotel in Detroit.

In addition to reaching a dead end in trying to tie him to the sport coat, Angel was questioned, and police found out he was arrested on Mackinac Island on July 14 for an outstanding warrant for bad checks in Montcalm County. He wasn't released from the Montcalm County Jail until July 28.

The second man who stayed in the room with Angel was checked, and he left the Island prior to July 24. He took a job in Ionia with a bread company and was working for six days straight. The only day he had off was August 14.

Both men submitted hair samples for comparison with the hairs taken from Frances Lacey's body. Even though it was clear neither one could have been involved in the murder, comparisons were still made with the evidence, and as expected, neither of the two men's hairs could be associated with the hairs taken from the body.

17: MRS. DECOURVAL

As summer's end rapidly approached, many of the local residents on Mackinac Island were convinced that the killer had to be a member of the MRA simply because Frances Lacey's body was found on the Stonecliff estate property.

Some of the MRA members had already been interviewed immediately after the body was found. A month after the murder, two detectives were assigned to begin tracking down which members had been working on July 24 and which ones weren't. They were given a list of fifty-four MRA members and told to check where they were on the day of the murder. They would have to check each person's story to verify it too.

The detectives began by interviewing some of the construction workers for the MRA including plumbers and electrical maintenance workers. Each member interviewed was either at home or had left the Island by July 24.

Throughout the week, police continued to concentrate their efforts on interviewing members of the MRA. Anyone associated with the MRA who might have been on the Island at the time was interviewed.

While MRA workers were being interviewed, so were more employees at the Grand Hotel. Many of the summer employees on the Island were college students looking to make money during their summer break. When Detective Hoffman interviewed a blue-eyed employee from the snack bar at the Grand Hotel, the young University of Michigan student said he'd worked until 3:00 a.m. on July 24.

Beyond that time, he couldn't recall anything else about that particular day. Hoffman, following up on the young man's story, could do nothing more than verify that he had, in fact, worked until 3:00 a.m. on the morning that Frances Lacey was murdered.

***

It was after 5:00 p.m. on August 17 when Sergeant Burnette's phone rang at the Coast Guard Station. It was George Beverly, and he was finally able to get a description of the watch that Frances had been wearing when she was murdered. He checked various jewelry stores in the Detroit area, and he discovered that Mrs. Lacey's watch had once been repaired at the Shaw Jewelry Store on Plymouth Road.

He gave a complete description of the watch to Burnette. While the sergeant appreciated the information, he still needed to verify it independently, so he called Operations in East Lansing to have a detective in the Detroit area double-check Beverly's story.

***

Bertha DeCourval and her teenage granddaughter, Christine, were enjoying their stay at the Grand Hotel as the fall season began to close in on the Island. After arriving on August 11 for their four-day vacation, the two stayed close to the hotel and only ventured short distances into town. Mrs. DeCourval had withdrawn two hundred dollars for their trip on August 4, and the pair set out by Greyhound bus a week later.

The sixty-nine-year-old widow heard about the Lacey murder while she was on the Island, and it was part of the reason she decided to stay so close to the hotel. She was heard making a lighthearted comment about the Island murder when she said it wasn't going to happen to her.

Only a year earlier, Mrs. DeCourval had been robbed of two thousand dollars when her home on Fleming Road in Flint was broken into while she was away for a couple hours.

When the grandmother and her granddaughter left Mackinac Island at 2:50 p.m., they started their return trip to Flint on a Greyhound. Eight hours later, the pair were picked up at the bus station by Mrs. DeCourval's son, Leo, and his wife. After dropping Leo's mom off at her modest, five-room home on Flint's northwest side, the small family left her standing at the front door as she waved goodbye.

When Leo arrived home with his family, Christine realized she'd forgotten the key to her suitcase. Her grandmother had it. She only lived six blocks away, but because it was late and she was tired, Christine decided to walk over to the house the next morning to get the key.

When the thirteen-year-old got to her grandmother's home the next morning, she noticed the front door was open slightly, and when she pushed it open, she saw her grandmother lying face down on the floor only a few feet away in a pool of blood. She was wearing her nightgown and slippers.

The teenage girl panicked and ran the entire six blocks back to her parents' home. She burst through the front door screaming to her mom that she thought her grandmother had been murdered. Christine's mother grabbed the phone and called her husband at the Flint factory where he worked, then called the Flint Police.

At the DeCourval home, the Flint Police Department discovered that three rooms in the house had been ransacked. The back door was ajar, and the theory was that Mrs. DeCourval was struck in the face when she answered the front door to her home after being dropped off the previous night. She'd likely been dead for at least ten hours before her body was discovered.

Tears streamed down Christine's face when she spoke to the police. "It was the worst thing I ever saw," she said.[83] When detectives asked if her grandmother knew about the Lacey murder on Mackinac Island, she said timidly, "She said she wasn't going to get herself killed in the woods . . . She said she was going to sit on the porch of the hotel, and that's what she did."[84]

During the investigation, police discovered a nylon stocking was stuffed in Mrs. DeCourval's mouth, but the autopsy showed her cause death was from a brutal beating.

Other than the rooms being ransacked, there were no other signs of a struggle in the home. Police couldn't find a murder weapon, and the elderly Mrs. DeCourval was still wearing a diamond ring on her finger when her body was found,[85] just as Frances Lacey was.

When the police questioned Leo about his mom's habits, he said she used to keep large sums of money in the home, but since the break-in a year earlier, she didn't do that anymore.

The Flint Police Department knew about the murder of the wealthy Dearborn widow on Mackinac Island. Since Mrs. DeCourval had just returned from a short vacation on the Island, and Mrs. Lacey's murder was only three weeks earlier, a detective from the Flint Police called MSP Detective Ralph Baney at the Flint Post. Baney was told about the circumstances surrounding the DeCourval homicide, and he wrote a supplemental report to forward

83. *The Herald-Press*, "Police Ponder Link Between Two Murders," August 16, 1960, p 14

84. *Lansing State Journal*, "Police Have Puzzle: Did Same Man Kill 2 Elderly Widows," August 16, 1960 p 4

85. *Detroit Free Press*, "Flint Widow Fatally Beaten in Home," August 16, 1960, p 1

to Bilgen on the chance that the two murders might be connected. It seemed too coincidental.

MSP investigators on Mackinac Island discussed the details of both murders with the Flint detectives by phone. While Frances Lacey was raped and strangled with her own panties in the morning while walking along Lake Shore Road, Bertha DeCourval was murdered at around midnight in her home. Mrs. DeCourval was beaten to death in her front doorway with a blunt object, she wasn't raped, and her house was ransacked.

Within a few days of Bertha DeCourval's murder, the Flint Police released a statement that they were satisfied the murders of Frances Lacey and Bertha DeCourval were not connected and were simply coincidental.

***

By mid-August, interviews about the murder of Frances Lacey had taken place all over Michigan and beyond, both with tourists and employees from various businesses on the Island. Some of the detectives assigned to the investigation immediately afterward had already returned to their assigned posts.

On August 23, Sergeant Burnette's phone rang, and Sheriff Garries in St. Ignace was on the other end of the line. There was someone in his office who wanted to turn himself in for the murder of Frances Lacey. Burnette had his doubts as he hurried to the Mackinac County Jail.

Looking very nervous, the man sat across the table from Burnette and a deputy. He was a kitchen helper at the Grand Hotel, and he said he heard from hotel employees on the Island and from a news broadcast that the police were going to pick him up for the murder. He wanted to clear himself from any suspicion, so he came to the sheriff's office in St. Ignace.

As they spoke with him, Burnette quickly realized the man was suffering from some emotional problems. He'd already been interviewed by Detective Hoffman a few weeks earlier. When some of the other employees at the hotel found out, they started to tease him, saying, "They're going to come after you."[86] Burnette was certain that the constant teasing led the man to believe that he might have misinterpreted a news report and thought the police were looking for him.

As long as he was willingly going to give them an accounting of his activities, Burnette listened closely and took notes as they spoke.

The man was off on the morning of the murder, and he told Burnette he either slept or read in his room. He shared his room with three other men, but he felt that his boss at the hotel could provide a better accounting of his time so he passed the name on to the MSP sergeant.

To be certain they didn't miss anything, Burnette decided to assign someone to verify the man's story.

***

Private Investigator Ralph Beverly was frustrated. He met with the MSP investigators, and during the meeting, he asked that he be allowed to review all of the reports that MSP had accumulated thus far in connection with the murder. He wanted to put some of his own men, working undercover, at the Murray Hotel and the Grand Hotel. He told MSP he had wiretap equipment, a polygraph machine, and bugging equipment that MSP could use if the need arose. While his offer was appreciated by the detectives, any decisions made regarding the private investigator would have to be made by someone higher up.

---

86. Burnette, George. "Supplemental Report." *Michigan State Police*, August 23, 1960

The next day, a detective from the Flint Police Department contacted Lieutenant Bilgen about the DeCourval homicide. He made sure Bilgen was aware of the details since Mrs. DeCourval had been on the Island just before she returned to her home in Flint. In turn, Bilgen briefed the Flint Police detective with details of the Lacey homicide.

Bilgen learned that one of the Coast Guard members on the Island had actually spoken with Mrs. DeCourval on her bus ride from Flint, so the service member was interviewed in the hope he might be able to offer even the smallest clue as to who killed the Flint widow. Their brief conversation was nothing more than that, and he had nothing to offer.

***

A little over a week after the DeCourval murder, Detective Spratto found out that one of Harold Asp's roommates, Clark Sutherland, had been found by the Indiana State Police working as a bartender at the Embassy Room in Indianapolis. Spratto drove to Lansing and flew to Indianapolis on an MSP plane to interview Sutherland.

Spratto knew Sutherland was working at the Grand Hotel on the morning of the murder. He made arrangements so the former bartender from the Island could be interviewed in the office at the Embassy Room.

Sutherland said that on July 24, he saw Asp and his other roommate at around 8:30 a.m. and didn't see him again until around noon when Asp was packing. He seemed extremely angry saying that he was going to quit. Sutherland saw him one more time later that night, and Asp was drunk. On the morning of July 25, Sutherland saw him at around 8:00, but he hadn't seen him since. He also remembered that Asp often wore a dark-colored sport coat.

Clark Sutherland said that Asp fancied himself a real ladies' man and said that his former roommate had a short fuse and was very cocky.

Spratto asked Sutherland if he would submit some body hair for comparisons with the hairs that were taken from Mrs. Lacey's body, and Sutherland willingly offered them.

***

Since much of Mackinac Island was a state park, Chairman of the Michigan State Park Commission W. Stewart Woodfill wanted to keep abreast of the investigation. On September 1, forty days after Frances Lacey's body was found, he wrote a letter to Lieutenant Bilgen regarding the report of the nude man seen several weeks earlier.

Woodfill had done his own investigation when he saw the story about the nude man in the *Mackinac Island Town Crier*, and he discovered the witness who confronted the man was Pete Marudas. When Marudas was contacted by Woodfill, he said he wanted to keep his anonymity about being the person who saw the nude man and spoke with him, but said he did report it to the state police.

Woodfill had had two detectives at his home a few weeks earlier, and asked them if the man who was seen nude on the beach near the pillared gates along Lake Shore Road was considered a suspect in the murder of Frances Lacey. One of the detectives said that they felt they knew who the man was, and based on their investigation, they didn't consider him a suspect in the murder.

The commissioner wanted to know conclusively because he knew Pete Marudas was leaving the Island for the winter, and Marudas had asked the state police if the man he saw on the beach had been cleared as a suspect. He was told that MSP detectives identified a nudist in St. Ignace, but still hadn't located the nude man on Mackinac Island, and whoever it was would still be considered as a suspect.

Woodfill didn't want to bother the state police with trivial matters. He wasn't certain how much information they could share with him without jeopardizing the investigation, but as chairman of the state parks, he was still confused about whether MSP had located the nudist on the Island, and whether or not he'd been cleared as a suspect.[87]

The letter from W. Stewart Woodfill attracted immediate attention. Three days later, Detective Spratto submitted a supplemental report. He'd spoken with a confidential informant, and the informant identified the man as a summer resident on the Island who enjoyed nude sunbathing on the beach. He was an attorney, spoke with an accent, and people could easily mistake him for being British.

Spratto wrote in his report that he spoke with the man, and he was certain that he had no involvement in the Lacey homicide. In his report, he added, "Due to his age and being feeble, he should not be listed as a suspect, and he should be carried on [the] inactive list."[88]

***

As Spratto was digging into identifying the nudist, several other reports of a suspicious person were coming in.

A boyfriend and girlfriend were on a late-night bike ride around the Island and were returning around 2:30 a.m. As they were returning to her home, a man stepped from the bushes. The boyfriend knew the man as Edward Pulaski*, a worker at the Grand Hotel. Startled, the pair of bike riders

---

87. Woodfill, W. Stewart, "Letter to the Officer in Charge," September 1, 1960

88. Spratto, Anthony. "Supplemental Report." *Michigan State Police*, September 4, 1960

watched Pulaski, and he stared back at the woman until she was safely in her home. As her boyfriend started to ride away, he saw Pulaski quietly slip back into the woods.

One of the barboys from the Grand Hotel had had a similar experience with Pulaski and had also reported it to the police. He said that he and some friends were having a beach party one evening, and just before midnight, he and his girlfriend began to walk back up the boardwalk. They were following the path from the beach that went by the Grand Hotel pool house where Pulaski was staying. As they neared it, Pulaski stepped from the woods in front of them, startling them. Pulaski simply stood there and grinned.

In yet another encounter, a tourist from Nashville, Michigan, had been riding her bike from Fort Mackinac to the carriage barns. She told police she'd been on the North Road that ran by the golf course, and as she neared a large pine tree, a man stepped from the shadows in front of her and simply stared at her. He said nothing and began to laugh eerily at her. She could only describe him as wearing a stocking cap.

Pulaski had been questioned only a few days after the murder. He was found in his room at the pool house where he lived. He told Detective McCluer that he was from Flint and worked during the summer on the Island painting the pool at the hotel for a month, then worked as a dishwasher at The Snack Shop. He got off work at 2:30 or 3:00 a.m. and went straight to his room and then bed. His alarm went off at 6:50 a.m. He got up, went to The Snack Shop, got his breakfast, and returned to his room, where he went back to sleep. McCluer asked if he had any roommates, and Pulaski said he had two, but they weren't around to confirm his story.

During the interview, Pulaski said he didn't hang around with any other employees because he didn't drink or smoke, and he had nothing in common with them. He admitted to the detective that he had one arrest in Flint for disorderly conduct, and he'd been court-martialed in the army for leaving his post but still received an honorable discharge.

McCluer spoke with the pool manager at the Grand Hotel, and he said he knew Pulaski's family because he was from Flint too. He brought Pulaski to the Island to work for the summer, and it was actually his second summer there. The routine Pulaski had described was exactly what he did each day, and the pool manager didn't think he could be involved in anything like the Lacey homicide.

A week later, the detective was able to contact both roommates of Pulaski. Neither one could say whether or not he was in his room sleeping in the early morning hours of July 24 because they were both gone. The pool manager was there when McCluer spoke with the roommates, and he said again that he didn't feel Pulaski could be involved because he'd never shown any interest in women. McCluer knew there was no way to confirm Pulaski's story about his whereabouts on the morning of July 24.

With the reports of his weird activities, Pulaski was picked up for questioning a second time and taken to the Coast Guard Station. It didn't take long for the detectives to conclude that he was mentally challenged. McCluer didn't mention that in his report. Pulaski said he only went as far as the eighth grade in Flint. He was on the Island for his second summer, and he was a dishwasher at The Snack Shop at the Grand Hotel.

Detective Harold Stock was questioning Pulaski and asked him about the activities that had been reported about him. He remembered some of them but added that he hadn't done anything wrong, and he just liked to look at girls. He said he slept most of the time but sometimes he would walk to the beach or into the city.

Detective Stock zeroed in on July 24. Pulaski couldn't account for his time but said that since he sleeps all the time, that must have been what he was doing. The MSP detective asked him specifically if he was involved in the murder of Frances Lacey. Pulaski didn't think he was involved but said he could have been. When some of the details of the murder were mentioned by Stock, he said he couldn't recall doing any of it.

Pulaski added that if he did kill Frances Lacey, he'd admit to it. He readily admitted to the detective that he masturbated on a regular basis, but he hadn't been with a woman in four or five years.

Stock and the other detectives were still suspicious of Pulaski. They asked if he'd go to the murder scene in hopes of jogging some of his memory, and he agreed. Four detectives accompanied him to the pillared gates along Lake Shore Road where Frances Lacey's body was found.

As Pulaski slowly looked around, he said he'd never been to that side of the Island, and nothing looked familiar to him. He was questioned again about his normal activities but didn't add anything new. When they took him back to the Coast Guard Station, he was questioned again, and his story never changed.

All the investigators working the case had become accustomed to obtaining hair samples from anyone they thought might be a potential suspect. Pulaski willingly gave them both head and pubic hair for comparison.

The hair samples were sent to Dr. Kivela at the crime laboratory in Lansing. On September 14, Kivela received the white envelope that contained Pulaski's head and pubic hair. The lab expert examined the samples microscopically comparing them with the hairs taken from the murdered Dearborn widow.

In his report to the director of the state police, he wrote that the hairs were not similar, and therefore, they could not have come from the same source, and Pulaski was cleared as a suspect.

***

While lab analysis was being done on hair samples at the crime laboratory, investigators on the Island were still tracking down people who might have known Harold Asp or his roommates.

A cashier from the cocktail lounge at the Grand Hotel was interviewed and asked about his own routine. He was a student at Western Michigan University, but his summer employment was at the Grand Hotel. He didn't have a girlfriend, and each night he'd finish his shift at 2:00 a.m. and head back to the Cottage House where he was staying.

He knew Harold Asp and described him as often being drunk. He heard a rumor that on the night of July 24, Asp had shown up drunk at the City Inn and got into a fight, but he didn't know what the fight was about. He simply heard that Asp was involved.

***

As MSP cleared Asp and Pulaski from any suspicion in the murder of Frances Lacey, they still worked under the assumption that there could be a connection to the murder of Bertha DeCourval in Flint, even though other investigators were sure there was no connection between the two.

18: NEW TIPS

In mid-August, tips continued to trickle in. Each one was still put on a tip card and assigned to a detective to follow up on, but the pace of the investigation slowed substantially.

A promising call came from the Island House Hotel when an employee reported that he'd seen a man at the Arnold Ferry Dock around 2:00 p.m. on the day of the murder. He thought the man looked pretty rough, and he noticed scratches on the man's face. He recognized him but he didn't actually know his name. As the two talked, the man said he came to the Island to work at the City Inn but ended up working at the Grand Hotel because he could handle heavier stuff than what one might expect at the smaller hotels. The tipster also recalled the man had made mention of being a bartender in the area of Gratiot and Ten Mile Road in Detroit. The conversation lasted only a few minutes until the ferry arrived, and it was the last the man was seen.

Maybe he was the killer. A rough-looking man leaving the Island on the day of the murder with scratches on his face piqued their interest. Were the scratches the result of a struggle with Mrs. Lacey as she fought for her life?

The detectives walked to the City Inn. The bartender recalled a musician named Al Banner who matched the description and had come to the Island to entertain. He described Banner as being red-faced, with a heavy build, and he played guitar. He'd been on the Island before and entertained at the Chippewa Hotel.

The manager at the Chippewa Hotel recalled Banner, and he found a photo of him posing with several other musicians who played at the Chippewa at some time in the past. The detectives showed the photo to the person who gave the tip, and he recognized Banner as the man with the scratches on his face.

The manager of the City Inn was contacted, and he was certain that Al Banner didn't arrive until after July 25. He remembered placing a phone call to Banner at his home in Detroit at around 12:15 p.m., and they spoke about arrangements for him on the Island and the amount of his salary. He'd be entertaining at the City Inn.

The detectives checked the phone records, and there was a call placed to Detroit on July 24 with a charge of two dollars and seventy cents.

Banner arrived on the Island on July 25 at 6:00 p.m. He'd been drinking, so he was put up at the theater for the night. The next day, he started drinking again and didn't show up for work, so the manager told him he didn't want him around anymore. He tried to borrow some money but ended up having to call his wife in Detroit for twenty-five dollars, and he left Mackinac Island on July 26 at 6:00 p.m.

Based on what they found out, investigators believed the date provided on the tip sheet was wrong. Since Banner didn't arrive on the Island until July 25, there was no way he could have been involved in Frances Lacey's murder.

***

The phone rang at MSP Operations in East Lansing at 12:20 a.m. It was Kay Sutter, and she was furious. She'd just found out that the Watts and Whalen Detective Agency was working on the murder investigation, and the Beverly Detective Agency had dropped their investigation when they heard about it. She hadn't hired anyone other than the Beverly Agency.

The next morning, Detective Spratto was told by Captain Grant of the phone call. It was the first he had heard about a second detective agency becoming involved, and he didn't know anything about it. Spratto suggested that Kay Sutter's brother, William, be contacted to see if he had hired them. A check was also made around the Island to see if anyone from the Watts and Whalen Agency had been asking questions, but it appeared they hadn't.

***

Each tip that looked as if it might have some substance to it seemed to fade as quickly as it was written down. Tip number three-thirty-three was received early in the investigation, and there wasn't a lot of validity given to it because the person calling in the tip thought it was a big joke, but it still had to be checked.

Calvin Land, a contractor on the Island, claimed to several coworkers that he had killed Frances Lacey. He said he strangled her with her own "Maidenform panties" and watched her eyes roll back in her head as she passed out. He said that he had intentionally gone out on Lake Shore Road to look for her because he'd been paid five hundred dollars, and he was going to get more money once the murder was complete. After telling the tipster about the murder, he showed him a large amount of cash in his wallet.

Police were skeptical, and they checked into his criminal background. Land had an arrest on his record for rape. It was unlikely that anyone who was the subject of an intense manhunt on the Island and around the state would admit to coworkers that he was responsible for the Dearborn widow's demise. But it also wasn't unheard of for someone to brag about a murder they'd committed. The police knew they had to talk to him.

The coworkers who heard Land claim responsibility for the murder were each questioned, and they recalled that Land confessed to the murder and described how he choked Mrs. Lacey with her own panties. Even though he said he had been hired to kill her, he told them he wouldn't have done it if she hadn't screamed. He said he received five hundred dollars up front, and he was supposed to get more the following month. Land seemed to have a lot of money in his wallet when he flashed it in front of them, and a traveler's check was visible too, but Land wouldn't let them count the cash.

The detectives were curious about the color of his hair, and they were told it was white and that Calvin Land had a very light complexion.

As police were starting to track down Land, his father-in-law heard about it and called him. He told Land that the police wanted to question him about the Island murder, so Land, now concerned about what he'd said to his coworkers, quickly returned to the Island and reported to the state police post. He told the police he was on the Island with his wife and kids, but he'd make himself available for an interview.

The detectives wasted no time. Land admitted he had told some coworkers he killed Frances Lacey and described how he strangled her with her panties while watching her eyes roll back in her head. He also admitted that as he was telling his colleagues how he committed the murder, he grabbed a coworker by the throat from behind just to scare him. From time to time, he'd bring up the murder again because he liked to see their apprehension and fear as a few of them took it seriously, but he also said it was all a joke.

Accounting for his time on July 24, Land said he left his home with his stepdaughter at around 10:00 or 10:30 a.m. They rode horses by the old cemeteries on the Island and down the old State Road to British Landing. They visited with his mother-in-law for a couple hours, then returned to their home near Lake Shore Road. He thought it was about 2:00 p.m. when they left British Landing.

Land admitted he had a couple misdemeanor arrests and had been arrested for statutory rape in Detroit when he was seventeen. The detectives were pretty certain he wasn't involved in the Lacey murder, but it had also become standard practice to get head hair and pubic hair from anyone who might even remotely be considered a suspect, and Land provided both.

Because Land had an arrest for rape in his past, they weren't simply going to take his word. His wife told them that she had been married once before, and Land was her second husband. She had heard that Land had confessed to the murder, and she confronted him about it. He told her that he did say it and didn't really know why. The Lands had been married for six years, he'd never been physical with her during an argument, and she didn't think he was capable of murdering anyone.

The detectives asked if she could recall him going horseback riding on July 24, and while she couldn't be exact on the date, she remembered that he left with her daughter to ride horses one day. She said they went to British Landing and visited the pop stand that her mother ran at British Landing.

The MSP detectives also spoke with her daughter, and she remembered going horseback riding with her stepdad, but she couldn't be sure if it was July 23 or July 24. She mentioned riding by the cemeteries, then taking the old State Road behind the golf course to British Landing before stopping to visit with her grandmother.

***

Late in the afternoon on September 23, two months after the murder, the phone in Corporal Louis Pantini's office rang at the St. Ignace Post. It was the auditor at the Grand Hotel, and he had received a letter from the Michigan Employment Securities Commission. They were trying to verify the employment of a man named Kemper at the Grand Hotel. Kemper, whose last known address was in Kalamazoo, was applying for unemployment insurance. On his application for the insurance, he wrote that he'd left the Grand Hotel over a salary dispute.

Pantini hung up the phone and immediately called Burnette to let him know they had a lead on where they might be able to find Kemper. Burnette received another call from an FBI Special Agent in Muskegon. A deserter from the military they'd been looking for who'd been on the Island at the time of the Lacey homicide had been picked up. He was serving six months for desertion, and he was going to receive a general discharge. He was court-martialed on August 31.

The FBI offered to interview him about his time on the Island on the weekend of the murder. Burnette didn't have the manpower to send detectives to Chicago for the interview, so he accepted their offer. He briefed the agent on the case and asked that he concentrate his questioning about the suspect's activities on the Island on July 23 and July 24.

***

By October, the case had stalled. Spratto and six other detectives met in Lansing at the MSP Headquarters to discuss other leads in the case that still needed to be explored.

It was time to step back and take a look at reinterviewing some of the key players. One of those was Frances Lacey's son, William. During his interview, William said that his mother's estate hadn't been settled yet but when it was, it would probably be worth around one hundred twenty-five thousand dollars.

He was asked to recap how he'd heard about his mom's disappearance on July 24, and he said he had received a call from his sister at around 5:00 p.m. telling him that his mom was missing. He told Kay to call him back at 11:00 if she still hadn't been located. There were a couple more calls in that time span from his sister, and by 11:00, he and his wife dropped their baby off at his mother-in-law's home and headed north.

William also said that his dad, Ford, had been married twice before he married Frances. He knew that after Ford's death, his mother would never remarry. He said she wasn't the type of person to go out to bars; he only recalled her drinking once when she had a glass of wine at his wedding. The only places that he knew his mother liked to go to were stores that sold funny postcards. She loved those and she'd even sent one to him during the short time she was on the Island. He said he'd look around for it and give it to them if he could find it.

The police asked about a potential boarder at his mother's house. William could only recall that the young man was going to stay at his mom's home, he was a friend of her twin brother, and he lived in Lake Odessa.

The police were looking for even the smallest of clues. Could the killer be someone close to Mrs. Lacey? Could the killer be from Dearborn?

Kay was reinterviewed again, and her recollection of the events on that fateful weekend never changed.

***

Police were leaving no stone unturned, and part of the investigation into Frances Lacey's financial situation involved looking through her checkbook. They were quick to notice a missing check. Detectives still wondered if there could be a financial element to her murder? Check number 121 was written to the Manufacturers Safe Deposit Company for six dollars and sixty cents. Check 122 was missing, and the next check to be written was 123. Kay said her mom cashed a check on the way to Mackinac, and she likely hadn't had time to record it in the ledger. That would account for check 122.

Police also discovered a sealed envelope in her purse when it was turned over to them, and the envelope was addressed to the Manufacturers Safe Deposit Company. They would have to open the envelope to see if check 122 was inside. A second sealed envelope was opened that was addressed to the Michigan Consolidated Gas Company. Their suspicions were confirmed when both envelopes were opened. The envelope addressed to the gas company contained check 121 in the amount of four dollars and thirty-seven cents. The envelope addressed to the safe deposit company contained check 122 in the amount of six dollars and sixty cents. Mrs. Lacey had recorded the wrong check number in her ledger.

***

The AWOL sailor from the navy who had been picked up was now at the Great Lakes Naval Station in Chicago, and during his interview with navy authorities, they discovered he'd been on Mackinac Island at the time of the murder. Since the time he'd surrendered himself to authorities, he tried to die by suicide twice. There is nothing in the police report to indicate if the second sailor was ever located and interviewed. Sergeant Burnette wondered why the sailor would try to take his own life after turning himself in. If he'd murdered Frances Lacey, was he afraid of being caught? At the sergeant's request, the FBI had agreed to interview him in Chicago.

Richard Baker* had left his ship with another sailor, and they headed for Mackinac Island, where they both got jobs as dock porters for the Grand Hotel while he stayed at the Marquette Hotel. After six weeks, he changed jobs when he was hired by the Island House, and he moved his temporary residence to Jack's Livery Stable. When he finally left the Island, he met a waitress from the Island House on the ferry. She was with her sister, and they both worked at Sammy's Restaurant. He ended up going to Detroit with the two women and staying for a short time at their home.

Baker said he left the Island in early August, and he didn't know anything about the murder, but he was good friends with one of the Mackinac Island police officers whose nickname was Junior.

The information gained from the interview was scant, but the FBI forwarded what little information they'd been able to get from Baker to MSP and added that he was being held in the brig at the Great Lakes Naval Station. There was no additional investigation noted in the police report regarding Richard Baker.

19: STALLED

The investigation into Mackinac Island's unsolved murder had stalled. Each tip that seemed promising had reached a dead end. The longer the investigation went on, the more police began to believe the killer had escaped the Island between the time of Mrs. Lacey's disappearance and the discovery of her body. If that were the case, her killer could be anywhere.

***

Bill Yates* had been with the Pennsylvania Railroad for over forty years. One of the perks he enjoyed with his seniority was being able to occasionally work as the conductor on the passenger trains, and just before July 4, he started on the railroad run from Grand Rapids to Mackinaw City and back. The schedule was set to run until the weekend after Labor Day.

On October 15, nearly three months after the murder, Yates was still working as the conductor, and the train had a stop in Kalamazoo. While waiting, he noticed MSP Trooper Don Tordel near the train station. Seeing the trooper reminded him of a man he'd seen on July 24, and he'd meant to share the information a couple months earlier. Now was his chance because he knew the murder of the Dearborn widow on Mackinac Island still hadn't been solved.

Trooper Tordel was assigned to a special work detail in Kalamazoo. Senator John F. Kennedy was in town for a speaking engagement, and Tordel's assignment was to cover the train station. The Kennedy detail hadn't arrived yet, so Tordel listened intently as Yates shared the information he'd been meaning to pass on for a couple months.

On July 24, Yates was working the run to Mackinaw City, and on the return trip to Grand Rapids, he'd noticed a man get on the train who seemed out of place. It was around 4:00 p.m. when the passengers boarded, and Yates quickly noticed the lone man didn't have any luggage. He carried a couple of magazines, and to Yates, appeared very nervous. The man took a seat in the middle of the passenger car away from the rest of the passengers, and he got up several times to walk back and forth in the train car.

Working as a conductor, Yates had learned to memorize where passengers sat, to know which luggage belonged to which passenger, and to be able to let them know if their stop was coming up. To Yates, the man seemed very suspicious. He tried to engage the man in conversation a couple of times, but the only thing he could gather was that he was from Detroit. As the train made one of the first stops in Petoskey, the man got off, and Yates last saw him on a street adjacent to the Perry Hotel. Bill Yates had planned to report the suspicious person when the train arrived in Rockford, but it had slipped his mind.

Tordel asked Yates for a description of the nervous train passenger, and he said the man was short and had a medium to stocky build. His hair was brown with some gray in it and was cut short. He described it as almost a butch haircut. He said the man was wearing black pants, a black sports coat with gray specks in it, and he described it as a salt and pepper suit. He was wearing dark brown loafers, and his clothes appeared to be well kept. Yates went on to say that the man had dark eyes and a dark complexion, and he thought it looked as if the man had been out in the sun quite a bit.

As the trooper was taking notes, the Kennedy detail was quickly approaching, so Tordel had to leave Yates. He made sure to tell him that he'd pass the information along to the detectives working on the homicide case.

Tordel's report about his conversation with Yates was sent to the Cheboygan MSP Post and was assigned to a detective for follow-up. The detective's first move was to check the guest registrations at the Perry Hotel. He was able to get a complete list for July 23 and July 24.

He also checked with the local police to see if anyone had been arrested on those days, but no one had. When the Petoskey Police heard the description, it matched one of their local residents, and they agreed to try to locate him to see if he could account for his time on July 24.

The detective also spoke with the agent at the train station to see if he could track the man down by checking the tickets for July 23 and July 24. He found one two-party ticket to Detroit, and a one-party ticket to Detroit. He also found one-party tickets to Saginaw and Cincinnati.

Five days after Yates had told the trooper in Kalamazoo about his passenger on July 24, Tordel's report had made it to Howard Whaley's desk. Whaley sent a memo to the MSP district commander in Traverse City. In the memo, Whaley asked that Detective Sergeant Bloomquist be allowed to do the follow-up and expand his investigation to the Mackinaw City and Petoskey areas in hopes of tracking the man down. If the suspicious man on the train was Frances Lacey's killer, Bloomquist knew all the details of the investigation.

Five days after Whaley's memo to the district commander, the Petoskey Police made good on their promise. They contacted the detective from the Cheboygan Post and said the man they were thinking might have been on the train was a sexual deviant. He lived in Petoskey, but he'd been prosecuted in the city of Gaylord, and they suggested that the detective contact Gaylord for more information about him.

The original complaint was from 1955. The man thought to have been the train passenger had pled guilty in circuit court to indecent liberties with a minor female. He wasn't sentenced to prison in the case, but instead was sent to the psychiatric hospital in Traverse City.

When the detective checked with the hospital, he was told the man had been released on leave. He also learned that one of the restrictions on his leave was that if he left his home in Petoskey where he lived with his eighty-eight-year-old mom, either she or his brother-in-law (who had also been a patient at the psychiatric hospital) had to accompany him.

The detective went to the house but no one was home. A neighbor said the first time they remembered seeing the man after his release from the hospital was around June 1, and each time they saw him, he was with his mom or his brother-in-law. Sometimes he was seen with his sister too. They also mentioned he didn't drive, and his mom didn't have a car anyway. If he did leave in a car, it was in his sister and brother-in-law's car, and one of them was driving.

After doing some initial checking, the MSP investigator contacted the Petoskey Police again. They'd been to the man's home only a few days before on another matter, and they saw him in the house. After speaking with them, the detective and the Petoskey Police were confident that the man they thought could have been the train passenger likely wasn't involved given his strict restrictions about leaving the home. There was nothing in the police report to indicate there were any additional attempts to learn the identity of the man on the train.

20: STARVED ROCK

While detectives and troopers were sifting through clues and interviewing possible suspects in the Dearborn widow's vicious murder, the Illinois State Police and LaSalle County Sheriff's Office in Illinois were still trying to solve the brutal murders of three socialites in Starved Rock State Park that had happened on March.

By mid-November, papers across the country carried the news of a suspect's arrest in the Illinois murders. He was a former dishwasher at the park lodge, and Howard Whaley took notice and drafted a letter to Illinois State Police Superintendent William Morris. In the letter, Whaley wrote:

> Many people are employed on Mackinac Island each summer as cooks, bartenders, dishwashers, waiters, etc., and it is possible that the subject of your arrest may have been employed or sought employment there.[89]

The murders in Illinois and Michigan were only four months apart, and they were both committed in state parks. With the arrest of a suspect in the Illinois triple murder, it seemed a promising lead to the Michigan investigators as they desperately searched for new clues in the Lacey murder.

LaSalle County Illinois Sheriff Ray Eutsey had years of experience in law enforcement. When the bodies of the three socialites had been found in the Starved Rock caves,

---

89. Whaley, Howard. "Letter to William Morris," November 17, 1960

it was Eutsey who had ordered the cave and surrounding area to be preserved until members of the Illinois State Police Crime Laboratory could search the area for clues six hours later.

After the bodies were discovered on March 16 at around 12:30 p.m., Sheriff Eutsey and Illinois State's Attorney Harland Warren headed the investigation, and Eutsey vowed to the public that the case would be solved.

"It only started as a robbery," the twenty-one-year-old former dishwasher told the sheriff.[90] Chester Weger was working at the Starved Rock Lodge in March. Early in the investigation, he'd come to the attention of the police when they checked his background and learned he was a suspect in a rape and robbery the year before in nearby Deer Park. Police had found heavy string in the kitchen where Weger had worked at the lodge, and it was matched with the string that was used to bind the three victims.

When the father of two small children was finally arrested, he was interrogated for five hours, and his parents and wife urged him to tell the investigators the truth. Chester Weger finally broke down and told the sheriff that he entered the canyon in the park during the afternoon of March 14, and he saw the women leaving. He noticed the camera carried by one of them and a purse carried by another.

Weger made the decision to try to grab the purse, but he grabbed the camera case instead. One of the three women took a swing at him and hit him in the head with the binoculars she was carrying. When he realized he hadn't grabbed the purse, he begged the women to walk back toward the end of the canyon so he could escape. They hesitated but finally agreed, and he walked with them back toward the end of the canyon. Weger used the string he'd taken from the kitchen at the lodge to tie the hands of two of the women together, and the hands of the third woman who

90. *The Times*, "Solve 3 Brutal Murders," November 17, 1960

sat only a few feet away. He assured all three that someone would be along eventually to find them.

Chester Weger continued his confession to the Illinois authorities when he said he left the three women in the cave, and as he walked down the trail, one of them had worked herself free from being tied up, ran up behind him, and started hitting him with her fists. He turned, pushed her away and reached for a nearby short tree limb lying on the ground. Swinging it at her, he hit her in the back of the head and knocked her out. Weger picked her up and carried her back to the mouth of the cave. When he laid her down, the other two women, still bound, tried to attack him with their hands and feet. The dishwasher took the club and started beating the other two women over and over. When Weger was certain they were dead, he turned, and the first woman had come to and tried to strike him with the binoculars. He still had the club in his hand, and he beat her with it repeatedly until she was dead too.

Weger told Sheriff Eutsey that he dragged the bodies back into the cave because there was a plane circling overhead, and he thought the bodies might be spotted. He dragged them in and to the back of the cave, then ripped off the women's underwear to make it look as if they'd been raped. He said his motive in the killings was nothing more than not wanting the women to be able to identify him.

The day following his late-night confession, Weger was taken to the cave by investigators, and while he was physically chained to Sheriff Eutsey, he reenacted the crimes to show how he'd murdered the three socialites.[91]

A month or so after Howard Whaley had asked the Illinois State Police to see if Chester Weger might be involved in the murder of Frances Lacey, he received his reply. After checking into Weger's background, the ISP discovered that he had been arrested in Illinois the night before the murder

---

91. *The Times*, "Solve 3 Brutal Murders," November 17, 1960

of Frances Lacey, and after being released on Sunday, the day of the Lacey murder, he still reported for work on Monday morning, July 25. The Illinois State Police were certain that Chester Weger wasn't involved in the Mackinac Island murder, and the Starved Rock murders weren't connected with the death of Frances Lacey. Chester Otto Weger was convicted of the Starved Rock murders in 1961. He was the third longest incarcerated inmate in the Illinois history. He was released from an Illinois prison in February 2020, at the age of eighty.

***

On the same day Whaley received the report from the Illinois State Police, Frances Lacey's twin brother was reinterviewed about his sister's murder. The police were still looking for any additional information that might help them solve the crime.

William said that he and Frances were raised in Barry County and grew up around the Ionia area. He and Frances were very close until she married Ford Lacey, and when she moved to Wayne County, it was more difficult for them to see each other on a regular basis so they drifted apart to some degree.

Frances Lacey's twin brother told the police he was on the Island for several days after the murder, and he was initially told of his sister's disappearance by his niece Kay.

William was impressed with the investigation into his sister's murder, considering the few leads the state police had to go on, but he still had no suspicion of anyone who might want to harm her.

The detective interviewing him asked about the potential boarder who was going to rent a room from his sister. The prospective renter was a graduate of Central Michigan University and was a high school social science teacher.

He'd just gotten a job at a high school in Dearborn and, through a family friend, had arranged a deal with Frances to rent a room from her.

Mrs. Lacey agreed to fix up a room and cook his breakfast and dinner. She also agreed to do some light laundry for him. The new renter told his friends and family that Frances Lacey was one of the nicest people he had ever met. For the eight dollars a week she was going to charge him, he would even be allowed to use half of the garage if he would keep the driveway shoveled in the winter.

After her initial disappearance and the eventual discovery of Frances Lacey's body, the new renter was very distraught, and after the interview with William Lacey, police doubted that he was involved in her murder. There was no indication in any of the police reports that he was ever interviewed about the murder.

***

Incoming tips became fewer and fewer. By early November, many of the detectives and troopers assigned to the case were now involved in other investigations. On December 8, a new lead developed from an interview with a suspect in Ionia, and MSP wasn't taking any chances.

The Ionia County Sheriff's Office arrested Cleon Brown for several break-ins, and he pled guilty to all of them. After receiving a sentence of three to five years, in a follow-up interview with a state trooper, he mentioned he'd been on Mackinac Island. When he was questioned later about his whereabouts on July 24, he changed his story and said that he never mentioned Mackinac Island, but he might have mentioned North or South Fox Island instead. He said he was doing some work there. When troopers pressed him about which island he'd mentioned, Brown maintained that he hadn't mentioned Mackinac.

Brown agreed to take a polygraph test and also gave investigators samples of his head, arm, and pubic hair for comparison. After his polygraph, the examiner wrote a written report stating he didn't believe there was any deception in his answers. Dr. Ed Kivela still had the hair samples he'd been given, but his report about the hair analysis didn't come out until December. After his laboratory examination and comparison with the known samples from Cleon Brown and the hair samples recovered at the Lacey autopsy, Kivela wrote:

> Microscopic examination of the hairs submitted discloses many similarities between the head hairs and pubic hairs of Cleon Brown and the hairs found on the clothing of Frances Lacey. It is my opinion that all could have come from the same original source.[92]

While Kivela believed they could have come from the same person, there wasn't anything other than that to hold Brown. He'd passed his polygraph and was already in prison. This was the only report that Dr. Kivela wrote mentioning that all of the samples could have come from the same source, yet there were no other reports indicating any type of additional investigation regarding Cleon Brown or his possible involvement in the murder of Frances Lacey.

***

In January 1961, the tourist season on the Island was virtually nonexistent. It had been almost six months since the murder, and the Michigan State Police didn't seem to be any closer to solving the crime than the day when Frances Lacey's body was found on the Stonecliff property along Lake Shore Road.

---

92. Kivela, Dr. Edgar. "Toxicological Examination." *Michigan Department of Public Health*, December 20, 1960

Each time a new tip was received or a new clue was uncovered, there was a small glimmer of hope that it might be the one bit of information that could lead to the killer. The investigation was largely being handled by detectives at the St. Ignace Post.

Troopers across the entire state were familiar with the killing on Mackinac Island, and each time an arrest was made in a violent crime, the officers checked into the person's background to see if there was any connection to the Michigan resort island.

In mid-February, Detective McCluer received a tip from a claims adjuster in Oscoda, Michigan. The adjuster had been at a friend's home, and he noticed a room key to the Murray Hotel lying on a bookcase. The key was to room twenty-six. Knowing it was the room Frances Lacey had stayed in, he asked his friend where she had gotten the key from. She said it was left in her husband's barbershop in Mackinaw City the previous summer, and her husband had told her it was the key to the murdered woman's room.

McCluer headed for Oscoda. When he sat down to interview the homeowner, she told the same story to him. She added that it was found in her husband's barbershop, he'd put it in a drawer with the rest of his odds and ends, and the first she'd seen it was after they moved to Oscoda. The detective needed to talk with her husband.

Since moving to Oscoda, Thomas McCoy* had taken up residence as a barber at a nearby beauty salon on Old M-171. There was a lull in business that day, and McCoy gladly sat down with the MSP detective to explain how he'd come across the key to room twenty-six.

In the summer of 1960, McCoy was leasing a barbershop on Central Avenue in Mackinaw City. He wasn't certain of the time period when he found the key but said it could have been around the time of the Lacey homicide. When he found the key, he threw it into a drawer full of odds and ends and joked with his wife about it being the key to the murdered woman's room. He also told McCluer that he had no idea who might have left it there.

It wasn't much to go on, but after the interview, McCluer called Howard Whaley. There was some confusion regarding who had stayed in room twenty-six, and when Whaley finally realized it was Frances Lacey, he wanted McCoy reinterviewed.

In early March, Detective McCluer sat down for a second interview with the barber. McCoy had been thinking about it, and he thought the key was given to him by a man who had come into the barbershop. He said the man was around fifty years old, had gray hair, and around five feet, ten inches tall. He gave McCoy the key and asked if he'd be willing to mail it back to the Murray Hotel.

McCluer asked the barber if the man had a car. McCoy couldn't recall a description of it, but he thought the car might have been parked in front of the barbershop.

The detective was still trying to pin down a date when the key was found in the barbershop, and McCoy said he was certain it was probably prior to Mrs. Lacey's murder or he would have made the connection as soon as he got the key.

After throwing the key in a drawer, he would come across it occasionally, and after the Island murder, he'd show the key to a few of his customers who were getting a haircut and joke with them by saying it was the key to Frances Lacey's room.

McCluer dug a little deeper into McCoy's background. He was originally from Coopersville. In the summer of 1956, he moved to Mackinaw City to live with his uncle, and after working on a ship that summer, he returned to Coopersville during the winter. In 1957, he did the same thing, and when he returned to Coopersville the following winter, he attended the Flint Barber School. After graduating in November 1958, he worked as an apprentice barber in Coopersville before marrying his wife and moving back to

Mackinaw City, where he was leasing a shop on Central Avenue with the option of buying it. In January 1961, they moved to Oscoda, and he was renting space at the beauty salon.

The MSP detective continued to dig. He asked the barber about his whereabouts on July 24, 1960. McCoy couldn't recall exactly where he was on the day of the murder. He said he didn't think he left Mackinaw City, and he hadn't been on Mackinac Island since 1959. He and his wife weren't married yet, and they'd gone with her brother and nephew and swam in the pool at the Grand Hotel. He said he never stayed at the Murray Hotel.

As McCluer was finishing the interview, he could see that McCoy had a large birthmark on the right side of his face, and the barber told him that he had numerous operations to have it removed. There was significant scarring that was evident on the barber's face, and McCluer was sure that if he'd been on the Island, he would have been noticed by someone.

21: TINY

While McCluer was digging into the mystery of the room key showing up in Oscoda, Sergeant Glen Dafoe at the MSP Petoskey Post received a call from the local chief of police. On February 25, a woman walking up to the entrance of the Little Traverse Hospital was attacked when a man got out of a car, ran up from behind and grabbed her. Covering her mouth, he told her not to scream or he'd cut her throat. He began choking her and forcing her toward the car. The woman wasn't giving up and fought for her life. He dragged her into the car, then pinned her down on the seat. As he loosened his grip around her throat to close the car door, she broke away and ran toward the hospital. He chased her for a short distance but quickly gave up, ran back to his car, and sped away.

The victim described the car as a 1954 or 1955 light blue Buick, and she said her attacker was wearing a gray jacket. It didn't take long for the Petoskey Police to find a car matching the description with the driver wearing a gray jacket. Police showed the car to the woman, and at first glance, she wasn't sure. She looked closer and saw a hole in the seat cover. She remembered seeing it as the man held her down inside the car.

The chief of police asked if an MSP detective could run a polygraph examination on the man they'd picked up because he was denying any involvement in the assault.

During the polygraph examination, Detective Sergeant Bloomquist was able to get a confession about the assault in Petoskey. The suspect said he didn't know why he'd done it, and he hadn't planned the attack. It just happened when she walked by his car. After the test, Bloomquist felt the man should be questioned regarding the Lacey murder.

The Petoskey police chief contacted the suspect's wife and asked her to come to the station for an interview. She was interviewed by the chief and Bloomquist, and she said that her husband was a very moody person and had a bad temper. She recalled that the previous year, they spent the Fourth of July with a relative, and after arriving back home, they had an argument. He grabbed her around the throat and was trying to push her out the window. She told the chief that it was the only time she felt that he was actually going to kill her.

Her husband would occasionally go fishing with her dad, but he was never away for more than four or five hours, and he never took a day to himself or left home for any substantial amount of time.

The chief asked if they had ever thought about getting away and going to Mackinac Island. Her husband only had one day off per week, and they talked about it at one point but never actually went there. She was pretty sure he'd been there as a boy.

Following up on the interview with the suspect's wife, the chief contacted the local auto dealership where he'd been working during the previous July. Their records showed he'd worked on July 23, but he was off on July 24.

The suspect was charged in Petoskey with assault with intent to do great bodily harm and was referred for a psychiatric evaluation. Although Sergeant Dafoe didn't feel the suspect would have enough time to get to Mackinac Island and murder Frances Lacey, he suggested in his report that he be interviewed about it. There was nothing in the entire report to indicate any additional follow-up regarding this person.

***

The Michigan State Police often keyed on specific details of an arrest that might indicate the person could have been involved in other crimes. Anything to do with a sex crime piqued their interest and often resulted in supplemental reports forwarded to the St. Ignace Post in the hope it might lead to the killer of Mrs. Lacey.

In early March, a trooper at the Mt. Pleasant Post made an arrest, and while he was searching the man, he discovered several pocket knives, a pair of female child's underwear, and a doll with the crotch cut out of it. The report done by the trooper was quickly sent to the post detective, and an interview was set up to see if there was any connection to Mackinac Island.

The suspect didn't deny having the items, and he admitted to having sex with the doll, but he also said that he was either in jail at the time of the murder or he was working at a car wash. When he was arrested, he was working as a clean-up man at a car dealership in Clare.

It didn't take long for MSP to follow up on his story. He was on parole, was arrested on May 1, 1960, and was sentenced to five days in jail. On July 24, the day of the murder, he was working at the Minit Car Wash in Bay City, and the records confirmed he had worked from 8 a.m. to 6 p.m. They determined that, while the man had some serious problems, there was no way he could have been involved in the murder of Frances Lacey.

***

Detective George Strong received an anonymous tip in the form of a letter. Whoever had mailed it didn't want to be identified, but they wrote that a man with the nickname Tiny was hired by the Chippewa Hotel as a dishwasher right after he was released from the Newberry State Hospital, a psychiatric facility in the Upper Peninsula. The only person who knew he'd been released from the hospital was the person who got him the job at the hotel. The owners of the Chippewa Hotel didn't know about the man's background nor did anyone else working there. Whoever wrote the letter also said that Tiny hadn't stayed very long; he quit the job, saying that the cook was mean to him. After he left his employment at the hotel, he stayed on the Island for a while. He was described as being nineteen years old and weighing almost three hundred pounds.

Whoever wrote the anonymous letter felt that he was on the Island at the time of Mrs. Lacey's murder, and he was now living in Sault Ste. Marie.

Later in the month, Strong met with Ed Hill at the St. Ignace Post, and they headed to Newberry to see what they might be able to find out about the tip. The doctor at the Newberry State Hospital was very familiar with Tiny and said he was capable of anything. Even though he was a patient at the hospital, he knew the difference between right and wrong and was admitted to the hospital on numerous occasions during 1960. After he was given a leave of absence on May 28, he left to work on Mackinac Island before returning to the hospital in March 1961, and he was still there. According to the doctor, Tiny never profited from any of his mistakes. He only had one record of being violent, and it involved him stabbing his brother many years earlier.

The doctor felt that Tiny had sadistic tendencies toward others and even himself. He was certainly capable of rape and would never feel any guilt if he were involved. He'd blame someone else, or he might even feel that the police were trying to frame him.

The two seasoned detectives still weren't sure if he'd been on the Island at the time of the murder. They headed to Sault Ste. Marie to speak with a local investigator and the Catholic Social Service Center. They knew it was a long shot, and their suspicions were confirmed. The Social Service Center couldn't release any information about Tiny unless a Circuit Court judge ordered it, but the investigators learned that their new suspect was in Marquette in late June and was already under investigation for a breaking and entering there. A request had already been made to the Circuit Court for a judge to review before any information could be released.

The detective in Sault Ste. Marie knew Tiny's family and contacted them to see if they might recall when he was on the Island. His family wasn't sure, but they thought he might have been picked up in Marquette around June 13 and returned to their home by July Fourth. He also returned to Marquette on at least two occasions to work for a man who cut and sold wood. Tiny's family was pretty sure that he didn't go back to the Island after he left around June 10 but added that they had no control over what he did when he wasn't at their home, so he could have.

As the police dug further into Tiny's background, they found an arrest on June 28 by the FBI in Marquette for failing to register for the draft but nothing beyond that.

The following day, detectives recontacted the Social Service Center in Marquette and found out they only had a record of Tiny being in Marquette on June 27 and June 28. He could have been there beyond that point and may not have checked in with their office.

The state police still couldn't determine if he'd been on the Island at the time of the murder. It was time for a face-to-face interview.

***

In mid-June, Ed Hill sat across the table from Tiny at the Newberry State Hospital for a formal interview.

For most of the month of June 1960, Tiny worked at the Chippewa Hotel on Mackinac Island. He got into an argument with the cook and ended up quitting his job. After quitting, he went to Marquette, where he stayed at the Catholic Orphanage for a few days and spent a night in jail after being arrested for failing to register for the draft. After the arrest, he headed back to Mackinac Island. He stayed with a family he knew on the Island who owned a dray business, and after a couple of days, he headed back to Sault Ste. Marie. He said he returned home by July 4.

Tiny returned to the Island again but said it was a week or two after the Lacey homicide. He'd already heard about it on the news before he went back. Back on the Island, he again stayed with the family he knew, and he left after a couple of days, returning to Sault Ste. Marie and stayed until just before Christmas.

Hill hadn't mentioned the murder. Tiny brought it up in his conversation, believing the police were questioning him about his whereabouts at the time of the break-ins in Sault Ste. Marie. When he mentioned the murder, Hill spent some time discussing it with him, and though he seemed genuinely interested in it, he didn't reveal any details that weren't already common knowledge in the media. He'd heard several things about the murder while he was on the Island and had read a lot of news articles about it.

Hill seemed satisfied that Tiny wasn't on the Island at the time of the murder, but he also needed to verify some dates with the family he stayed with. When the detective contacted the family, he found the dray service was owned by an elderly man who knew Tiny. He remembered his stay there but couldn't recall the dates.

Hill spoke with the man's daughter-in-law, and she recalled Tiny being there. He stayed one night sometime between late June and July 3. She said he returned for a second short stay, and she knew it wasn't until mid-August because it was her sister's birthday. Her aunt had come to the Island. As she was seeing her aunt off at the ferry docks, she saw Tiny arriving and getting off the boat. Hill also spoke with the woman's husband, and he recalled Tiny staying with his father, but he couldn't recall which dates he was there either.

Detective Hill was reasonably sure that Tiny hadn't been on the Island when Frances Lacey was murdered but couldn't say it with absolute certainty.

***

It had been eleven months since the murder when Sheriff Garries of Mackinac County had someone stop by the sheriff's office and turn in a woman's sandal that was found along the west side of the Island just one mile north from where Mrs. Lacey's body was found. The woman who turned it in said she was walking along the beach with her grandson when he found it.

Sheriff Garries contacted Detective Hill and turned the sandal over to him. Hill could see it was a woman's sandal with a wedge sole. It had two adjustable buckle straps around the toe and one buckle strap around the ankle. It looked weathered, and there was no brand name visible on it.

Hill went back to the area where the sandal was found to see if there might be any other things of interest to the investigation, but he found nothing.

The detective knew the only footwear found at the murder site were the shoes found under the old boat. One of those was in a plastic bag, while the other was lying near it on the ground. There were two theories: Mrs. Lacey could have been carrying that pair with her when she was attacked. She also could have been wearing them and slipped them off and into the bag while she finished walking to British Landing in her bare feet. If she was wearing anything other than the shoes found under the abandoned boat when she was murdered, they still hadn't been found.

Sheriff Garries had already taken the sandal to a local shoe store to determine the size; it was the same size that Mrs. Lacey would have worn.

Detective Hill packaged the sandal and had it sent to Detective Craft at the Detroit Post, along with a copy of his report. He asked that the sandal be shown to Kay Sutter in an attempt to identify it. When the detective received it, he tried to contact Kay, but Wesley said she was out of town until late June. Craft wrote in a supplemental report that when Kay returned, the sandal would be shown to her to see if it belonged to her mother. There was nothing in the entire report to indicate any additional follow-up regarding the sandal.

22: MURDER IN MINNESOTA

Imposing sentence, the Ramsey County District judge in Minnesota said, "It is not possible for me to understand an individual with such a complete disregard for human life as had been manifested by you." The judge looked directly at the defendant standing before him. "I am informed you faced three possibilities of execution in other jurisdictions for other wanton killings." He continued, "Whether or not the sentence I am about to impose will affect the possibility or probability of any of these being carried out by trial and conviction, I do not know." The defendant stood motionless. "Your conduct indicates a complete lack of conscience. Whether or not you can make peace with your creator is up to you."[93] With that, Hugh Bion Morse was sentenced to two life terms in a Minnesota prison.

Morse seemed gentle and was remembered for his blue eyes and boyish smile by his friends. Some thought he was well mannered and a good worker.[94] But he was also one of the FBI's Ten Most Wanted fugitives, and before his arrest and conviction, he was on the move.

Serial killer Hugh Bion Morse had been abandoned by his father while he was an infant. Growing up, his grandmother was exacting over both him and his mom. She left him scarred for life after hitting him with a hammer

---

93. *The Minneapolis Star*, "Slayer of St. Paul Woman Gets Life," December 15, 1961, p 8

94. *The Lexington Herald*, "Story of Killer Hugh Bion Morse Casts Light on Nationwide Problem," November 5, 1961

at the age of four. His childhood was extremely unhappy, and he developed both admiration and hatred for women because of it, with sexual uncertainty and violence being the end result.

While in the service and stationed in North Carolina, the killer's first arrest was in 1951 for indecent exposure and assault. He received a dishonorable discharge, and more arrests followed in the mid-1950s.

He was committed to a state hospital in California after he molested two eight-year-old girls in 1955, and he was released in 1957 after being "cured." After his release, he received one year of probation, and he moved to Spokane, Washington, where he married, but the romance didn't last.

Morse had an overpowering urge for sex, and after his release, he began to prowl neighborhoods at night as a peeping Tom and break into the homes or apartments of women. In 1959, he raped and murdered twenty-eight-year-old Gloria Brie in Spokane.

His second known victim was sixty-nine-year-old Blanche Boggs, who was raped and beaten with a pipe wrench in September 1960. A third woman managed to survive an attack by Morse two weeks later.

Neighbors tipped off police about Morse as a possible suspect, and he fled the state, heading back to Southern California.

Eight days after his last assault in Spokane, his ex-wife, Virginia, living in Reseda, awoke to find him standing over her with a knife. Virginia's mother screamed when she saw him on the verge of stabbing her daughter and the attack was thwarted. He fled the state afterward as police charged him with burglary and attempted murder.

When California authorities realized he'd left the state, the FBI was brought in.

Morse worked his way across the country, financing himself with menial jobs. He stayed in St. Louis and became a suspect in a rape and murder there but denied any involvement. Leaving St. Louis, he stayed in Indianapolis, Miami, and Atlanta.

During a later interview with police, he said he'd raped two girls and broke into a home where he threatened a woman and molested one of her daughters.

Morse moved on to Birmingham, Alabama, and jimmied the door of twenty-seven-year-old Bobbi Ann Landini. Intending to commit rape, he found her sleeping and crushed her skull with an iron pipe. Instead of raping her, he took her ring and fled.

The killer ended up in Nashville, Tennessee, where he pawned the ring he'd taken from his last victim. He used the fifty dollars to move on to Louisiana, Iowa, and Minnesota.

During his cross-country crime spree, he traveled to Ohio, where he attacked a woman in Dayton and left her for dead. His travels also included Michigan.

Morse's last stop was in Minnesota. Living in St. Paul under the alias of Darwin Corman, he prowled apartments, copying the telephone numbers of the women and later making lewd telephone calls to them. During one of those calls, he became even more aroused and went back to the woman's apartment.

Five blocks away from his rooming house, he entered the apartment through an unlocked door and found Carol Ronan asleep. He struck her with a padlock, knocking her unconscious, then raped her, and when she began to awaken, he strangled her with a stocking.

A few weeks after the Ronan murder, a young couple from St. Paul was on their honeymoon to Washington, DC. On a tour of the FBI headquarters, they were invited to look at a wall with the FBI's Ten Most Wanted fugitives. They initially chuckled at the prospect of identifying anyone, and as the newlyweds looked, the new bride's attention was quickly drawn to only one photo. It was the man who lived across the hall from her at her St. Paul rooming house. She knew him as Darwin James Corman.

Hugh Bion Morse was arrested later that afternoon.

The trail of rape and murder for Morse stretched from the Pacific Northwest to the Deep South, up to the northern Midwest, and became national news. When the FBI learned he had traveled through Michigan at one point, they remembered the Island murder. They knew the Dearborn widow was raped and strangled with her own panties. A call was made to Howard Whaley, and he gave them the specific details of the investigation. Whaley asked for the FBI to interrogate Morse.

Special Agent Dennis Gibbs, assigned to the FBI's Lansing office, contacted Whaley after the interview. He handed Whaley an FBI memo, dated November 13, 1961. It read:

> Re victim Mrs. Frances Lacey: Morse advised that in July 1960 he was either in Van Nuys, California employed by the Bones Hamilton Buick Co. or else he was living in Spokane, Washington and employed by the Desert Hotel in that city.[95]

In his report about the interview and memo from the FBI, Whaley wrote that because Morse had admitted to several other murders across the country and was being prosecuted for the murder in St. Paul, it was unlikely that he would withhold information about the murder of Frances Lacey.[96] There is nothing else in the original police reports to indicate any additional follow-up investigation regarding Hugh Bion Morse.

***

95. Whaley, Howard. "Supplemental Report." *Michigan State Police*, November 22, 1961

96. Whaley, Howard. "Supplemental Report." *Michigan State Police*, November 22, 1961

Throughout the year, MSP had continued to follow up on possible leads. This included checking on an Island employee who was charged with indecent liberties in St. Ignace. He had a fourth-grade education and had worked on the Island in 1960. When police discovered he was on the Island the day of the murder, his work records were checked but he was quickly discounted as a suspect when they found out he had worked the entire day.

In another tip, a man was being held for rape in the city of Hancock. A quick check by investigators showed he wasn't on the Island on July 24.

Tip after tip led nowhere.

It had now been almost eighteen months since Frances Lacey was murdered, and MSP was still no closer to solving the crime.

Detective Edwin Hill was at his desk in St. Ignace when his phone rang. It was one of the town's local barbers. He found a suitcoat in his barbershop, and it looked like it had blood on it. He thought it might be related to the Mackinac Island murder.

On that cold January day in 1962, Hill wondered why the barber thought it was related to a murder committed two years earlier. He listened as the barber explained that he found the suitcoat hanging on a hook in his shop. When no one returned to claim it, he hung it in a closet at the barbershop and forgot about it. Now, he was cleaning out the closet and found the coat again. When he started to look it over, he noticed what he thought was blood on the inside of the coat. Hill asked when the coat was left there, and the barber was certain that it was left around the time when Frances Lacey was murdered.

Detective Hill stopped by the barbershop to pick it up, and he spoke with the second barber. He also remembered the coat hanging in the shop for three or four weeks, and he was also certain it was left around the time of the murder.

He and his colleague had checked the pockets and found a crumpled piece of paper with a phone number on it.

Hill looked the coat over. It was a solid tan coat with dark brown leather patches on the elbows. The inside label was black with white lettering and read HARPER INCORPORATED, DETROIT. The detective noted the bloodstain on the inside near the left armpit area of the sleeve.

Hill knew he would be forwarding the coat to the crime laboratory, but he would also try to track down the phone number on the crumpled piece of paper. The number exchange was from Ontario, Canada, so Hill enlisted the help of the Royal Canadian Mounted Police in checking it. The RCMP traced the number to a man at the White Birch Hotel in Sault Ste. Marie, Ontario. The man, a freezer salesman from Hamilton, Ontario, was about forty years old and around six feet tall with broad shoulders. The suitcoat was much smaller, and it was obvious it was made for a much smaller person than the man described. When the RCMP checked with him, the man said he only had the number since November 1961.

Still trying to track down the owner of the number, the RCMP checked with the telephone company, but they were unable to track who had the number the previous year.

While the RCMP was conducting their investigation, Detective Hill forwarded the suitcoat to Dr. Ed Kivela at the MSP crime laboratory. Kivela received the coat on February 10. The bloodstains on the inside of the left upper sleeve area were obvious.

Serologic tests of the stains were done, and Kivela first determined the bloodstains were human. He was trained to look at bloodstain patterns as well, and after closely examining the staining pattern, he concluded they were caused by whoever was wearing the coat. They weren't caused by an outside source, and there was no evidence of any tearing or holes in the material that would be indicative of any violence. He also couldn't find any evergreen needles, twigs, or other types of wood debris that would be consistent with the area where Mrs. Lacey's body was found.

Like all of the other evidence turned in for analysis in the Lacey homicide, Dr. Kivela retained custody of it for future comparisons, or until he was instructed to dispose of it. There is no indication in any of the police reports of an identification of the person assigned to the phone number found inside the suitcoat.

23: THE JUNGFRAU

Two years after Frances Lacey's murder, Detective Anthony Spratto retired after a decorated career with MSP. That October, he was appointed to the Marquette County Friend of the Court office by Michigan Governor John Swainson.

As troopers and detectives were promoted, transferred, or retired, the murder of Frances Lacey was still being investigated, though oftentimes it was new investigators who had nothing more than the original reports to go by.

In the fall of 1962, Howard Whaley, now captain, received some information from a man who served as the chief steward on a yacht called the *Jungfrau* during the Chicago-to-Mackinac Race in July 1960. The informant thought that one of the members of the crew might be a suspect in the Lacey homicide because he had borrowed a bike from the harbor master on several occasions and had ridden around the Island. There was more to the story, but he wanted to meet with the detective face to face.

Whaley asked Detective Hill in St. Ignace to research who the harbor master would have been at the time of the Lacey murder so a list of all the boats that were docked there on the day of the murder could be located.

Hill discovered that prior to 1960, management of the state dock was done by the State Park Commission, but it changed that summer. Management was turned over to the State Waterways Commission, and there was a logbook kept of all the boats docked but it was kept in Detroit.

The harbor master, whose parents lived on the Island, was living in Arlington, Virginia, and working for a state senator while attending Catholic University Law School.

Hill found out that when the state dock was full of boats, many would tie up at the Arnold Ferry docks, so there might not even be a record of the *Jungfrau* on the Island.

While the detective was doing his follow-up in St. Ignace, Whaley asked Captain McPhail to check with the State Waterways Commission to see if he could find out the names of all the yachts docked at the state dock during the weekend of the Lacey murder. It was something that had been overlooked in the initial stages of the murder investigation. The logbook would have the names of the crew members from each vessel.

A check was made for several days before and after July 24, 1960, and McPhail confirmed the *Jungfrau* was docked at the state dock from July 20 to July 28 with a six-person crew. He also found there were two harbor masters on duty during that time period. One was listed as living on the Island while the other lived in Detroit.

Captain Whaley and Detective Strong tracked down the chief steward for the *Jungfrau*. He had worked in that capacity for several years prior to 1960, and he told them the information he had to pass along had been bothering him since the time of the murder.

The *Jungfrau* was owned by a contractor in Flint, and in July 1960, it was only the second trip to Mackinac Island. Just a few days after the murder, the boat left the Island and sailed to Harbor Springs.

On the morning of July 24, the boat was tied at the state-owned dock on Mackinac Island. Because of his own duties that morning, the chief steward didn't have time to leave the boat to run into town for supplies, so instead, the captain did. The captain left the boat at 8:00 a.m. and took the harbor master's bicycle, which wasn't unusual for him to do. At around 11:00 a.m., the steward found the captain back on the boat taking a shower, which seemed odd. "What the hell are you taking a bath for at this time of the day?"[97] the steward asked. He said the captain looked at him as if he'd been caught doing something wrong.

Later that day, as word spread that a tourist was missing on the Island, the captain said, "I think that's the woman I saw over on the dock getting on the ferry."[98] When her description was published in the paper, he repeated the statement several different times, and when Frances Lacey's photo was finally published, he repeated it several more times over a period of time.

The steward knew the captain lived north of Owosso with his parents, that he'd never been married, and he also had a temper. He once told the steward that he'd beaten up a detective in Florida who tried to serve a warrant on him. According to the steward, the captain was very well known around the Island, and he talked with numerous boat owners up and down the docks.

Whaley asked if the captain was a drinker. According to the steward he wasn't. He'd served in the navy for fifteen years and was receiving an eight percent disability for his time in the service. A background investigation on the captain showed he'd been arrested at least four times; in Owosso, St. Johns, Miami, and Waukesha, Wisconsin.

On June 25, Detectives Sobolewski and Hoffman went to the home in Henderson, where the captain lived with his parents. They asked that he come with them back to the MSP Headquarters in East Lansing to answer some questions, and he agreed without any hesitation.

When the three men sat down for the interview, the captain was asked to tell them everything he knew about the murder of Frances Lacey in July 1960.

97. Whaley, Howard. "Supplemental Report." *Michigan State Police,* June 4, 1962

98. Whaley, Howard. "Supplemental Report." *Michigan State Police,* June 4, 1962

The captain had come to the Island on the *Jungfrau*, and the boat was tied at the state dock. The first time he heard about Mrs. Lacey's disappearance was when he was stopped by a police officer and shown a photo of Mrs. Lacey during the afternoon of July 24 and was told she was missing. He told the officer he thought it was the woman he'd almost run into with the bike. At the time he spoke with the officer, he was with two women from a nearby boat.

Frances Lacey's picture hadn't been circulated until Monday morning, July 25. When he was asked about which day it was that he was shown the photo, he said he couldn't recall which day, but it could have been four or five days after her initial disappearance.

The detectives wanted to verify his story, so they asked about the women he was with. He only knew the name of one of them. He said she was around twenty at the time, and she used to work at the Saginaw County Prosecutor's Office.

When Sobolewski asked him to describe the woman he'd almost hit when he was on the bike, he said she was around fifty years old, and he thought she was wearing a gray suit of some sort. Her hair was worn in a bun on the back of her head, and she reminded him of an old maid. He couldn't recall if she carried anything but remembered that she spoke with a British accent. He told both detectives that he was from Britain, and he quickly recognized her accent when he apologized to her for almost hitting her.

Pressed for the date and time when he spoke with the woman, he said he couldn't recall, but he was sure it was before he'd been shown a photo of Mrs. Lacey, and he was certain it was the same woman he'd spoken with.

The detectives switched their questioning to the captain's knowledge of Mackinac Island. They wanted to know the various locations he'd been to. The furthest he'd been on the west side of the Island was just beyond the Grand Hotel. Sometimes he would use the dock master's bike, and sometimes he would walk. On the morning he was with the two young women, he walked around the Grand Hotel with them, but never went up Lake Shore Road.

It was the captain's belief the murder occurred on the MRA property along the east side of the state park. He'd read the newspaper accounts, and that's how he knew the location. He'd been in that area several times, both on foot and on bike. While he put himself in the area where he believed Frances Lacey's body was found, he wouldn't commit to putting himself in the area where she was actually found, and it was clear that he didn't know about the MRA property on the west side of the Island.

The questioning circled back to the topic of the bike trip on the morning that Mrs. Lacey came up missing. He couldn't recall it. He used the harbor master's bike on several occasions, and he never had to ask permission. He didn't admit or deny taking a shower on a late July morning two years prior. He simply said he couldn't recall.

When he was arrested in Waukesha, he was committed to the Veteran's Hospital, and he ended up walking away from there. He was being treated for tuberculosis, was an alcoholic at the time, and had given up drinking after he'd had a lung and five ribs removed at the Veteran's Hospital.

The detectives had done their homework before the interview. They asked about the rape allegations that had been made against him, and he admitted he'd been picked up by the Shiawassee County Sheriff's Department in 1950 and was questioned briefly but he was released after the woman admitted it was a hoax.

The captain was asked if he'd take a polygraph test, and he agreed, but he was very nervous when he took it. Afterward, the examiner wrote:

> The subject was examined on June 24, 1962, and the erratic nature of this subject's polygraph responses precluded a definite determination. This

subject alleges that he was an alcoholic, that in 1947 he had tuberculosis and now has only partial use of the left lung and has a nerve condition.[99]

No further information was available in any of the police reports indicating additional investigation into the captain of the *Jungfrau* as a suspect.

***

Searching for a way to generate new tips or leads, the state police began appealing to the public through the media. An article was published in the *Detroit News* in 1962 about the murder.[100] Asking if anyone knew of Frances Lacey's murder two years earlier, the article mentioned that the state police were convinced that several people likely saw the killer. With anywhere from six thousand to ten thousand people on the Island on any given day during the busy summer season, police were certain the killer simply "lost himself in the crowd."[101] With three hundred seventy-eight people interviewed thus far, the state police were hoping the article might generate new clues.

A second article titled "MICHIGAN'S NO. 1 MURDER MYSTERY" appeared in *True Detective* magazine. In cooperation with the state police, the article was written by Charles Remsberg and published in the hope that someone might recall something about the two-year-old murder and contact the police. A quote in the article from Michigan Attorney General Frank Kelley read:

99. Petzke, Jack. "Supplemental Report." *Michigan State Police*, June 28, 1962

100. *The Detroit News*, B. Simmons, "Mystery Witness Needed to Solve Mackinac Murder," August 11, 1962

101. *The Detroit News*, B. Simmons, "Mystery Witness Needed to Solve Mackinac Murder," August 11, 1962

The murderer of Mrs. Frances Lacey, who met her death on one of Michigan's most beautiful vacation spots, Mackinac Island, is still at large. I have examined the records of our Michigan State Police thoroughly in hopes of finding a clue, and I have instructed this splendid organization to continue to give this case high priority. I sincerely hope that the publicity given this case by True Detective may unearth some new clue or may alert some person with information which will be brought to our attention, so that whoever is responsible for this vicious crime can be brought to justice.[102]

In late September, after the article was published, Frank Kelley's office received a letter postmarked from Sulphur, Oklahoma. Kelley's office contacted Whaley in Detroit, and Whaley passed the information on to Detective Hill. The letter referred to the discovery of Frances Lacey's wallet near the Grand Hotel on August 10, 1960, seventeen days after the murder. The writer felt the gardener who discovered it should have been looked at more closely as a suspect. It read:

Dear General,

That fellow McKay was he physically able to commit such a crime? He, a gardner, found the purse, stuck in his pocket until he quit work then delivered it to employer. How much time elapsed from the time he found it until he delivered it, or how long was it in his pocket? If it was in his pocket any length of time, then he evidently was trying to make up his mind whether to deliver it at all or not. He knew of the crime, knew that

---

102. Remsburg, Charles. "Michigan's Number One Murder Mystery." *True Detective Magazine,* 1962.

every one was excited about it, and if innocent his natural instinct would have been to deliver it immediately after finding it. The purse was found 17 days after the crime, that's a long time for the locality and so many people around as the story indicates, perhaps he had it all along and dident want any one to find it on him. did he ask him if he saw Mrs. Lacey on the morning of the 24th? Did you put him on the lie-box to see if was telling the truth about finding the purse? Did you snoop his room, apartment or home, if that were possible, in trying to locate some jewelry or perhaps something else that might give a lead? A man delivering a purse might be under strain and want to alley supiciton of innocence or guiltness, they do some crazy things at times. To deliver the watch and jewelry, he might think would be a dead give-a-way. It would appear that the crime was committed by some one of the help or a guest or visitor and who would be in a better position than some of the help. I'm not accusing just suggesting and do pardon my instrusion.[103]

There was nothing in any news reports stating that any jewelry was missing from Mrs. Lacey. In fact, when her body was discovered, she was still wearing her diamond ring. The only thing missing from her body was her watch. After reading the letter, Detective Hill and Sergeant Burnette both reviewed the reports about the wallet's discovery. Hill recalled that the gardener was an elderly man who needed glasses just to read things. Because he didn't have them with him when he found the wallet, he wasn't able to discern who it belonged to. After finding it, he finished his work for the day and turned it over to his

103. Letter to Mr. Frank J. Kelley, September 29, 1962

supervisor. It was then they discovered that it belonged to the murdered woman.

Hill recalled that not only was McKay elderly, but he was also short and didn't weigh very much. He had suffered from severe asthma for several years, characterized by his difficulty breathing. Based on all of those factors, it was pretty obvious that McKay couldn't have been involved in Mrs. Lacey's murder.

There were several employees at the Grand Hotel who weren't interviewed after the murder because they were working at the time when the police believed it occurred. McKay was only interviewed in a general sense afterward because he was the employee who found the wallet. Now that someone was questioning whether or not there was more to McKay's story, Detective Hill did some checking and found that he was living in Sault Ste Marie.

In a follow-up interview, McKay said he worked on Mackinac Island in the summers of 1959 and 1960. Prior to '59, he worked for Union Carbide in the Soo for fifteen years before retiring. In spite of his asthma, he took the gardening job at the Grand Hotel because he could work outside at a leisurely pace. He never went anywhere on the Island other than to work because of his asthma. It was very difficult for him to walk from the Marquette House, where he stayed, to the Grand Hotel.

After interviewing McKay for a second time two years after the murder, Detective Hill was convinced that because of his age and his physical condition there was no way he was involved in the murder. They weren't so certain about the captain of the *Jungfrau*.

There's no indication that MSP ever attempted to identify the author of the letter.

24: FISHER

Kay and Wesley Sutter's marriage had fallen into disrepair. In 1963, they were living in New Mexico, and on May 1, they were granted a divorce.[104] Wesley joined the army, and later that year, Kay remarried.

In the fall, Sergeant George Burnette was preparing to be transferred from the St. Ignace Post to MSP Operations in East Lansing as a staff sergeant. Transfers to other posts around the state weren't uncommon, and Burnette was looking forward to it.

***

Like so many other times, the battered woman threatened to call the police when Clayton Fisher lost his temper. "I've killed one woman, and I don't care if I kill another," he yelled at her, slapping her again as he moved toward her. It was a vicious, endless cycle the woman endured while living with Fisher. She knew his temper could flare like the flip of a switch, and the red mark on her cheek was proof of that.

The couple lived near Gaylord, and in August 1963, Trooper Robert Johnson was investigating the theft of a Winchester .32-caliber lever action rifle when he developed a suspect; it was Clayton Fisher. Before interviewing him, he wanted to talk with Fisher's brother-in-law to get some background information. As the two were talking, Fisher's

104. *Albuquerque Journal*, "Divorces Granted," May 1, 1963

brother-in-law mentioned the assault on his mother-in-law only a month earlier. He said Fisher mentioned having already killed one woman and he wasn't afraid to do it again. Knowing of the unsolved Lacey homicide three years earlier, Johnson wondered if he was referring to the widow's murder. After all, Gaylord was less than an hour from Mackinac Island.

Johnson gathered all of the information he had about the theft of the rifle to pass on to a detective for follow-up, and when he met with Detective Goodrich, he told him about the statement made by Fisher as he assaulted his wife.

Like so many other tips and leads, maybe this would be the one tip they needed to solve the case. Maybe Fisher had murdered Frances Lacey.

Clayton Fisher had come to the Gaylord area in August 1960, shortly after the murder of the Dearborn widow. He was living in the St. Ignace area prior to the move. Wearing an old sailor's hat, he had some old clothes and two hundred dollars to his name. Some neighbors believed that Fisher had done time at the Detroit House of Corrections for assaulting women, but no one really knew for sure.

Trooper Johnson told Goodrich that Fisher was now living in the Holland area south of Grand Rapids, but he didn't have any information on where he might be working. The information about Fisher was passed on to the Sixth District Post and assigned to Detective Guzin.

Guzin began digging into Fisher's background, and he was able to locate the daughter of the woman who was assaulted by Fisher in Gaylord. She hated Fisher. He had a short temper, and the assaults on her mother happened repeatedly. Her mom had worked at a local restaurant in Gaylord, and that's where the two met. When he was sober, he was a nice guy, but when he was drinking, he was vicious and sadistic. After the last assault, her mom moved to Holland, but Fisher followed her there, and she believed he was still in the area. She said he was very elusive and seldom spoke about where he had lived in the past. She learned he had served time in Detroit for an assault, and he still had several other women who he saw on a regular basis. Some of them were still living in the Gaylord area. She also considered Fisher a thief because he took her mother's television set and several other items after they separated.

As she described Fisher to Detective Guzin, she said, "He's over-sexed, and he's a sex maniac."[105]

Guzin asked her to describe the other times when he had assaulted her mother, and she said on one occasion he had choked her to the point that his fingernails dug into her throat. In another assault, he came into the bedroom with a wire wrapped around both of his hands in the form of a garrote, but her mom had managed to escape.

After the murder of Frances Lacey, her mom had asked Fisher if he'd killed the woman on Mackinac Island. He answered, "If I've done anything, it's because the service has taught me to kill with my hands."[106]

When Clayton Fisher was living west of Otsego Lake near Gaylord, another woman was living with him who'd come from Detroit. One day, she simply disappeared, and when people asked Fisher about her whereabouts, he said she'd left him and gone back to Detroit.

Guzin watched Theresa's daughter closely as she continued describing Fisher. She said that after the woman who'd been living with him disappeared, her mom would occasionally stop over to his trailer, and she saw several pieces of women's clothing and shoes still laying around the trailer.

Her mom was definitely fearful of him. Her mom left her dog with him one time, and when she returned, the dog was

105. Guzin, Bruno. "Supplemental Report." *Michigan State Police*, August 23, 1963

106. Guzin, Bruno. "Supplemental Report." *Michigan State Police*, August 23, 1963

gone. He told her the dog had died, and he buried it by a large pine tree near his trailer. He also made sure to tell her it was his private burial ground.

Describing another incident, her mom told her that someone stopped near his trailer one night, and he grabbed his rifle and took a shot at the person.

Guzin asked her to describe her own feelings about Fisher. She felt that he liked to womanize with widows until he could get anything and everything out of them.

She knew he served in the navy, and he told her mom that when he was a baby, his mother had tried to drown him. On another occasion she had tried to smother him with a pillow.

The detective asked about other weapons that he might have, and she said he had several knives hidden around whatever room he was living in.

After Guzin finished the interview, he did a check on Fisher's background. He discovered four arrests, but none appeared to be felonies. He also found Fisher's fingerprints were attached to a 1958 application to be a special deputy in Michigan, and he made an application to obtain a concealed weapon permit two weeks later.

Two weeks after Guzin interviewed the woman's daughter, Detective Hofmann located the sister of the woman Fisher had made the statement to. Hofmann interviewed her at her home in Howell.

Hofmann wanted to know if her sister was married to Clayton Fisher, and she said they were married in Ferndale. She attended their wedding. The couple even lived with her for a short time, and she suspected that he was abusing her sister, Theresa, but she'd never gone to the hospital. She knew her sister hadn't seen him for a few years but also knew there wasn't a divorce either. She said her sister worked at a credit bureau in Howell, and they could go ahead and contact her there.

During the interview with Theresa, it was difficult for her to speak about Fisher, both out of fear and out of her own feelings of guilt.

Theresa and Clayton Fisher were married in 1954, and she said they were still legally married. There was no divorce. She said she hadn't seen him in four years, but she tried to locate him at one point to settle up some property in the Gaylord area but couldn't find him. The detective asked her about Fisher's background, and she said he sold real estate in past years, and he also worked in retail.

Fisher was a smooth talker, and that's what led to their marriage problems. She said on Christmas Eve 1959, they were having a Christmas party in their apartment, and she noticed he was missing. She had seen him paying close attention to a female neighbor, and she decided to check the woman's apartment. Since she was managing the apartment building, she used her pass key to let herself in, and she found Fisher and the woman naked in bed. Even after she caught him with the other woman, he insisted he hadn't done anything wrong.

Hofmann asked her about the assaults, and she said he'd never beaten her up, but he had slapped her on numerous occasions. She said that when he lost his temper, he typically broke up furniture.

Hofmann wanted to know if Fisher had ever been to Mackinac Island, and she said he never mentioned it during their marriage but she hadn't seen him in the last four years either.

As Hofmann was finishing his interview, Theresa mentioned that Fisher was bitter toward women and seemed to enjoy hurting them.

By mid-September, Detective Guzin received the report from Hofmann's interview with Theresa and tracked down the location where Fisher was working.

The detective was told that Fisher worked at the Warm Friends Hotel in Holland from February to September

1960. As Guzin dug further into his background, he found out that Fisher had worked there, but it wasn't in 1960; it was in 1961.

Hofmann traveled to meet with Guzin in Holland, and along with a Holland police detective, the three men located Fisher and asked him to come to the Holland Police Station for an interview.

When the questions began, Guzin quickly told him that he determined Fisher hadn't worked for the Warm Friends Hotel in 1960.

Fisher thought for a moment, then told Guzin that in 1960, he worked in the Gaylord area at Bob and Stan's Gas Station from mid-July through the Christmas season. He could have even started as late as August 1. Prior to working at the gas station, he was a truck driver working at the Rehabilitation Center for the Salvation Army in Detroit. At the same time, he was also managing an apartment complex in Detroit. In May 1960, he was arrested for assault and battery in Detroit, and he served ninety days at the Detroit House of Corrections.

On June 29, he was in jail. He remembered because it was his birthday, and he was released a few days later. He went right back to work at the Salvation Army, and he told the three detectives that they could check with the major at the Salvation Army to verify his story.

After he left the Salvation Army job, he moved to Gaylord, and within three days, he started his new job at the gas station.

Hofmann asked if he'd ever been to Mackinac Island. He said he hadn't and was willing to take a polygraph test if they wanted him to.

While the detectives were encouraged by his agreement to a polygraph, they were more interested in physical evidence. Clayton Fisher agreed to give them samples of his head hair and pubic hair for comparison with the evidence taken from Frances Lacey's body.

The detectives knew if Fisher was employed in Detroit through late July 1960, the chances of him being involved in the Mackinac Island murder were slim. Detroit Police records showed his arrest on May 15 for assault and battery with a deposition in the case on June 4. He was sentenced to the Detroit House of Corrections for the first thirty days and two years of probation.

Following up on his claim of working at the Salvation Army as a truck driver, they checked with Major Briggs. Briggs said Fisher worked as a truck driver for the Salvation Army in the late 1950s for a couple of years before leaving for another job. He was rehired on July 5, 1960, as a beneficiary. He was paid five to eight dollars per week, and he was provided room and board. He lived at the Salvation Army Center until July 31, when he was listed as absent without leave. As a beneficiary, Clayton Fisher was subject to a bed check each night at 11:00 p.m. If he was not there, he would have been listed as being absent without leave, and according to the records kept by the Salvation Army, he wasn't listed that way until July 31.

Fisher's work records showed he worked until 4:00 p.m. on July 22, two days prior to the murder, but he also worked on the morning of July 25 at 8:00 a.m. The only way he would have been absent for a bed check and not listed as absent without leave was if he'd been granted a weekend pass. Unfortunately, the Salvation Army didn't keep any records of the passes issued, so there was still a possibility that Fisher could have been on Mackinac Island on July 24, 1960.

On October 2, 1963, Dr. Edgar Kivela submitted a brief report to MSP Commissioner J.A. Childs. He compared the head and pubic hair of Clayton Fisher to the hairs found on Frances Lacey's body. Kivela wrote: "Microscopic examination of the head and pubic hair does not show any similarity to the hair available from the Frances Lacey murder."[107]

107. Kivela, Dr. Edgar. "Toxicological Examination." *Michigan Department of Public Health,* October 2, 1963

25: THE THOMPSON MURDER

By late September 1963, Sergeant Burnette was transferred to East Lansing and had settled into his new position at Operations. The new sergeant in command at St. Ignace was William France.

The majority of summer tourists disappeared and fall colors started to overtake the Island. Jack Welcher was the new Mackinac Island Police chief and, much like Burnette, he settled into his new job quite nicely. He was well aware of the unsolved murder from three years earlier, and as he sipped his morning coffee, the owner of Alford's Drug Store walked in. He told Welcher that he recently read an article in the news about a brutal murder in St. Paul, Minnesota, and he thought one of the men arrested might be the same man who passed a fraudulent check on the Island in 1960. Welcher picked up the phone and immediately called Sergeant France.

***

On Monday morning, March 6, 1963, Carolyn Thompson said goodbye to her husband, and like every other morning, she got her kids off to school before she headed back to bed for a little more sleep. It was her normal routine. Police theorized that at around 9:00 a.m., she got back up and was standing in her bedroom when she was attacked from behind. It was clear from the evidence that she fought with her attacker, struggling to break away and running toward the front door. He caught her before she could open it and began beating her, hitting her repeatedly with a pistol he had in his hand until she was unconscious.

Fearing she may not be dead, the killer went to the kitchen, grabbed a paring knife, went back to the front door where Mrs. Thompson was lying and stabbed her twice in the neck. One of the stab wounds nicked her trachea. When the man plunged the knife into her neck a second time, the blade broke off. He was certain she was dead. There was so much blood that he didn't realize the plastic grip on the handgun had broken and pieces of it were lying on the floor. His hands were covered in blood and he knew he'd have to wash it off before he left the house, so he headed for the bathroom.

Mrs. Thompson, bleeding profusely from the vicious beating and stabbing, wasn't dead and began to regain consciousness. She could feel the knife blade lodged in her throat, and now, clad only in her blood-soaked robe, was able to barely escape through the front door. Leaving a trail of blood, she made her way across neighborhood front yards as she went from house to house pleading for help. There was no answer at the first home. She staggered to the next but there was still no answer. She made it to the third house before someone came to the door. The neighbor knew Mrs. Thompson, but there was so much blood covering her she didn't recognize the woman frantically begging for help at her door. "I've got a knife stuck in my throat. A man came to the door," she managed to get out before collapsing and losing consciousness.[108]

A doctor who lived in the neighborhood rushed to the neighbor's home to help until an ambulance and the police arrived. Carolyn Thompson was taken to the local hospital, but by 1:00 p.m., she was dead.

---

108. *Star Tribune*, "Slaying," March 7, 1963

Her killer, realizing she wasn't dead and had escaped, fled the house.

When the St. Paul Police began their investigation into the Thompson murder, they recovered the pieces of a pistol grip from the Thompson home, along with three unfired bullets lying near the front door where Mrs. Thompson had been brutally beaten and stabbed. The house had been ransacked.

Mr. Thompson was a prominent criminal defense attorney in St. Paul, and one of the first theories discussed by the police was a robbery gone bad. Was the Thompson home targeted by someone thinking that no one would be there and there might be a large sum of money kept in the home?

In the first few weeks of the investigation, the pieces of the broken pistol grip were sent to the FBI Laboratory in Washington, DC. They were unique because they were made of plastic and had a black and white color combination. The FBI determined the grips had come from a 7.65-millimeter Luger pistol that originally had wooden grips.

With information about the type of gun likely used in the murder of Mrs. Thompson, a media blitz began, asking for anyone with information about a gun that might match the description to contact the St. Paul Police.

Wayne Brandt was a traveling salesman living in St. Paul, and when he returned from one of his business trips, a friend told him the police were looking for a gun like the one he owned. Brandt had a 7.65-millimeter Luger with homemade black-and-white grips, but it had been stolen in February during a break-in at his apartment.

At around the same time, a civilian police informant contacted a detective at the St. Paul Police Department and said that a local burglar by the name of Bill Ingram had been seen with a gun similar to the one police were looking for. Ingram, along with a man known as Hank Butler, had been arrested a few days earlier after a robbery at local tavern.

Ingram and Butler were still in jail, and when detectives interviewed the two men, they said they had the gun at one point but had given it to two other men identified as Norman Mastrian and Richard Sharp.

The interrogation of Ingram and Butler continued as police began asking about the murder of Carolyn Thompson, and the robbery suspects finally admitted they had been asked if they were interested in killing a woman. They said they weren't going to kill anyone, and when asked who had made the offer to them, they said it was Norm Mastrian. Even though they had turned down the contract on Mrs. Thompson, they knew who had actually taken the job and killed the housewife. The man who committed the actual murder was Dick W.C. Anderson.

Anderson was a familiar name to the St. Paul Police. He'd been arrested eighteen months earlier on a bad check charge. Police took his photo when he was arrested but when he made restitution, the hotel where he'd written the bad check dropped the charges.

Two weeks after the murder of Mrs. Thompson, police felt they had enough evidence and began to make arrests. Norman Mastrian was arrested at his home in St. Paul after a brief standoff. Police were certain that Anderson, along with another suspect who'd been identified, had fled to Arizona, but law enforcement officials weren't sure where the men were.[109]

That afternoon, Dick Anderson placed a call to his former boss in Minnesota at around 3:45 p.m. from a hotel south of Phoenix. Having already been contacted by the police because they expected Anderson might contact him, Anderson's former boss quickly called the police.

---

109. *The Minneapolis Star*, "Detectives Kick in Door, Nab Thompson Suspect," April 19, 1963, p 1

The killer was arrested when police staked out the Tropic Motor Hotel where he was staying.

A close friend of Anderson's was also arrested at a trailer park south of Phoenix, and police identified him as Richard Sharp. When he was arrested, he denied knowing Anderson but later admitted he'd met him in a Minneapolis bar, and police believed that Sharp was driving Anderson's wife and children to Phoenix from Lansing, Michigan, but Sharp denied it.[110]

Dick W.C. Anderson was born in Alden, Michigan, along the west shore of Torch Lake, only ninety miles southwest of Mackinaw City. Both Anderson and Norman Mastrian were charged with first-degree murder in the Thompson homicide. In follow-up interviews, Mastrian, who'd been represented by Carolyn Thompson's husband, T. Eugene Thompson, in a prior case, said the murder of Mrs. Thompson was orchestrated by her husband. Mastrian was the middleman, and after offering the job to Ingram and Butler, he'd finally gotten Dick W.C. Anderson to commit the murder.

Police were also searching for a material witness in the murder. His name was Sheldon Morris, but went by Shelly. Morris had handled the gun used in the Thomson homicide and disposed of it for Anderson. Morris knew the police were looking for him, and after turning himself in to law enforcement, he was charged as an accomplice in the murder of Carolyn Thompson.

***

By September 1963, while MSP Detective Guzin was investigating Clayton Fisher, Mackinac Island Police Chief Jack Welcher was reading the article in the paper mentioned

---

110. *Star Tribune*, "2 City Men Held in Phoenix in Thompson Slaying Case," April 20, 1963

by the owner of Alford's Drug Store about the arrest of Shelly Morris. Welch recalled that a man named Morris had passed a bad check on Mackinac Island sometime during 1960, and he wondered if there might be a connection. Welch began to look at the original check complaint.

On September 8, 1960, a man had walked into Alford's Drug on the Island and said he was selling souvenirs to various businesses on the Island, claiming to be from the Far East Import Company in Detroit. The owner of the drugstore ordered some of the trinkets to offer for sale in the store. The man, who identified himself as Shelly Morris, said he was the owner of Far East Imports, and he cashed a check for seventy-five dollars while he was at the drugstore. The owner described Morris as a fast talker and said he walked with short stride. The check was returned several times after that, and in 1961, the owner of Alford's Drugstore filed a bad check complaint with the Mackinac Island Police.

Police from the Island contacted two import companies in the Detroit area looking for Shelly Morris, but one of the companies had never heard of him. Checking further, investigators found out there wasn't even a company in Detroit called the Far East Import Company.

Police checked another import company with a different name and found that Morris did make some purchases from the company in April, May, and June 1960. They also learned that the Far East Import Company was Morris's own company, but he'd given the address of a different business as his own. Morris would make purchases from the import companies then resell the items to vendors on the Island. He'd even left behind a briefcase at one of the import companies, but it was the last time anyone had seen him. Police checked the briefcase but didn't find anything to indicate where he might have gone.

Sheldon Morris was apparently living out of his car. Police found two former addresses for him; both of those were motels. They also found that several other checks had been passed around Michigan, and the bogus checks written by Morris were drawn on an account through the Detroit Bank and Trust, but police couldn't find any information because Morris had used a fictitious bank branch.

By June 1962, warrants for fraud were authorized for Sheldon Morris.

Detective Hill, still working the case, received information about Morris possibly being on the Island at the time of the Lacey homicide. He checked to see if his name was listed anywhere in the index files of people associated with the murder investigation, but he wasn't. That still didn't mean he couldn't have been on the Island at the time of the murder. A quick call was placed to St. Paul Police Department, and Chief McCauliffe said that Sheldon Morris was arrested on April 22, 1963, and he was charged as being an accomplice to first-degree murder in the Thompson homicide. McCauliffe told Hill he'd have their Detective Lieutenant George Barkley contact him.

When Barkley called Hill, he didn't have much information to pass on to MSP because the St. Paul Police file on the murder was at the prosecuting attorney's office, but he did know that Morris was one of the pay-off men involved in the Thompson murder. Morris was given the gun after the murder and disposed of it, but he led St. Paul investigators to the swamp where he threw the gun and it was recovered. He cooperated with the police and testified before their grand jury. He also had a criminal history beginning in 1946, when he served three years in prison for transporting a stolen car across state lines. Barkley added that when Morris was arrested, he was running a bar about thirty miles from St. Paul, but prior to that, he was selling insurance in North Dakota.

A few weeks passed, and Detective Hill received a letter from Chief McCauliffe in St. Paul. McCauliffe wrote that in an interview, Morris said he was employed by the Benefit

Association of Railway Employees in 1960, and he was in North Dakota. Morris also told his interrogators that he was only in Michigan as a child, had no connections with the Far East Import Company of Detroit, and he'd never heard of the company. Morris was willing to provide handwriting samples if it became necessary. He also said they could check with his former employer to determine his whereabouts in 1960.

A request was sent to the MSP Headquarters to have a detective contact the Benefit Association of Railway Employees about Sheldon Morris to see if he was employed and if they might be able to account for his whereabouts from July 20 to August 1, 1960.

In a letter dated October 29, 1963, the Association wrote that Sheldon Morris had been employed from May 1958 to November 1961. There was no way to track his movements during that time period, and he was only licensed to sell insurance in the state of North Dakota. Morris was considered self-employed so he worked on commission, and the only way to determine his location would be by the number of new insurance applications he would turn in to the company. Based on the insurance applications the Association had received from him, it appeared he must have been in North Dakota.

The Michigan State Police couldn't exclude him as a suspect based solely on the letter because his physical description matched that of the man named Sheldon Morris who passed the no-account seventy-five-dollar check on Mackinac Island in September 1960. MSP mentioned the possibility of getting handwriting samples from Morris, and during his interview with police in St. Paul, he offered to provide one to prove he wasn't responsible for the murder of Frances Lacey. There's no further mention of Morris in the police report. While police looked at Sheldon Morris as a possible suspect in the murder of Frances Lacey because he'd been arrested as an accomplice in the Thompson murder, it doesn't appear that they looked at Dick W.C. Anderson as a suspect. At the time of the Lacey homicide, Dick W.C. Anderson was living in Lansing, Michigan, and his mother was still living in Alden, Michigan, only ninety miles from Mackinaw City.

26: PAUL STRANTZ RETURNS

Another year passed, and there were still no new leads in the Mackinac Island murder. New tips were few and far between. By early 1964, the case was at a virtual standstill.

In Traverse City, another of Michigan's premier vacation destinations, Detective Sergeant Ernest received an anonymous tip about a possible suspect.

The anonymous tipster said that in 1960, a man was traveling through the Traverse City area and had a young blonde woman with him. The woman appeared to be in her early twenties, and the couple had been seen in a Ford Falcon with Ohio license plates. The tipster found out later that although they had claimed to be married, they really weren't.

Rick Gray was the man the anonymous tipster had referred to, and Gray wasn't afraid to let everyone know he was an actor. He loved to tell people that he was in show business and was going to have his own television show in the fall. He also mentioned that he and his wife had just returned from a Hawaiian vacation. He seemed to think of himself as a real ladies' man. He liked to brag a lot, and to most people, he appeared to be a con man. The more he talked, the more suspicious people became of him. He mentioned that he had no family in the area, but then said that his mother operated a beauty shop on Mackinac Island. He also gave the impression that he had plenty of money, yet before he left the area he tried to borrow some cash.

The informant told Ernest that four or five days before the murder on the Island, Gray was seen washing dishes at a hamburger place on the Island and when asked about it, he said that he was researching a part for his career, and he introduced a woman with him as his mother.

Ernest listened intently as the informant described Rick Gray. The informant even provided a picture that was taken of him on the Island in July 1960.

Ernest tried to trace the Ohio license plate but found out that all vehicle records for Ohio in 1960 had been destroyed (it's unknown if this was standard procedure or if the Ohio motor vehicle records were destroyed accidentally) so he took the information he'd gotten from the informant and passed it on to Detective Hill at the St. Ignace Post.

When Hill got the information from Ernest, the first thing he did was check to see if Rick Gray's name had appeared in any of the files related to the Lacey homicide. Gray hadn't been listed in the name card file or on any lists of employees.

Hill began to check the hair salons on the Island. He found the beauty salon at the Chippewa Hotel had a woman with the last name of Gray who had worked there, and she had a son named Rick. The owner didn't think that Rick Gray was on the Island at the time of the murder, though. He knew Gray had played some bit parts in Hollywood, and he was certain that he couldn't have committed the murder.

Chief Welcher also checked his records, but he couldn't verify whether Gray had been on the Island four years earlier.

The investigation was back to square one with no one being able to determine with any certainty the correct dates that Rick Gray was or was not on Mackinac Island. There was no further information in the police report regarding whether investigators attempted to contact Mrs. Gray or her son.

***

Another tip in September seemed promising when an Island police officer heard that some local women had recently seen Paul Strantz at one of the local bars and heard him say, "I wouldn't have strangled her if she hadn't yelled so loud." They knew Strantz had been arrested almost immediately after Frances Lacey's body was found and was released shortly afterward due to lack of evidence. The information about seeing him at a local bar and hearing his admission to the murder was passed to Trooper Ken Yuill.

Trooper Yuill had been assigned periodically to the Island since 1960, and in 1962, he took the summer MSP job on the Island and was assigned there every summer from June to September. Each summer, he moved his family to the Island, and he became the full-time summer trooper on the Island in 1963. His primary assignment while on the Island was the convenience to the governor when he visited, but he also assisted the city police on numerous occasions and was literally on duty twenty-four hours. He could be called at any time, night or day. When he took the full-time assignment for the summer months, he reinstated the mounted patrol rather than a bike patrol simply because of the back trails across the Island, and he was proud to say that he was the only mounted state trooper in the entire state of Michigan.

During Yuill's interview with one of the local women, she said she heard Strantz make the statement about two years prior. Yuill checked with the other women but none of the other three could remember it.

Trooper Yuill was able to track down Strantz because he was still a transient summer worker and was on the streets all the time doing odd jobs. He was staying at the LaSalle Hotel. During the interview, Strantz denied ever making the statement and didn't want to talk about the murder, but he did agree to take a polygraph exam. Yuill passed his report on to Detective Hill at the St. Ignace Post, and a polygraph was set up for the following week.

When Strantz showed up for his test, the examiner quickly noted his mental capacity. He discovered that Paul Strantz had been going to Mackinac Island for the previous fifteen years but changed his routine the year following the Lacey murder. Instead of going to the Island in 1961, he went to Petoskey and worked before returning to Mackinac Island in 1962.

At the conclusion of Strantz's polygraph, the examiner wrote:

> Tests were conducted on the above subject and there were significant emotional disturbances in this subject's polygraph records on the relevant and irrelevant questions. Therefore, the examiner, because of these ambiguous disturbances, is unable to state whether or not the subject is guilty or innocent of the matter under investigation. The subject's true mental status is somewhat of a question.[111]

The examiner had good reason to question Strantz's ability to understand the seriousness of the matter. While he was in the washroom cleaning the polygraph instrument pens after the test, Strantz came in. He asked for a bar of soap and said, "I want to remember this momentous occasion." A short time later, he reappeared in the polygraph exam room with a school bus safety pamphlet he'd taken from the lobby and asked the examiner to autograph it.

A day after Frances Lacey's body was discovered, Detective Spratto felt there was reason to believe Paul Strantz might be connected to the murder and even ordered him held for questioning. Not having enough evidence to

---

111. Simmons, William. "Supplemental Report." *Michigan State Police*, September 11, 1964

hold him, Strantz was released. Even with the polygraph exam four years later, police couldn't be certain, and Paul Strantz is never mentioned again in any of the police investigative reports.

***

Throughout the early sixties, an occasional tip still trickled into the Michigan State Police. All of those tips quickly faded.

In April 1965, three men were arrested in South Haven, Michigan, for breaking and entering, and they admitted to a break-in at a jewelry store in Escanaba.

When pictures of the three men showed up in the *Escanaba Daily News*, a former fire tender at the Grand Hotel thought he recognized one of the men. He contacted an MSP detective at the Gladstone Post, and in his statement to the investigator, he recalled that on July 25, 1960, he was out in the back of the hotel when a man rode up on a bicycle early in the morning. It was clear the man had been drinking.

As they conversed, the man on the bike asked if he could get some breakfast, and the fire tender told him he couldn't do that but there was a restaurant in town. They talked a little more, and the man admitted that he'd stolen the bike from somewhere on the Island.

Their conversation only lasted a few minutes before the man rode off. The fire tender was certain the man who had ridden up on the bike was one of the three men arrested for the break-in at the jewelry store in Escanaba.

The MSP detective began to do some follow-up investigation but it was another dead end. There is nothing in the MSP investigative file to indicate what the disposition of this tip was.

27: LONG-TERM STORAGE

As the years passed, Frances Lacey's death was moved to the cold case files as fewer and fewer leads developed. Staff Sergeant George Burnette, assigned to Operations in East Lansing, retired in 1966.

***

Five inmates made their escape from the Saginaw County Jail on September 11, 1966, and one of them was awaiting trial for the murder of his stepfather, a gas station owner, in Bridgeport just five months earlier. The twenty-five-year-old didn't make it far before he was recaptured the next day in Midland and was locked up at the Midland County Jail.

A retired school principal from Midland, divorced and living with her mother in Saginaw, watched the evening news and the reports of the escape. As pictures of the wanted men flashed across the television screen, she quickly recognized one of them.

During the summer of 1965, she had been invited to stay on Mackinac Island at a friend's home. They wouldn't be there but their home was being repainted and the man they hired to do the painting and general cleanup, Frank Williams*, was staying there. The homeowners contacted him and told him about their guest arriving on Wednesday and leaving on Sunday. She had been looking forward to her trip because her adult son was staying on the Island and working for the summer repairing carriages.

On the evening before she had planned on leaving, the house painter arranged a party and invited several of the college students working on the Island. By midnight, the crowd had left but a few lingered. By 3:00 on Sunday morning, the noise from the party picked up again with someone playing the piano and someone else strumming a guitar. She was frustrated and hadn't gotten much sleep, so she confronted Frank and told him to keep the noise down.

Around 5:00 a.m., there was a knock on her door, but she didn't answer. A moment later, someone burst into her room. She was scared beyond belief as she jumped out of bed and ran to another room to get to a phone. She told the intruder she was calling the police, and he made a quick exit.

After the police arrived, arrangements were made for her to stay at a hotel. Police knew who the suspect was, tracked him down, and tried to question him about what had happened. He was belligerent and refused to answer any questions. The investigating officer didn't make an arrest, though he tried to convince her to press charges against him for assault with intent to commit rape. She refused because she didn't trust the Island police.

As she watched the news reports of the escape in 1966, the entire incident came back to her, and she wondered if he might have been on the Island in 1960 when Frances Lacey was murdered. She made a phone call to a former state trooper who was married to her cousin, and the information was forwarded to the St. Ignace Post.

A detective at the MSP Bridgeport Post checked the state system to see if he might have been locked up somewhere in 1960; he hadn't been. The detective also knew he'd be uncooperative in the investigation because when he had been arrested for the murder of his stepdad, he had refused to make any statements.

Bilgen, now a captain and commanding officer for the Upper Peninsula, received the supplemental report with the new information and possible suspect. By December, he'd already passed the information to two detectives at the St. Ignace Post.

Investigators knew their suspect had spent time on Mackinac Island within the previous few years, but they weren't sure if he was there in 1960. The card file that was compiled showed everyone who had been questioned in the murder didn't have his name.

The woman's friends who owned the home on the Island where she'd stayed in 1965 had since moved, and detectives began checking with some of the local residents who knew the suspect. They were pretty certain he hadn't been on the Island in 1960.

There was only one thing left to do. Just two days before Christmas 1966, a detective sat down with the murder suspect at the Midland County Jail for an interview.

The only time he had been on Mackinac Island was in the summer of 1965 when he was hired to paint a house and do minor repairs to it. He told investigators that there had been a house guest there. He couldn't remember her name, but on Saturday night, he had a party at the house and around 3:00 a.m., she complained about the noise. Later that morning, he went into her room, though he never said why, and she called the police. He was pretty sure that if she hadn't complained about the noise, no one would have known she was up there.

The detective asked if he'd been on Mackinac Island in 1960, and he said he hadn't been. He was working in Saginaw building homes. He lived with his parents until October of '60 when he got married. He was certain he didn't leave Saginaw in 1960 (and no further information was offered in the police report regarding any additional interviews to verify his story). His alibi was easy enough to check, and police dropped him as a suspect in the unsolved Island murder.

***

It had been two years since there was any active investigation into the murder of Frances Lacey when a letter sent to the Michigan Attorney General's Office, signed and dated October 28, 1967, was passed down to the detective through the chain of command and read:

> Dear Sir. At the time of the murder on Mackinac Island there was a tree trimmer in this vicinity that was nothing but mean. He always professed to prefer "older women." He was employed here in Cheboygan. This morning I heard via radio a former tree trimmer was picked up in Chicago for the murder in New Jersey. I have always had a lurking feeling that this man could very well have been on the Island the day of the murder there, now I feel guilty because I haven't written you sooner if by the merest chance it is the same man, one more murder could have been averted. I am writing this in the hospital, so writing is pretty illegible.[112]

Detective Seppanen, now assigned to do follow-up on the Lacey homicide when the need arose, was able to interview the letter's author, and when she wrote the letter, she was a patient at Cheboygan Community Memorial Hospital for several days. She had heard the news report of the killer's capture in Chicago, and when she heard he was a tree trimmer, her mind flashed back to 1960 when she lived in Cheboygan.

She was a barmaid at the Gateway Bar when Frances Lacey was murdered. On half-a-dozen occasions, she frequented Guyette's Bar on State Street and would see a man who also frequented the bar while she was there.

---

112. Seppanen, John. "Supplemental Report." *Michigan State Police*, December 14, 1967

He was employed somewhere nearby as a tree trimmer in Cheboygan, and she didn't know who he was working for. She described him as about five feet, eleven inches tall, with a slender build. He had sandy-colored hair and ruddy complexion, but she didn't know his name. She described him as a hillbilly, and he spoke with a Southern accent. To the best of her memory, he was only there for about a week, and she knew he was staying at the Charles House Hotel.

A few of the times that she was at the bar with her girlfriends, he was obnoxious and wouldn't hesitate to come up to various women and make lewd comments and tell them he preferred older women. On at least two occasions, he was thrown out of the bar by the owner.

Seppanen tracked down a former employee from the bar, but they couldn't remember the man. He also spoke with the owners of the Charles House Hotel and examined the hotel register too but it was of no help. It was an odd ending to his supplemental report when he wrote:

> [She] has been having pangs of conscience for not reporting her information when there was a possibility of it being checked out. At this time, it is too ambiguous to be checked further.[113]

There was nothing to indicate the detective ever tried to obtain a photo from the Chicago Police to see if the witness might be able to identify him as the same person from Cheboygan.

***

In September 1969, Robert Bilgen retired from the Marquette Post after twenty-nine years of service to the department. In March 1970, he accepted a position to coordinate the Upper Peninsula Committee Law Enforcement Planning Program.

---

113. Seppanen, John. "Supplemental Report." *Michigan State Police,* December 14, 1967

He'd be assisting law enforcement agencies in the UP to plan new programs and improve crime prevention while improving the enforcement of criminal laws.[114] Almost two months later, and only eight months after his retirement, Bilgen suffered a heart attack while inspecting his newly built home in Hancock and died.[115]

***

In July 1976, sixteen years after Frances Lacey's murder, all the evidence in the Lacey homicide was transferred from the St. Ignace Post to MSP's long-term storage in Lansing. There is nothing in the police reports to indicate what happened to the trace evidence held by Dr. Edgar Kivela when the Crime Laboratory was located at the Michigan Health Department. In a brief paragraph, the report stated:

> All evidence held by the post on this complaint was turned over to the Headquarters Evidence Storage Facility on July 9, 1976. Due to the lack of a suspect this complaint is being closed at this time, however if further information is obtained this complaint will be reopened at that time.[116]

There were no new leads in the case, and many suspected that it would never be solved. Much like many of the original detectives assigned to the case in 1960, those in later years believed the suspect quickly escaped the Island before Mrs. Lacey's body was found.

With the evidence being moved from St. Ignace to a long-term storage unit, police knew that unless new information

114. *The Escanaba Daily Press,* "Former Officer to Direct UP Law Program," March 3, 1970, p 1

115. *The Escanaba Daily Press*, "Robert Bilgen Taken by Death," April 28, 1970, p 2

116. Nowak, Joseph. "Supplemental Report." *Michigan State Police,* July 30, 1976

was received, the evidence would sit on a shelf in a secure evidence room and collect dust.

28: PROFILES

In the 1950s, MSP began criminal profiling by collecting behavioral data on sexually motivated crimes in the form of a Sex Motivated Crime Report. If a crime involved a sexual assault of some sort, a special report was filled out indicating specific details about the attack itself, the victim, the suspect, and a host of other information in the hopes of identifying a suspect. The FBI was mainly using fingerprints as the most effective means of identifying criminals.

By 1972, with the rise in reported sexual assaults and homicide cases, the FBI established the Behavioral Science Unit. The unit was originally made up of ten agents, and in 1976, Special Agents John Douglas and Robert Ressler began visiting prisons across the United States to interview predatory killers with multiple victims and begin building a centralized database. The information contained in the FBI database included motives, planning and preparation, specific details about the offense, and the disposal of evidence. That included information about the types of weapons used and the victims' bodies.

Three years after beginning the research, agents started working in the field to provide consultations on active criminal cases involving serial predators around the country.

Five years later, the BSU was split into two separate units. The BSU continued to train profilers, while the Behavioral Science Investigative Support Unit (BSISU) became responsible for consultations and active investigations.

In 1984, the National Center for the Analysis of Violent Crime (NCAVC) replaced the BSISU, comprising of three divisions—the Behavioral Analysis Unit (former BSU), the Violent Criminal Apprehension Program (VICAP), and the Child Abduction Serial Murder Investigative Resources Center (CASMIRC)—and provided behavioral-based investigative and operational support. In addition, VICAP included Agents Douglas and Ressler's data regarding serial offenders. The database also included crime scene descriptions, victim and offender information, lab reports, criminal history information, court records, media information, crime scene photographs, and victim statements. All of the information in that database involves homicides, missing persons, unidentified victims, and sexual assaults.

The instruction arm of the unit has members of the FBI with advanced degrees in psychology, criminology, sociology, and conflict resolution, and they provide training to both domestic and international law enforcement partners.

"If you want to understand the artist, you have to look at the painting."[117] In a book titled *Mind Hunter,* former FBI profiler John Douglas wrote:

> You have to be able to re-create the crime scene in your head. You need to know as much as you can about the victim so that you can imagine how she might have reacted. You have to be able to put yourself in her place as the attacker threatens her with a gun or a knife, a rock, his fists, or whatever. You have to be able to feel her fear as he approaches her. You have to be able to feel her pain as he rapes her or beats her or cuts her. You have to try to imagine what she was going through when he tortured her for his sexual gratification.

117. John Douglas & Mark Olshaker, *Mind Hunter,* 1995, p 21

You have to understand what it's like to scream in terror and agony, realizing that it won't help, that it won't get him to stop. You have to know what it was like.[118]

Most of all, the FBI profilers understand that what they do is an art and not a science. Often, after a suspect is arrested, many investigators say it was the profile that caught the killer; profilers disagree. To say the profile caught the killer is never true. Killers aren't caught because of a profile. It's the uniformed cop and the detective working the street that catch the killer through their training, experience, and good, old-fashioned police work. It's knocking on doors, talking to witnesses, following up on leads and even a little bit of luck. A criminal profile is nothing more than an investigative tool, much like a composite sketch done by a police artist based on the witness description. The investigative tool simply helps narrow the search.[119]

***

The information provided to MSP Detective Sergeant Robin Sexton in 2007 was by no means conclusive. Sexton asked the FBI to create a profile of Frances Lacey's killer based on the photographs and police reports. The detective knew the report wasn't a replacement for a thorough criminal investigation, but after forty-seven years, maybe it would help. As he read through the report from the FBI supervisory special agent, Sexton noted that the report was based on probabilities and that no two criminal acts or criminal personalities are exactly alike. The offender might not fit every aspect of the FBI's analysis. Sexton was hoping an analysis of the offender's behavior toward Mrs.

118. John Douglas & Mark Olshaker, *Mind Hunter*
119. Robert K Ressler & Tom Shachtman, *Whoever Fights Monsters*, 1992

Lacey might provide the FBI with some insight into his personality traits and characteristics.

A distinct disadvantage for the profiler is the time between the murder and when the profile of the killer is created. For a criminal profiler, being able to visit the murder site shortly after the murder has a distinct advantage because the profiler can orient themselves and see relationships between things that otherwise might be missed.

In his report to Sexton, the special agent noted that Mackinac Island experiences very little violent crime, and since the murder of Frances Lacey, no other similar crimes have been committed on the Island. Based on the knowledge the FBI had in reviewing the reports, it was assumed nothing had been stolen from Mrs. Lacey's purse except her wallet, and while she was the focus of the crime, whoever was responsible didn't have to murder her. She was a victim of opportunity and looking at both the crime and Frances Lacey's background didn't show anything to indicate she was specifically targeted for murder. As the FBI looked at her past, it became clear that she was considered low risk in terms of being the victim of a violent crime but by being alone on a remote part of the Island, her risk was somewhat elevated.

In the analysis, the NCAVC looked at Frances Lacey's autopsy and noted she had no defensive wounds. She was likely struck from behind in a "blitz-style" assault, manually strangled, and her panties were then ripped off and used as a ligature to ensure her death. Whoever had killed the Dearborn widow had to conceal her body to allow his escape from the Island.

The FBI concluded that at the time of the murder, the killer was inexperienced because he tried to strangle her with his hands before resorting to ligature strangulation.

Considering the manner of the attack on Mrs. Lacey, it was likely that the killer wasn't socially competent because he attacked her from behind to gain control of her. That suggested to the profiler that the killer was immature and unsophisticated in the act. He was likely a blue-collar worker or had some menial labor job and was likely a substance abuser of either alcohol and/or drugs.

Whatever his fantasy was, it was never mentioned in the profile. The expert in behavioral science purposely avoided commenting on it. It's their rule. Commenting on it simply encourages the killer to continue.[120]

After analyzing the killer's behavior, suggestions were listed that could aid the state police detective in his investigation of the Lacey murder. One of those was to use the television show *America's Most Wanted* to generate new leads. Use of the media might produce new tips. Another suggestion was made to look closer at members of the MRA since Frances Lacey was assaulted and murdered on the MRA property, and her body was concealed there.

***

In 2008, David Minzey, who had retired from MSP as a detective first lieutenant, was asked to analyze the case. Minzey joined the state police in 1978 and was assigned to the Niles Post, which was near Michigan's state line north of South Bend, Indiana. After his promotion to detective sergeant, he was reassigned to the Jackson Post and eventually moved to the Violent Crime Unit in East Lansing as the chief criminal personality profiler for the entire state. In 1997, he was promoted to detective first lieutenant and was in charge of the Investigative Resources Section. That included the Violent Crimes Unit, the Criminal Intelligence Unit, and the Investigative Training Unit.

In his report to Detective Sergeant Sexton in St. Ignace, Minzey wrote that it was possible that suspects might not fit each aspect of the assessment, and a suspect shouldn't be

---

120. Robert K Ressler & Tom Schachtman, *Whoever Fights Monsters*

eliminated just because he or she didn't fit every descriptor in his report.[121]

Minzey recapped the known facts in the murder investigation from the existing police report.

In his report, the retired MSP detective mentioned that there was some speculation that Mrs. Lacey had partied the night before she was murdered and may have had sex with an unknown male, but Minzey felt that given the information about the victim, it was highly unlikely. Mrs. Lacey was a solitary person and didn't have any history of one-night stands, and if she had, in fact, met someone and they ended up in her room, it's more than likely she would have been murdered there. Someone would likely have seen the killer at some point, either in the hotel or somewhere on the Island. There wasn't any information uncovered in the investigation indicating she had been with a man prior to her murder, in spite of the information about beer cans being located under the bed in her room. In fact, there was nothing in the police report to indicate that those beer cans were ever checked for fingerprints or preserved as evidence.

Minzey's analysis had to be viewed in the time frame when it occurred. In 1960, almost ninety percent of murders in the United States were solved, whereas in 2008, only about fifty percent were solved.[122] Whoever killed the Dearborn widow was a complete stranger to her, and given the circumstances of her death, she likely hadn't perceived the suspect as a threat.

Whether the killer was walking behind her or lying in wait, he probably didn't possess strong verbal skills. Minzey felt that Frances Lacey probably didn't anticipate the attack, and the killer had overpowered her rather quickly.

---

121. Minzey, David. "Report to Detective Sergeant Robin Sexton." *Michigan State Police*, January 23, 2008

122. Minzey, David. "Report to Detective Sergeant Robin Sexton." *Michigan State Police*, January 23, 2008

Not everything in the investigative report made sense to the seasoned MSP profiler, and that included the fact that Kay Sutter and her husband took the long way around the Island to look for her mother. Wesley didn't seem to have a close relationship with Frances, yet by demanding that tracking dogs be brought in to search and that money was no object, he made it appear to the police that he did have a close relationship with her. The fact remained that neither he nor his wife had large sums of money immediately available to them, and at the time he demanded the dogs, his mother-in-law was simply late in arriving to British Landing. It would have made more sense if they had returned to the cabin to see if Kay's mom had returned before contacting the police. Still, even if Wesley disliked her, it was very unlikely that he would have sexually assaulted her.[123]

Minzey believed that Frances Lacey never saw the attack coming, or saw the killer but didn't feel threatened by him. The killer knew he could use his fists to overpower her, and he had the ability to strangle her into submission. He'd probably been involved in fistfights at some point in his life prior to the murder and could even have been the target of bullies. He probably lost those fistfights but still felt confident in his ability to overpower Mrs. Lacey because of her size.

Based on the injuries to Mrs. Lacey, the killer was likely right-handed. His excessive use of violence suggested his expression of rage, and the homicide was consistent with power and control.[124]

As part of the profile, Minzey looked at the killer from two perspectives: what his personality traits were at the time of the murder and what he might look like in 2008.

---

123. Minzey, David. "Report to Detective Sergeant Robin Sexton." *Michigan State Police*, January 23, 2008

124. Minzey, David. "Report to Detective Sergeant Robin Sexton." *Michigan State Police*, January 23, 2008

In 1960, he probably behaved like an adolescent. He was disorganized, withdrawn, antisocial, and had low self-esteem. He wouldn't have had any sort of job dealing with the public because he had poor interpersonal skills. His likely job would have been doing manual labor, and he wouldn't have had much interaction with others. He could have been a dishwasher, stock boy, maintenance, or even a busboy.

He came from an environment where the woman in his life was dominant. If his father was there, he would have had a very weak personality.

While Mrs. Lacey's violent murder had a sexual element to it, the underlying issue in her death was a hatred toward women. Minzey wrote, "Sex was, in essence, used as a weapon to demean and denigrate the victim."[125]

> When it comes to females, the offender will have great difficulty establishing relationships. When he does, the female will likely represent his mother (or the dominant female that raised him). He is dependent upon it . . . Their sexual relationship will be unusual and at the discretion of the female. While most people couple their sexual aggression with pleasure to create a love-making experience, this individual couples his hatred for women with pleasure.[126]

The killer's behaviors before the murder began developing in his childhood because he never understood the world around him in anything other than egocentric terms, most likely because his mother never taught him properly regarding it.

125. Minzey, David. "Report to Detective Sergeant Robin Sexton." *Michigan State Police*, January 23, 2008
126. Minzey, David. "Report to Detective Sergeant Robin Sexton." *Michigan State Police*, January 23, 2008

The Island was the perfect environment for the killer to get a job because of the large, transient work force coupled with thousands of tourists. It provided him with an ability to remain solitary in his off hours without drawing attention to himself. It was likely that he didn't socialize after work, and to those who did know him, they'd describe him as quiet, quirky, and a man of few words.

Because of the deep-seated hatred for women, he would have learned to self-medicate in the form of alcohol. If he did go to a bar, he'd sit by himself, or he'd drink by himself wherever he was living.

If he had any contact with the police, it was likely to be as a suspicious person or being drunk in public. He might have been involved in window peeping, or he could have simply been in an area where he didn't belong. If he'd come to the attention of the police about the murder of Mrs. Lacey, he was dismissed as a suspect early on because he wouldn't appear as the monster who murdered the widow.

The Mackinac Island murder could have been precipitated by some sort of negative event involving a woman who was in a position of authority over him, and while he was unable to take his anger out on that person, he'd be able to take it out on someone physically weaker than him and in a vulnerable position.

David Minzey described the attack on Mrs. Lacey as swift and violent. It was based simply on the fact that her dental plate had been knocked out. Once she was rendered helpless, the killer picked her up and carried her up the hill into the wooded area, but he only carried her a short distance—enough to accomplish his goal—and that was representative of his physical strength.

Not only was the murder quick and violent, but the killer also vented his rage for older women. He was a man who had few, if any, sexual relationships with a woman. It was poorly planned and impulsive. By lifting Mrs. Lacey's clothing, Minzey believed the killer hadn't seen very many nude women in person, and his voyeurism is what likely caused him to spend more time with Mrs. Lacey, which allowed the couple from Detroit to get as close as they did.

After returning to his room, which would have been considered his safe space, the killer would have behaved in a manner that was even more strange. It would have suggested something was bothering him, even though the disappearance of Mrs. Lacey wasn't common knowledge yet, and while he might have been interested in conversations about her disappearance, he wouldn't have participated in them.

Knowing she'd be found, the killer probably fled the Island suddenly, leaving any friends to wonder why he'd left. Given his day-to-day odd behavior, his sudden departure would be quickly forgotten. Even after Frances Lacey's body was located, any involvement in the murder wouldn't be associated with him.

After leaving the Island, his behavior would have become even more reclusive.

Since the time of the murder, the killer would have continued jobs with little interpersonal skills. Since the murder was about power and control, he could have sought jobs that gave him power. Minzey wrote that investigators should look at people in positions such as a security guard or something in a related field.

Forty-eight years after the murder, the killer's behavior would have become more rigid. If he was married, his wife would be much like his mother. The relationship between the two would be based on need, not love. She needs a husband, and he needs someone to take care of him. Their sexual relationship would be almost non-existent and precipitated by her.[127]

---

127. Minzey, David. "Report to Detective Sergeant Robin Sexton." *Michigan State Police*, January 23, 2008

A daily routine will control the killer's life. He'll get up every day at the same time and will like his coffee made the same way and at the same time every day. His routine won't vary, and he'll wear the clothing that his wife gets for him. Since he's not a social person, he'll dress for comfort, not fashion. He's a person who will wear the same coat for years and will only buy new shoes when the soles wear out on the ones he wears each day.

Describing the killer's home life, Minzey believes the killer not only has limited social life but that it's dictated by his wife. If they have children, she's the dominant personality in their lives, and the family vehicle will likely be plain and practical. It might even be a previously owned vehicle.

What if the killer isn't married? If that was the case, his living conditions will be substandard. Mrs. Lacey's killer won't be concerned about cleanliness, and his home would likely be messy. He could be the type of person who saves everything. He might only wash the dishes or his clothing out of necessity, and the exterior of his home will appear unkempt. He might even be living in a rental home or an apartment.

The older he's become, the more difficult it will be to control him. He might have avoided law enforcement for years simply by being institutionalized, and might even be back in society.

In 1960, the killer was most likely in his late teens to early twenties with a high school education, GED, or trade school certificate, and probably single. His physical stature would have been five foot, eight to five foot, ten with a slight, unathletic build. Based on the hair recovered from Mrs. Lacey's body, his hair color would have been light to medium brown and unkempt in its appearance.

By 2008, Mrs. Lacey's killer would be in his late sixties to early seventies. He might have acquired some type of training through the military or trade school, and if that was the case, he would have been goaded into doing it by whomever he was dependent on.

When David Minzey profiled the killer's criminal history, he wrote that in the time span between the Lacey murder and his analysis forty-eight-years later, the killer likely acted out against other women on more than one occasion. If his significant other is alive, she would have protected him, and he likely evaded law enforcement because DNA wasn't an investigative tool for much of his life. He might even have turned to sex workers in his later years.

Finally, the retired detective lieutenant felt the killer was psychopathic, and he wouldn't feel any emotion about the Lacey homicide or any other crimes he might be involved in.

Much like a composite sketch of a suspect is simply a tool to use an investigation, so were the profiles done by the FBI and MSP. The profiles are strikingly similar. They're not released to the public and are used as another investigative tool to help narrow down their search for individuals with those specific traits named by the profiler.

29: LOST

A person who commits a crime against a person for anything other than monetary reasons is a different type of criminal altogether. Their motivation isn't profit, and even though it's likely that Frances Lacey had money in her wallet, both profiles suggest the motive in her murder was more than monetary. Someone who is a killer, or a rapist, or a child molester, is seeking emotional satisfaction in a perverse way.

If the eighteen-year-old male walking along Lake Shore Road seen by witnesses was the killer, the Lacey murder could have been his first. Given that scenario, it's possible the killer wasn't satisfied with the killing because it wasn't perfect compared to the fantasy he'd created. Afterward, he might have imagined how the murder could have been better, and when he's thinking like that, he imagines the next murder and how it can be done more efficiently. It's an improvement continuum.[128] Obsessed with his fantasy, the killer strives to better it, and it drives him to his next murder. In his next murder, he'll include details of the first murder. While his first crime may have been spontaneous, future victims will likely be sought out, and by the next murder, he will have improved.

***

---

128. Robert K Ressler & Tom Schachtman, *Whoever Fights Monsters*

While he knew it was a long shot, Detective Sexton hoped the profiles by the FBI and Dave Minzey might lead to the identification of a new suspect. He also knew it was time to release specific details about the murder that the public was never made aware of; he provided a complete description of Frances Lacey's missing watch to the media.

The watch was a Ladies Elgin Model 619. It was 14-karat yellow gold, and the production year was 1945. The size of the watch was 21/0s and it contained 19 jewels. It was manufactured from 1940 to 1948 with a run quantity of ten thousand. There was no second hand, and the movement setting was wind and set. The serial number, located on the inside, was E804949, and there was a jeweler's repair number on the back of the casing that read L8933. The number 8933 was inscribed in the lower left corner of the L.

***

Sexton had other cases he was working on at the same time, and one of those included another cold case from forty-two years earlier, though it had no connection to the Lacey homicide.

In the northern Michigan backwoods in 1966, a body was found by a group of deer hunters at the base of a pine tree near the town of Trout Lake in the Upper Peninsula. It was the body of a man; he'd been shot five times and been left there for several months.

When the body was found, investigators believed the man was likely Canadian because there were several Canadian coins found in his pocket, and there was also a specific type of key ring found that was very commonly used in Canada.

Detective Sexton hoped to solve the case, but he quickly became frustrated, and his frustration seemed valid. Sexton said that in 1989, evidence gathered at the scene in 1966, including the victim's clothing and personal possessions, were taken from MSP's storage and destroyed.

It would later be echoed by the next detective at the St. Ignace Post. A reporter wrote that Sexton characterized it as the destruction of vital evidence in an office cleanout twenty years earlier.[129] Sexton, with years of experience, knew there was a family out there missing one of their own. "As far as I'm concerned, every case is solvable," he said. "Detectives—we collect everything. We're pack rats. We just don't get rid of things. Other people charged with administrative matters say, 'we've got to get rid of things.'"[130]

"I'll be real candid about it. It was not handled properly. It was closed, and it shouldn't have been," he said. "With DNA, we probably could have solved this. But now we don't have that either."[131]

Detective Sexton had made his point. If his understanding was correct, evidence in an unsolved homicide forty-two-years earlier near Trout Lake was destroyed in the late eighties.

***

By June 2010, Robin Sexton had retired from MSP, and a new detective hadn't been assigned to replace him at the St. Ignace Post.

In the middle of the month, the great-niece of Frances Lacey was visiting Mackinac Island with her husband for a weekend getaway. Sitting in a local bar, they were talking about the 1960 murder when they were approached

129. *Ottawa Citizen*, "Michigan Detective Reopens Cold Case with Canadian Connection," October 28, 2008, p 13

130. *Ottawa Citizen*, "Michigan Detective Reopens Cold Case with Canadian Connection," October 28, 2008, p 13

131. *Ottawa Citizen*, "Michigan Detective Reopens Cold Case with Canadian Connection," October 28, 2008, p 13

by a man who appeared to be quite drunk. He went by the nickname of Bub*, and he told them he knew something about the fifty-year-old murder. He wouldn't tell them what he knew while he was in the bar but asked to meet them the following day at his office.

Word filtered to the couple that the man they'd been talking to was an alcoholic, and although they were somewhat hesitant to meet a complete stranger, they agreed, with the hope of gaining some information about the murder, and the meeting was set up behind the police department for the following day.

Mrs. Lacey's great-niece and her husband met with the complete stranger the following afternoon. He'd clearly recovered from his intoxication the previous night and seemed quite articulate and very confident when he told them that his uncle had passed away two or three years prior, and on his deathbed, he'd identified Frances Lacey's killer. The couple listened intently, and Bub said he'd tried several times to tell the local police, but they didn't do any follow-up that he was aware of.

As the couple thought about it, they were hopeful that maybe they could pass the information on and have the investigation into the murder of their great-aunt reopened. The woman held off for a short time before calling the police because she wanted to check with some family members and make sure it was okay to pass the information on.

On July 28, they contacted MSP and spoke with a trooper. The information was passed on to Detective Sergeant Richard Rule.

Detective Rule interviewed the great-niece of Frances Lacey about the new information she'd obtained from Bub while on the Island, and afterward, he called Bub and asked him about what he'd told the couple.

The Island native made a minor change from his original claim as he spoke with Rule. He said he wasn't at his uncle's deathbed when the statement was made about who committed the murder, but that he'd heard it from both his father and his brother about who had killed the Dearborn widow.

Now having two different accounts about who may or may not have heard the statement, Rule decided to set up an interview with Bub at the Mackinac Island Police Department.

At that interview, Bub told the detective that he'd misspoken when he told members of the Lacey family that he'd heard it from his uncle as he lay on his deathbed. He'd embellished the story a little to make himself look good. His brother had told him that their Uncle George was spreading the word that a man named Harry Vance* was the actual killer. He claimed he never heard any other information regarding why Vance had killed Mrs. Lacey. Since that time, his uncle had passed away, but his brother was living in Denver, Colorado. He also said he was sorry he misled the Lacey family when he told them he'd heard his uncle identify the killer on his deathbed. He admitted to Rule that when he drank, he forgot things.

Rule set up a second interview with another of Bub's relatives who had also heard the same story. He said he heard that Vance had admitted to the murder at a party in St. Ignace at some point, but he couldn't recall exactly when it was. He'd passed the information on to Detective Sexton before he retired, and they wondered if Vance would have even been old enough in 1960 to have committed the crime because he would have just turned fifteen.

Rule decided to contact the Denver Police Department to see if they might be able to help in the investigation by talking to Bub's brother. Rule wanted him interviewed to see if he could verify what he'd been told.

A detective from the Denver Police interviewed Bub's brother, and he said that he'd been told by his uncle that Harry Vance had murdered Frances Lacey, but his uncle hadn't offered any information as to what the motive for the murder was. He also said his uncle was an alcoholic and had trouble remembering things.

Rule knew there was evidence collected in the Lacey homicide, but he wasn't sure where it might be located after fifty years. It would surely be of some use with DNA technology now being used on a regular basis in criminal cases. In an e-mail dated January 12, 2011, Rule wrote:

> The report indicates that hairs and semen were recovered, apparently being sent to the lab for analysis. Recently a family inquiry into the case was made due to the relative having contact with someone on the Island who mentioned a subject who may have been involved. Upon doing some inquiring, I was told that all of the property that the post sent to long term storage was no longer available. It was not determined what happened (lost during move/destroyed/located elsewhere). I was hoping that maybe the lab had sent items to the lab long-term storage and that those items may be of some investigative assistance. I am requesting that I be sent copies of our lab files/reports and a list of any property that is still present, if any.[132]

Almost three months later, Rule received a fax from the Lansing MSP laboratory that included eight pages from the original police report. Those eight pages included Detective Myre's supplemental report from August 2, 1960, describing the discovery of Mrs. Lacey's body; a request for laboratory examination form listing Mrs. Lacey's billfold; an Inter-Office Correspondence Memo to Lieutenant Robert Bilgen dated August 1, 1960, that listed the newspaper article Paul Strantz had in his room when Spratto and the other detectives searched it; and a copy of the article itself.

---

132. Rule, Richard. "Email to [REDACTED]." January 12, 2011

There was no mention of any other evidence, but in a fax received three months later, Rule wrote in a supplemental report that the Latent Print Unit at the crime lab re-examined photographs of fingerprints that had been lifted during the investigation and a match to Mrs. Lacey had been found.

One latent fingerprint observed in the photo marked, '83-862-60, photo of latent lift' was identified as bring made by the Left Thumb, digit #6 of Frances Lacey. Two latent fingerprints of suitable quality were searched in Michigan's AFIS (Automated Fingerprint Identification System) and the FBI's IAFIS (Integrated Automated Fingerprint Identification System) with no subject being developed.[133]

Detective Rule had run into a brick wall. Much like the Trout Lake murder that Detective Sexton had spoken about, it appeared the evidence in Frances Lacey's murder was either lost, misplaced, or destroyed.

While Rule was trying to determine whether Vance was involved in the murder, he learned that at the age of fifteen, Vance was sent to the Boys Vocational Training School in Lansing because of his troubled youth. There was speculation that he returned home at some point for his brother's funeral on the Island, but Rule learned that his brother died in 1961, not 1960. The detective knew that if Vance was at the Boys Vocational School in 1960, he couldn't be involved in the murder. He had a subpoena sent to the Library of Michigan Archives to see if the new suspect was confined in Lansing at the time of the murder.

While waiting for a response from the Library of Michigan, Rule was in Dearborn for a conference in May and was contacted by a woman who was a friend of the Lacey family and familiar with the case. The woman

---

133. Daniels, Gary. "Laboratory Report." *Michigan State Police,* April 22, 2011

had been watching news reports of a man being tried for murder in Oakland County, Michigan, and the jury was still deliberating the case. While she kept her identity anonymous, she wondered if there was any chance the man, Nolan Ray George, could have been involved in the death of Frances Lacey in 1960 because his crimes in Oakland County involved the rape and strangulation of his victim. To kill his victim, he strangled her with her own panties.

Rule began checking with the Oakland County Task Force, and he learned there were several assaults and strangulation murders where the victims were strangled with their own undergarments. George was on trial in Oakland County for the rape and murder of Gwendolyn Perry in Pontiac. The murder was in 1968, and George had knotted her stockings around the woman's neck as he raped her. He'd been a suspect, but at the time, police didn't have enough evidence to arrest him. After the murder of Gwendolyn Perry, George murdered two more women, strangling one with her undergarments. He beat another woman to unconsciousness and left her to die in a field. He was released from prison after twenty-two years because of plea bargains and appellate decisions. After his release from prison in 1992, the Perry case was reopened, and George was eventually charged with her murder.[134]

One of the task force members forwarded a photo of Nolan George from an arrest in the 1960s, and Rule wanted to have it shown around Mackinac Island to see if anyone might be able to recognize Nolan George as a seasonal Island worker from that era.

A month after beginning to look at George as a possible suspect, Rule was able to contact George's brother for a phone interview, who said that he and his brother were split and raised by different families when they were young, and

---

134. *Detroit Free Press*, L. L. Brasier, "Oakland County Jury Convicts Serial Killer Nolan Ray George in 1968 Pontiac Slaying," April 28, 2011

he didn't know if his brother had ever been to Mackinac Island. He was hesitant about answering any other questions because he couldn't identify Rule by a simple telephone call, and he said he doubted any family members would have any information about his brother's whereabouts in 1960.

Detective Rule knew that the Richmond Police in Indiana had arrested Nolan George in 1960, and when he contacted them, he was told they had a photo of George dated from that arrest. They were going to send the picture to Rule, and the detective also asked if they had any contact information that might indicate where he was in the summer of 1960. Knowing that the regular population of Mackinac Island was very small, he still hoped that by showing the photo of Nolan George from 1960 to the locals, someone might recognize him.

The Hamilton Police Department in Ohio was investigating Nolan George in their jurisdiction for two homicides, and Rule also contacted them to see if they might be able to review everything they had to see if they could verify where George had been in 1960.

In an e-mail from one of the agencies investigating George in Indiana, Rule learned that in February 1960, he'd been arrested in Richmond, Indiana, for disorderly conduct, and in February 1962, he was arrested in Frankfort, Kentucky, for auto theft. The first record of Nolan George being in Michigan was in February 1963, when he was arrested by the state police from the Holland Post for larceny.

By September, Detective Rule found out that none of the agencies in Ohio had any other information to tie Nolan George to northern Michigan fifty years earlier, but that didn't mean he hadn't been to the Island.

On January 19, 2012, Detective Rule, actively investigating the murder of Frances Lacey on Mackinac Island fifty-two years earlier, drove into the Alger County Correctional Facility just south of Munising, Michigan. At eleven degrees below zero with twenty-six-mile-per-hour wind gusts, it was frigid when he stepped from the car.

Inside the prison, the detective was led to a general-purpose room off the main control center. At around 2:15 p.m., Nolan George was led into the room by corrections officers. Rule noticed he wasn't handcuffed.

Detective Rule had a plan for his interview with the serial killer, but he also knew that because George was in custody, he'd still have to advise him of Miranda warnings. He told George that he was investigating a serious felony, and that's why he had to read his rights to him. After the Miranda warning, the detective asked the killer if he had any objections to the interview being recorded, but George had no objections.

Rule's plan of attack for the interview was to ask some basic biographical questions to see if he might mention being in northern Michigan at some point in his life, but George said that when he was growing up, he'd been in Kentucky, Ohio, Chicago, and Pontiac, Michigan.

The year was 1968 when Nolan George moved to Michigan at the age of twenty-five. Rule tried referencing certain events to see if George could be more specific. He mentioned the riots in Detroit and the Detroit Tiger's World Series win, but George couldn't recall those events. He simply thought it was during the mid-sixties when he came to Pontiac.

George moved to the Pontiac area with his wife. She had several children when they settled there, and he worked at either a foundry or a truck stop. He couldn't recall exactly, but remembered he'd become a Pontiac city employee and drove a garbage truck.

When Rule asked him if he'd ever traveled to the Flint area or anywhere north of Pontiac, George said he hadn't. Rule had done his homework, and he knew that George would have been seventeen at the time of the Lacey murder. George had trouble recalling what he was doing at the age of seventeen but remembered dropping out of school at the age of thirteen.

Nolan George's first stint in prison was for stealing cars, and he served his time at the Terre Haute State Prison in Indiana. He also served time in Kentucky and Illinois. Prior to being transferred to the Alger County Correctional Facility, he served his sentence at Jackson Prison.

Rule listened intently to Nolan George's responses to the questions. He asked the killer several times if he'd be honest and admit to any other homicides in Michigan if he'd been involved, and George told him that if he'd been involved in any, he'd tell him.

Detective Rule couldn't pick up any signs of deception on George's part about whether or not he'd ever been to Mackinac Island. He knew there was a possibility that he might have to question him sometime later, so he stopped the interview to end it on a positive note. Rule knew there was no evidence to support questioning Nolan George any further about the Mackinac Island murder. Rule had already worked with the Pontiac Police and Hamilton Police in checking George's background, and neither agency had found any connection to northern Michigan.

In his supplemental report about the Lacey homicide, Detective Rule wrote: "At the next bi-annual review a decision can be made whether or not to close the case as there is no evidence retained in long-term storage and no property retained at the post."[135]

***

By fall, word had started to spread that Detective Rule was looking into the fifty-year-old murder and wanted to talk to

---

135. Rule, Rich. "Supplemental Report." *Michigan State Police*, October 10, 2011

Harry Vance. On October 10, the two men finally connected for an interview at Vance's apartment on the Island.

Sitting at Vance's kitchen table, Rule said he was investigating an incident that had occurred in 1960, and Vance immediately asked him if it had to do with the murder of Mrs. Lacey. The detective hadn't mentioned any specifics about which incident he was investigating, but he quickly learned that all of the Island residents were still very familiar with the unsolved homicide.

Vance was pretty sure that he'd been confined at the Boys Vocational School in Lansing during the summer of 1960. He recalled being released temporarily to come back to the Island for his brother's funeral, but he couldn't recall if it was in '60 or '61. He said he recalled being on the Island at the time of the murder after having just returned from St. Ignace. Rule noted it, but also knew he could be mixing up dates because of his age.

Rule questioned him a little more about being on the Island, and he said he remembered being approached by two officers in plain clothes. They mentioned a couple specific names and asked if either of the men mentioned could have done something to Mrs. Lacey.

The detective could tell that Vance was having a hard time recalling dates. He seemed to recall that he might have painted the Lacey cottage, but then couldn't be sure because it might not have belonged to the Lacey's, and he seemed to recall Frances Lacey's daughter having a cabin on the Island somewhere.

Rule asked Harry Vance what he thought happened on July 24, 1960, and Vance said that the talk on the Island was that it was an insurance fraud and that someone had come up from Chicago and killed her for a life insurance payout. With nothing more to go on, and no evidence at that point, Rule suspected the case was going to remain unsolved.

In the middle of the month, he received a garbled voice mail from Harry Vance. In the message, Vance suggested that Rule contact his cousin because she'd been on the Island at the time of the murder. Rule took him up on the suggestion. Now somewhere near seventy-one years old, she would have been around twenty at the time of the murder.

The detective was very open with her and told her he was checking on some information regarding the murder in 1960. She had been on the Island at the time of the murder, and she worked for the MRA in the laundry department. She'd gone out with some of the other residents of the Island to check areas where they felt Mrs. Lacey could be, and that included an area that was close to where her body was eventually found. She described looking under an old boat along the inside of Lake Shore Road, and the group had used an inner path to get there. While they were in the area, a man approached them, but he didn't say anything. He was wearing clothing that resembled prison garb with boots, and she was quite intimidated by him. Asked specifically about the clothing, she was certain it was prison clothing he was wearing.

It was later that night, after they'd left the area, that she heard about the discovery of Frances Lacey's body. She thought Mrs. Lacey had been found under the boat that they looked under, so she was quite surprised. She reported it to the police, but she couldn't recall which agency it was at the time. She knew they weren't wearing uniforms, and she was certain they'd mentioned the suspicious man they'd seen. She told Rule that she thought the men she'd spoken with could have been with the FBI.

Detective Rule asked if her cousin, Harry Vance, could have been on the Island at the time, having come home for his brother's funeral. She said he could have come for the funeral because it was around that time, but she couldn't be more specific about the date.

Other than the woman's recollection that Vance could have been on the Island for his brother's funeral, there was nothing really useful to the detective in her statement.

30: A NEW PERSON OF INTEREST

After sixty years, the murder of Frances Lacey remains one of Mackinac Island's greatest mysteries, and there are numerous theories about who might be responsible for her death.

At one time, some local residents on the Island were certain that the tourist's murder was committed by a member of the MRA. Many suspected the killer could have been cloistered by the organization at Stonecliff and quickly removed from the Island before being identified. With Mrs. Lacey's wallet being found near the Grand Hotel, in addition to her watch and some cash missing, it seems unlikely that a member of the MRA, an organization with principles based on honesty and mutual respect, could be involved in such a vicious murder and cover-up. But even long after his retirement, Anthony Spratto still believed the killer was part of the MRA.[136]

Another theory pointed toward the murder being tied to Wesley Sutter, Frances Lacey's son-in-law. Her real estate holdings and life insurance were the basis to this theory. While the police were trying to develop a suspect and conducted hundreds of interviews that stretched across the entire country, the Lacey and Sutter families were still considered suspects in the murder too, and they weren't privy to any information about the investigation. Their sole sources of information were newspapers and the article printed in *True Detective* magazine two years

---

136. Cawthorne, *Mackinac Island: Inside, Up Close, and Personal*

after the murder. When police interviewed Wesley, he told them the entire family was together at British Landing on the morning of Mrs. Lacey's disappearance waiting for her arrival, and the only person that left was Marvin. He left British Landing to look for Frances after she failed to arrive on time, and everyone corroborated Wesley's account.

Years after serving the community of Mackinac Island, a former city official believed the murderer was a local resident on the Island. In a very small and close-knit community made up of generations of families, he believed the person responsible for Frances Lacey's murder has been shielded by some of their own in the years since the murder.

***

Mere speculation won't solve the murder of Frances Lacey. To prove a crime, an investigator looks for data that, when presented to a court or jury, proves or disproves the facts at issue. It may include the testimony of witnesses, records, documents, or objects.

To solve the murder of Frances Lacey, the key is to not only look at the physical evidence collected by the state police in 1960, but to look beyond that. Former FBI profiler John Douglas said:

> Behavior reflects personality. The best indicator of future violence is past violence. To understand the "artist," you must study his "art." The crime must be evaluated in its totality. There is no substitute for experience, and if you want to understand the criminal mind, you must go directly to the source and learn to decipher what he tells you. And, above all: Why + How = Who.[137]

---

137. John Douglas & Mark Olshaker, *Mind Hunter*

When Mrs. Lacey's body was found concealed under a fallen cedar tree on the MRA property four days after being reported missing, police scoured the area for clues not once, but several times.

The police recovered bits and pieces of a broken dental plate that was likely knocked out of Mrs. Lacey's mouth when she was attacked. They also found a pen, but there are no measurements noted of the pen's location, and no fingerprints were found on it. Other evidence recorded at the scene included a hair strand on the inside of a fence that started just inside the gate to the MRA property. That hair strand belonged to Mrs. Lacey, and it was stained with blood. Light brown to blond hair strands were removed from her body at the autopsy and didn't belong to her. Those hair strands, both head and pubic hair, likely belonged to the killer. Mrs. Lacey's purse and wallet were missing, as was her Ladies Elgin watch.

Mrs. Lacey's own panties were used as a ligature around her neck after the killer first strangled her with his own hands.

During the autopsy, the doctor noted a deep, jagged laceration on the upper left side of her head and opined that this injury was caused prior to her death. There was also a small laceration on her chin. In addition, vaginal smears showed the presence of sperm.

Mrs. Lacey's purse was literally found at the time of the murder but after being taken as found property by a well-meaning couple, it wasn't turned in until four days after her disappearance. Her wallet was found two weeks later near a trail leading through the Grand Hotel's tennis courts and ending at the pool.

Over the course of the investigation, known hair samples were taken from several men in the hopes they might match the hairs taken from the body. Several men were cleared through comparison with those hairs, but with at least two of those, Dr. Ed Kivela wrote that the known samples submitted could have come from the same source as those found on Frances Lacey's body.

Police interviewed hundreds of people, and some of those people were students at the University of Michigan who were working on the Island for the summer. During the course of the investigation into the murder, several polygraph tests were given to various men considered suspects. In most cases, those polygraph exams showed no deception, and they were cleared of any involvement.

With all of those meager clues, could the murder still be solved? Is it possible that Mrs. Lacey was the victim of a serial killer, and more importantly, could her killer still be alive?

***

A person with a psychopathic personality could be described as a person who has a personality that is amoral and antisocial. The person lacks the ability to love or establish meaningful personal relationships and may have extreme egocentricity.

As an example of compensation, a color-blind person sees things in different shades and has learned to function without seeing true color. The person has difficulty talking about true color but has learned to compensate for it. Because that person has learned to compensate, even people who know the person may not know that they can't see colors.[138]

Much like a color-blind person, a psychopath has learned to use ordinary words and repeat them while imitating true feelings without those feelings being legitimate.[139] He can separate his in-control personality from his criminal side. The criminal side is always there but he successfully hides

---

138. Hare, Robert D., *Without Conscience*, p 129
139. Cleckley, Hervey, *The Mask of Sanity*, 1976; 5th edition, p 230

it. Because of that, a psychopath may be able to defeat a polygraph examination. Through years of study, it's been learned that oftentimes nothing will be gained from a polygraph exam with a psychopathic personality because of the person's ability to compensate. The polygraph simply enforces the suspect's ability to cope with the interrogation process.[140]

Detective Sexton believed that Frances Lacey's Ladies Elgin watch was still missing and released a complete description to the media in the hopes that someone might have it because of the recurring trait among serial killers to take a trophy item from their victims. It could be in the form of an earring, bracelet, or even a watch. It could be given to the killer's girlfriend, wife, or even the woman who was the source of his anger. By seeing that person wear the item, the killer experiences the excitement of the murder and "mentally reasserts domination and control."[141]

***

As the star athlete in the small town where he attended high school, senior Jerald Wingeart lettered in track, football, and basketball. His constant smile and easy-going nature were traits that stood out. When asked about their former classmate, many said he was quiet, polite, even-tempered, and undemanding. They spoke of him as gentle and considerate.[142]

Wingeart was tall and muscular with blond hair, and he was set to attend the Michigan Institute of Mining and Technology in Michigan's Upper Peninsula after marrying his high school sweetheart in 1959, but instead, a

140. John Douglas & Mark Olshaker, *Mind Hunter*
141. John Douglas & Mark Olshaker, *Mind Hunter*
142. *The South Bend Tribune*, "From Role Model to Killer," December 2, 2001, p 20

scholarship at the University of Michigan seemed a better fit for the engineering student and the struggling young couple lived on the U of M campus in 1961.

It didn't take long for the relationship to begin crumbling, filled with violent disagreements over religion, children, and home management issues.

In late August 1960, they had their first child, a son, who died eight months later.

In stark contrast to the memories of his high school friends, forty years later, Wingeart was described by the media as brutal, calculating, and predatory.[143]

***

A young couple sat parked along the dark country road in the very early hours of a Sunday morning in July 1961. At nineteen years old, she had been blind since birth, and the two were talking when an approaching car stopped, facing theirs. The driver walked toward the car with a rifle and forced both of them out at gunpoint. He tied her companion's hands and feet with the rope he'd brought with him and stole two dollars from the young man. He tied the blind woman, forced her into her companion's car, and drove off, leaving his own car at the scene.

She was certain that he fully intended to kill her. A few miles from where he'd left her companion, he stopped the car and raped the blind coed before forcing her out of the car as he sped away. Perhaps the fact that she was blind and couldn't identify him saved her life.

Dazed and wandering down the road, she was found by a passing motorist and taken to the hospital, where the police were called, and she was so distraught that officers initially couldn't speak to her.

---

143. *The South Bend Tribune*, "From Role Model to Killer," December 2, 2001, p 20

As police arrived at the crime scene where her companion was still bound, they discovered the suspect's car. Following a quick check of the license plate number, a four-state manhunt quickly materialized. Police were searching for nineteen-year-old Jerald Wingeart.

Inside the suspect's car, police found rope and maps, and they theorized that he was out hunting for a victim when he came across the couple.

Near Chicago the next morning, still in the car he'd stolen, the suspect awoke. Listening to the radio, he learned he was a wanted man. Considering running, he instead decided to drive back to his hometown where he abandoned the car, and through a local attorney, he turned himself in to law enforcement claiming he had no memory of what happened.

Before his trial on the armed robbery and rape charges, he tried to plead insanity, and at his trial, psychiatrists testified that they believed he was temporarily insane at the time of the assault because of severe pressures and restrictions that included the loss of his young son in April 1961. The presiding judge believed that Wingeart had lied to the psychiatrists examining him, and the doctors had given too much weight to his claim that he couldn't remember what happened.

After a six-day non-jury trial, he was ultimately convicted of armed robbery and rape. Prior to his sentencing, the judge said, "The function of this court will not be substituted by the theories of psychiatrists."[144] The defendant was sentenced to two terms of ten to thirty years in prison.

In April 1962, Wingeart's wife divorced him and wrote in her complaint that prior to the rape he was convicted for in July 1961, he'd already told her that he didn't love her and wanted to be free.

---

144. *Ann Arbor News*, "Old Adversaries to Battle for Collins' Freedom," September 18, 1969

By 1963, the convicted rapist was already appealing his case and asking for a new trial after his first attempt at an appeal was denied at the circuit court level in 1962. The 1963 appeal was denied by the Michigan Supreme Court in a seven-to-one decision when the chief justice wrote that the trial record supported the judge's reluctance to accept the opinions of the psychiatrists. The dissenting judge argued the case should have been remanded for a new trial and that the prosecution had failed to prove the defendant's sanity beyond a reasonable doubt.

In December 1969, Jerald Wingeart was released from prison.

Within a few years, he became a computer programmer and garnered a job helping to set up the Michigan Lottery. By 1973, he was hired by the state of Michigan and bought a home in Eaton Rapids.

***

It was a spring-like day in mid-Michigan. January temperatures were usually much colder, but on this day in 1973, the high temperature reached into the forties.

Dressed in her brown suede jacket with fringed sleeves, blue slacks, and a black sweater, twenty-year-old Dawn Magyar, married just two years with a one-year-old baby, borrowed her father-in-law's pickup truck to run some errands. She headed for the J.C. Penney store to buy some clothes, and at around 5:30 p.m., she stopped at the grocery store.

The truck was found later in the store parking lot with the driver's door unlocked, and the keys were found under the vehicle. Her groceries and purchases from J.C. Penney were still on the front seat, but the young mother was nowhere to be found.

There was nothing in the woman's background leading police to believe that she had voluntarily disappeared. They suspected foul play and felt the case was similar to the abduction and murder of a Lansing woman who was last seen at the Meijer Thrifty Acres store in Eaton County's Delta Township six months earlier. Her body had been found the next day near Hastings. She'd been stabbed four times and strangled with her own belt. The abduction and murder of Betty Jean Goodrich remains unsolved.

As police focused on the most recent disappearance, an MSP helicopter searched the area with no luck, and a ground search was organized with volunteers. Police expected several thousand volunteers to help in the hunt for the missing mother while having the Civil Air Patrol, the Michigan Air National Guard, and the Dawn Patrol spotting from the air.[145] It was one of the most intense searches in mid-Michigan history, and a ten-thousand-dollar reward was offered for information about her disappearance.

Three months later, while police were still actively investigating the young mother's disappearance, a nine-year-old boy and his twenty-one-year-old brother were out tapping maple trees when they discovered the body of a woman in a wooded area fifteen miles from where the abduction had taken place. Even with warmer-than-normal temperatures, the body remained well-preserved because of the cold, and police were certain it was Dawn Magyar. It was confirmed through an autopsy, and police discovered that she'd been shot with a .22-caliber weapon—twice in the back and once in the back of the head. At the autopsy, police were able to preserve evidence that could lead to a conviction if a suspect was identified.

---

145. *Lansing State Journal*, "Grim Search Slated Today," February 3, 1973, p 7

After months of searching for the young mother's killer, leads became fewer and fewer, and the murder was relegated to the cold case file.

Just nineteen months after the discovery of her body, teenage boys were swimming in the Shiawassee River when one of them stepped on something in the water. Curiosity got the best of the teen, and he reached under to find out what he'd stepped on. It was a .22-caliber revolver with so much rust on it that the cylinder couldn't even be opened.

After it was turned over to the police, investigators suspected that it could be related to the unsolved murder almost two years prior. There were no shell casings found at the murder scene of the young mother, and police felt the killer had likely used a revolver.

At the crime lab, firearm experts were able to open the cylinder after soaking the weapon in hydrochloric acid. There were two spent cartridges, a misfired round, another spent cartridge, and two more unfired rounds. They also found the serial number under the layers of rust.

The gun was traced to a pawn shop in Arizona, and police found out the name of the buyer from 1968. The name of the owner was just too common, and there were thousands of people with the same name. There was no way the police could check the thousands of people with that name. The murder was once again relegated to the cold case file.

Two years after the discovery of the revolver, a purse was found along the banks of the Shiawassee River a mere two hundred yards from where the revolver was found by the teens. The finder unzipped the purse and found the identification. It belonged to the young mother who'd been murdered four years earlier, and the purse was turned over to the police.

Detectives were now confident that since the victim's purse was found so close to where the teenage boys had discovered the handgun that it had to be connected to the murder. Unfortunately, it didn't restart the investigation into the young mother's murder.

***

The seventeen-year-old boy told police he last saw his sixteen-year-old girlfriend, Laura McVeigh, jogging down Main Street on her way to the store. Three hours later, she was missing. Living in a very rural community, the teen was going to jog five miles to Carson City, Michigan. Her boyfriend told police, "I saw her around three o'clock Saturday. She said she was going to some stores in Carson City to buy some paint brushes and some material to make a bathing suit."[146]

The young athlete, nicknamed "Munchkin" by her friends, was last seen between five and six o'clock wearing a blue jogging suit with a white stripe, and as a member of the Carson City High School Track Team, she loved to run, ski, bird watch, and paint.[147]

After doing her shopping, she ran into some friends and tried to get a ride back, but her friends weren't ready to go. She'd told her boyfriend that if she couldn't get a ride back from friends, she'd hitchhike because she had to be back by 6:00 p.m., but she never arrived.

The rural community she lived in was near the intersecting jurisdictions of four counties, and law enforcement from all four counties, in addition to state troopers from several posts, fanned out in a massive search to find the petite, blue-eyed sixteen-year-old.

146. *Lansing State Journal*, Mark Nixon and Dick Frazier, "Search Area Widens for Laura May McVeigh," April 11, 1979, p 1

147. *Lansing State Journal*, Mark Nixon and Dick Frazier, "Search Area Widens for Laura May McVeigh," April 11, 1979, p 1

After stopping at a grocery store and florist,[148] her friends last saw her in an alley behind Gamble's Hardware Store. Police were looking for a brown van that was seen in the area where she disappeared. A witness thought the van might be a Ford, and it had a sliding door and several windows. Investigators were certain she hadn't run away because she had no problems at home and was a straight-A student.

Her dad told police, "She has hitchhiked before. She would not get into a car unless she knew who was driving."[149]

While police were searching for Laura, they also began to look for connections to the attempted kidnapping and stabbing of a fifteen-year-old girl in Dewitt and the murder of another fifteen-year-old girl near Harrison. By mid-April, they couldn't establish any sort of link between the three cases,[150] and mid-Michigan was gripped in fear.

On May 12, 1979, exactly five weeks after Laura McVeigh's disappearance, mushroom hunters discovered a badly decomposed body in a grove of Christmas trees near the intersection of M-55 and M-37, west of Cadillac. The state police were certain it was Laura because the body was clad in a blue jogging suit like the one she was wearing when she was last seen, but it took dental records to confirm their suspicion. The only thing that could be determined at the autopsy was that she'd been strangled with a rope that was knotted so tightly around her tiny neck that it cut through her skin and rested against her spinal column. Because the body was in a state of decomposition due to exposure to the

---

148. *Detroit Free Press*, "Expanded Hunt for Girl Jogger," April 10, 1979, p 3

149. *The Herald-Palladium*, AP, "Search Widens for Girl Jogger," April 10, 1979, p 1

150. *Detroit Free Press*, "Stab Cases Not Linked, Police Say," April 15, 1979, p 7

elements, it was difficult for the pathologist to determine if Laura had been sexually assaulted.[151]

A week after the discovery of her body, police held a press conference to show ten separate items Laura was carrying in a paper bag when she disappeared. The hope was that by showing duplicate items to the public, it might jog someone's memory. The items included painting supplies and sewing fabric, an Easter card, and a small ceramic duck. None of the items were found with the body, and her glasses were missing too. The police were still focused on finding a brown van, possibly a 1977 model, that was seen in the Carson City area during the late afternoon on the day Laura disappeared. When her friends saw her behind Gamble's, she was petting a large dog that was inside a brown van.

By the time police held the press conference to disclose the items Laura had in the bag, they had already executed at least one search warrant and questioned several suspects, but no arrests were made. The lead investigator for MSP was asked if one of the suspects being questioned was a high-ranking state official living in the Eaton Rapids, Michigan, area, and he refused to comment on the report, but it was common knowledge that police had executed a search warrant on a van in Eaton Rapids. The warrant was authorized on April 9 in Eaton County and was signed by Paul Berger, the Eaton County Prosecuting Attorney, just two days after Laura's disappearance. Police didn't release information that a witness saw the van with a large dog in the area where Laura had been jogging and wrote down the license plate number. The van was registered to a man named Jerald Wingeart.

Items seized during the search of the van included contents of the ashtray, in addition to animal hairs and blue fibers from the interior of the vehicle and three sleeping

---

151. Hornus, Anthony. *An Ordinary Killer*

bags. Police refused to say whether Laura's body had animal hair on it that could be matched with the evidence taken from the van.[152]

***

It was two years after the murder of Laura McVeigh when the forty-year-old former Michigan man named Jerald Wingeart was arrested in Niles and charged with her murder on June 13, 1981. He was arrested by MSP after the Wexford County Prosecutor's Office in Cadillac authorized a warrant charging him with first-degree murder. The former Eaton Rapids resident lived in New York but had come back to lower Michigan to check some property he owned near Niles, and he'd been a suspect in the McVeigh murder since the very beginning.

When Laura disappeared, Wingeart was living in Eaton Rapids and had already been through two divorces. Shortly after her body was found, he moved to Albany, New York. A detective with MSP told the media, "We knew he was in Albany. We knew he went there shortly after the girl's body was found, and we've been in touch with the police there on and off."[153]

Police already knew much about their murder suspect. He had attended the University of Michigan in 1960, and Laura McVeigh's murder wasn't his first arrest. In 1961, he'd been convicted of the rape and armed robbery of a blind woman and her friend in Ann Arbor.

Since his move to Albany, he'd become a computer software specialist and worked for a corporation that had contracts for computer installation services around

152. *Lansing State Journal*, Mark Nixon, "McVeigh Slaying Probers 'Go Public' in Evidence Search," May 24, 1979, p 13

153. *Detroit Free Press*, Harry Cook, "Ex-Eaton Rapids Man Mute in Ionia County Girl's Slaying," June 16, 1981, p 10

the northern portions of New York state. The company he worked for dealt with the design, development, and implementation of computer-based systems, including insurance information and payroll information.[154]

He travelled around New York often, and because of that, Wingeart's access to small villages, towns, and cities throughout the state was virtually unlimited.

***

As word of the arrest spread, MSP told the media that because Laura disappeared in Montcalm County, a warrant was sought for the man's arrest earlier in the spring, but the prosecuting attorney refused to issue it. Since her body had been found in Wexford County, the arrest warrant was issued there.

During his preliminary examination, a hearing to determine if there was enough probable cause to believe a crime had been committed and whether there was enough probable cause to believe the man had committed the crime, the prosecuting attorney tried to introduce testimony from a witness who was hypnotized after Laura's disappearance. During the hypnosis, he told investigators that the man in the courtroom, Wingeart, was the same man he'd seen in a van alongside the roadway in the area where Laura was last seen. The judge denied the prosecutor's motion to have the testimony introduced. It was a crucial blow to the prosecution, and according to his defense attorney, James Theophelis, a crucial boost to his client's defense.

The prosecutor spent the rest of the day trying to show Laura's final movements on the day she disappeared, and he introduced a credit card receipt the man had signed showing he was in Carson City at the time of the teen's disappearance. The testimony also centered on where

---

154. Hornus, Anthony. *An Ordinary Killer*

Wingeart had been just prior to her disappearance and his familiarity with the area where her body was found west of Cadillac.

Over the previous two years, there hadn't been any new evidence uncovered, and anything the prosecution had at the man's preliminary examination was the same evidence they already had two years prior when she disappeared.

After a decision by a district court judge to forward the case to the circuit court, there were pre-trial motions made by Theophelis in early 1982. One of those motions was to quash the search warrant that a Montcalm County detective had obtained three years earlier after Laura's disappearance. As a result of the 1979 Eaton County search warrant, police seized hair, fibers, and other debris that tied Laura McVeigh's body to the inside of the van.

By February 24, the judge had made his decision. The search warrant for the van was thrown out, and because of that, all the hair and fiber evidence obtained as a result of the search warrant became inadmissible at trial. Without the evidence, the case against Wingeart collapsed. The decision to dismiss the case was made by the Wexford County prosecutor after the judge ruled the search of the van, made just two days after Laura's disappearance, illegal. The judge wrote a fifteen-page opinion saying the state police and Ionia County Sheriff's Office had illegally seized the van and false statements had been made on the affidavit for the search warrant.[155] The judge went further to say the seizure of the van was "so patently illegal as to require no further comment."[156]

The judge's decision was based on statements attributed to two witnesses used to obtain the search warrant, and

155. *Lansing State Journal*, "Wingeart Free; Case Collapses," February 24, 1982, p 11

156. *Lansing State Journal*, "Wingeart Free; Case Collapses," February 24, 1982, p 11

their testimony in court contradicted the information in the document.

As Jerald Wingeart was released from custody and walked out of the Wexford County Jail wearing the same suit he'd worn for all of his court appearances, he was chain smoking and smiling. "It feels good to be out here. It feels very good," he said. "And I want to add I am not guilty. I did not kill that girl."[157]

***

The murder of twenty-year-old Dawn Magyar in 1973 remained a mystery even after a gun was found in the Shiawassee River, and her purse was found two years later in the same river.

Twenty-two years after her murder, while reviewing cold case files, detectives submitted some of the evidence in the case to the crime lab in the hopes that DNA might exist on the items. They were successful. A DNA profile of the killer was established, but it was still a dead end. They had no known DNA samples from any suspects for comparison.

Four years later, while the case was still considered cold, detectives began to focus on the gun that had been found in the river. In 1973, police didn't have the technology that was available in 1999. Using it, they were able to identify a person in the mid-Michigan area who had the same name as the person who purchased the handgun in 1968 in Arizona.

Their newfound suspect was questioned, and the heat was on. After being questioned about the gun, he was certain he'd be charged with the murder. He was puzzled and still didn't quite grasp why he was being questioned. He admitted owning the handgun, but he'd lost track of it at some point after returning to Michigan from Arizona. He

---

157. *Lansing State Journal*, "Wingeart Free; Case Collapses," February 24, 1982, p 11

quickly learned about the murder during the interview, but the investigators never mentioned that the young mother had been raped. They simply asked if he'd allow a blood draw, and he agreed.

The DNA analysis of the blood proved his innocence. It seemed they were back to square one. They'd taken blood samples from several other suspects and all of those men were cleared too. The detectives still felt the former owner of the gun was the key to solving the murder, and a decision was made to reinterview him.

At his home, the three men sat at a kitchen table, and the detectives began to ratchet up their questioning. The man, in an emotional state, finally recalled a detail he'd forgotten to mention in the previous interview.

Sometime in the early seventies, he had come home during the afternoon and found his wife in bed with another man. That man was Jerald Wingeart. His wife worked with Wingeart, and according to her, the relationship between the two had "just happened." During the resulting divorce, she still had a key to the home and would come by in the afternoon to remove some of her belongings. She eventually began to remove some of the furniture, and he wasn't sure if Wingeart had ever come with her to help during the move. His ex-wife ended up married to Wingeart, and they had a child together, but he eventually divorced her.

It was the information the detectives had waited for. They were one step closer to solving the 1973 murder.

Wingeart was nothing more than a quiet neighbor who kept to himself. He was married to his fourth wife in Sterling Heights, Michigan; his yard was immaculate. At work, he was the perfect employee, he donated to the United Way with each paycheck he received, and even participated in blood drives. [158] He was quiet, and he didn't socialize

---

158. Hornus, Anthony. *An Ordinary Killer*

afterward with any of his coworkers. He was just nine years away from retirement.[159]

The detectives knew that if Jerald Wingeart was their man, they'd need to get a DNA sample to prove their case. Their surveillance began on a Friday as they waited patiently watching him at work. On Saturday and Sunday, they surveilled his home but never saw him leave. They'd have to come up with another way to get a DNA sample.

One of the detectives had looked through the window into Wingeart's truck during the Friday surveillance and could see the brand of cigarettes he smoked.

On Monday morning, they waited until their suspect left for work at 7:30 a.m. There were two trash bags at the end of Wingeart's driveway, and after he left, the detectives pulled up and put the trash bags into their car before driving away. After searching through the trash, several cigarette butts were retrieved, carefully packaged as evidence, and driven to the MSP crime lab. One week later, scientists at the crime lab confirmed thirteen out of thirteen genetic markers in the DNA analysis.[160]

Jerald Wingeart was arrested for the 1973 murder and his trial was one of the first in the state of Michigan to use DNA technology.

It was billed as one of the most high-profile murder cases in Shiawassee County's history. Twenty-eight years after the abduction and murder of twenty-year-old Dawn Magyar, an arrest had been made, and the man's third trial was set to begin. His past included the conviction for kidnapping and raping a blind woman and robbing her friend near Ann Arbor in 1961. He was also the prime suspect in the abduction and murder of sixteen-year-old Laura McVeigh in 1979 between Carson City and Hubbardston. Though

159. Hornus, Anthony. *An Ordinary Killer*
160. Hornus, Anthony. *An Ordinary Killer*

that case had been dismissed, authorities were certain he was Laura's killer.

Now, in 2001, represented by a young defense attorney named Vince Green, he would face a jury after being charged for the abduction, rape, and murder of the young mother in 1973.

After a lengthy trial, the blond-haired former University of Michigan student who, in 1959, had planned on attending the Michigan Institute of Mining and Technology in Michigan's Upper Peninsula, was convicted for the murder of Dawn Magyar twenty-eight years earlier and sentenced to life in prison without parole.

AFTERWORD

The possibility exists that Frances Lacey was murdered on July 24, 1960, by a young serial killer who, after fleeing the Island, continued to kill throughout the years and has never been identified. Perhaps the killer is still alive.

Much like W. Stewart Woodfill, it's difficult to believe Frances Lacey's killer lived on Mackinac Island. It's also difficult to believe the killer was Wesley Sutter. Mr. Sutter told investigators that the entire Sutter party was together at the beach waiting for Mrs. Lacey to arrive on the morning that she disappeared, and the rest of the family confirmed that.

***

John Douglas says, "The public is often our greatest partner. Once all logical and reasonable leads have been exhausted, give ordinary citizens a chance to help the case."[161]

I first heard the name Jerald Wingeart in 2007 and knew nothing about his background until I started researching this book. His case was the subject of a true crime television documentary showcasing the 1973 murder of Dawn Magyar and Wingeart's conviction for the murder twenty-eight years later. Between that murder and his conviction, he was the prime suspect in the abduction and murder of sixteen-year-old Laura McVeigh in Montcalm County, Michigan. While he was awaiting trial in that murder, the case was

---

161. John Douglas & Mark Olshaker, *Mind Hunter*

dismissed based on discrepancies in the search warrant, and he walked away a free man. To this day, Laura's murder is classified as unsolved.

There are too many things to simply dismiss Wingeart as a suspect in the Lacey homicide.

Wingeart was married in 1959, and in a marriage announcement from a local Niles paper, it was mentioned that the young graduate from Niles High School was going to continue his education in Michigan's Upper Peninsula at the Michigan College of Mining and Industry in Houghton, now known as Michigan Tech. It leaves little doubt that he was familiar with northern Michigan.

At the time of Frances Lacey's murder in 1960, Wingeart would have been nineteen years old. Witnesses described an eighteen- to nineteen-year-old man walking along Lake Shore Road with his shirt open at the time of the murder.

Just one year after the Lacey murder, Wingeart was arrested for the kidnapping and rape of a blind college coed near the University of Michigan. At the time of his arrest, he was a sophomore. It's unknown if he attended his first year at the Michigan Institute of Mining and Technology or if he attended the University of Michigan as a freshman. There were numerous students from the university employed as seasonal workers on Mackinac Island at the time of the Lacey murder, and several of those students were identified and interviewed. In the police reports researched by the author, all names were redacted.

Based on the hairs removed from Mrs. Lacey's body, police theorized the killer had light brown to blond hair. Wingeart had blond hair.

Frances Lacey's watch has never been found. It's quite possible the watch might still exist in someone's jewelry box, or in some antique store, perhaps given as a gift to someone by the killer.

The trace evidence recovered from Frances Lacey's body and the information about Jerald Wingeart are meager clues, but oftentimes that's how a cold case is solved. If there are no definitive MSP records indicating a disposal of the evidence in this murder from 1960, is it worth the time for MSP to search from box to box at the St. Ignace Post or the district headquarters to see if it still exists and may have simply been misplaced?

***

Manipulation, domination, and *control* are the buzzwords when one thinks of a serial offender. Every thought and every action that makes up a serial killer's day is centered around fulfilling their inadequate lives, and the one factor that's crucial in the development of a serial killer is fantasy.[162]

Absent information of a killer's early years, there will always be questions about his motives and reasoning. If one looks at the person's family life, they might find a distant mother or a father who's either abusive or absent. Other factors might include abusive siblings or even the absence of siblings. A school system that doesn't intervene or a social services system that's inadequate can be contributing factors, as well as the person's own inability to relate sexually with others in a normal way.

Having the ability to research the background of a suspected killer is paramount to understanding his artwork; or better said, the murder. Criminal profilers agree on a simple equation: Why + How = Who.

In trying to understand the criminal mind, a psychiatrist looks at an individual's personality and infers their behavior, while at the same time, a criminal profiler looks at the person's behavior and infers their personality.[163]

---

162. John Douglas & Mark Olshaker, *Mind Hunter*
163. John Douglas & Mark Olshaker, *Mind Hunter*

In truth, after sixty-plus years, the rape and murder of Frances Lacey on Mackinac Island may never be solved. There may not be anyone still alive who knows the identity of the killer. Yet it's also entirely possible the killer may still be alive as of this writing and likely would be in his eighties. If that's the case, we owe it to Frances Lacey and her family to pursue the man responsible for her murder. Her family deserves justice. It's not an impossible task. All the reader has to do is check the daily headlines about cold cases being solved using DNA technology and suspects being cleared. There's no question that DNA might contribute to solving this case.

Does the evidence still exist? With the murder of Frances Lacey still classified as unsolved, MSP is reluctant to discuss it, and Jerald Wingeart died in August 2022.

BIBLIOGRAPHY

Barfknecht, Gary W. *Unexplained Michigan Mysteries: Strange but True Tales from the Michigan Unknown*, 1993

Cawthorne, Dennis O. *Mackinac Island: Inside, Up Close, and Personal.* Arbutus Press, 2014

Cleckley, Hervey, *The Mask of Sanity*, 1976; 5th edition, p 230

Douglas, John & Mark Olshaker, *Mind Hunter,* 1995, p 21

Hare, Robert D., *Without Conscience*, p 129

Hornus, Anthony. *An Ordinary Killer*, 2008

Ressler, Robert K & Tom Shachtman, *Whoever Fights Monsters*, 1992

Albuquerque Journal, "Divorces Granted," May 1, 1963

Ann Arbor News, "Old Adversaries to Battle for Collins' Freedom," September 18, 1969

Battle Creek Enquirer, "No Suspects Left in Widow's Slaying," August 1, 1960

Chicago Tribune, "Mass Finger Printing May Find Triple Killer," March 17, 1960, p 1

Detroit Free Press, "Find Widow Was Attacked," August 1, 1960

Detroit Free Press, "Shoes May Prove the Key to Mystery on Mackinac," August 2, 1960

Detroit Free Press, "Grim Paradise," August 3, 1960

Detroit Free Press, "Flint Widow Fatally Beaten in Home," August 16, 1960, p 1

Detroit Free Press, "Expanded Hunt for Girl Jogger," April 10, 1979, p 3

Detroit Free Press, "Stab Cases Not Linked, Police Say," April 15, 1979, p 7

Detroit Free Press, Harry Cook, "Ex-Eaton Rapids Man Mute in Ionia County Girl's Slaying," June 16, 1981, p 10

Detroit Free Press, L. L. Brasier, "Oakland County Jury Convicts Serial Killer Nolan Ray George in 1968 Pontiac Slaying," April 28, 2011

The Detroit News, "Widow Vanishes; Dogs Join Hunt on Mackinac," July 26, 1960

The Detroit News, "Trail Lost: Fear Widow is Drowned," July 27, 1960

The Detroit News, "Skin Divers Search for Missing Widow," July 28, 1960

The Detroit News, "Find Widow Strangled in Mackinac Myst," July 29, 1960

The Detroit News, "Killing Hard to Believe, Victim's Neighbors Say," July 29, 1960

The Detroit News, "Woman's Trip to Tragedy is Retraced on Mackinac," July 30, 1960

The Detroit News, "Mackinac Slaying Search Shifts to Wayne County," July 31, 1960

The Detroit News, "Murder-Stunned Mackinac Clings to Storied Ways," July 31, 1960

The Detroit News, "Slain Woman's Relatives First Tenants in Cottage," July 31, 1960

The Detroit News, "Mrs. Lacey Got $109,000 From Estate," August 1, 1960

The Detroit News, "Woman's Shoe is New Clue in Widow's Slaying," August 1, 1960

The Detroit News, B. Simmons, "Mystery Witness Needed to Solve Mackinac Murder," August 11, 1962

The Escanaba Daily Press, "Former Officer to Direct UP Law Program," March 3, 1970, p 1

The Escanaba Daily Press, "Robert Bilgen Taken by Death," April 28, 1970, p 2

Galesburg Register, "Police Search for Murder Clues, Use Flame Thrower," March 17, 1960, p 1

Galesburg Register, "Two Face Questioning for Triple Slayings at Park," March 19, 1960, p 1

The Hartford Courant, "Mackinac Island Mingles History, Charm, Leisure," June 5, 1960, p 44

The Herald-Palladium, AP, "Search Widens for Girl Jogger," April 10, 1979, p 1

The Herald-Press, "Police Ponder Link Between Two Murders," August 16, 1960, p 14

Mackinac Island Town Crier, "Big Story Puts Town Crier Staff in Tizzy, But It Still Scoops State," August 7, 1960

Mackinac Island Town Crier, "Murray Pianist Here for Seventh Season," July 24, 1960

Mackinac Island Town Crier, "Gough Resigns as Chief of Police," July 17, 1960

Mackinac Island Town Crier, "Widow's Beaten Body Found," July 31, 1960, p 1

Mackinac Island Town Crier, "Manhunt Blankets Mackinac," August 7, 1960, p 1

Mackinac Island Town Crier, "Stonecliff is Setting for Murder Mystery," August 7, 1960

Mackinac Island Town Crier, "Hunt Spreads to Other States," August 14, 1960

Mackinac Island Town Crier, "Former Island Employee Cleared of Connection with Lacey Case," August 28, 1960

Moline Daily Dispatch, "Blood-Stained Limb and Cord Are Only Clues," March 17, 1960, p 1

Mt. Vernon Register, "Melt Snow for Murder," March 17, 1960, p 1

Ironwood Daily Globe, "No Trace of Woman Found," July 27, 1960

The Minneapolis Star, "Slayer of St. Paul Woman Gets Life," December 15, 1961, p 8

The Minneapolis Star, "Detectives Kick in Door, Nab Thompson Suspect," April 19, 1963, p 1

Lansing State Journal, "Mackinac Mystery Unsolved," July 28, 1960

Lansing State Journal, "Police Have Puzzle: Did Same Man Kill 2 Elderly Widows," August 16, 1960 p 4

Lansing State Journal, "Grim Search Slated Today," February 3, 1973, p 7

Lansing State Journal, Mark Nixon and Dick Frazier, "Search Area Widens for Laura May McVeigh," April 11, 1979, p 1

Lansing State Journal, Mark Nixon, "McVeigh Slaying Probers 'Go Public' in Evidence Search," May 24, 1979, p 13

Lansing State Journal, "Wingeart Free; Case Collapses," February 24, 1982, p 11

The Lexington Herald, "Story of Killer Hugh Bion Morse Casts Light on Nationwide Problem," November 5, 1961

Ottawa Citizen, "Michigan Detective Reopens Cold Case with Canadian Connection," October 28, 2008, p 13

The South Bend Tribune, "From Role Model to Killer," December 2, 2001, p 20

Star Tribune, "Slaying," March 7, 1963

Star Tribune, "2 City Men Held in Phoenix in Thompson Slaying Case," April 20, 1963

The Times, "Solve 3 Brutal Murders," November 17, 1960

Langberg, Robert. "Homicide in the United States 1950-1964." *National Center for Health Statistics,* October 1967

Remsburg, Charles. "Michigan's Number One Murder Mystery." *True Detective Magazine,* 1962

Burnette, George. "Supplemental Report." *Michigan State Police.* August 10, 1960

Burnette, George. "Supplemental Report." *Michigan State Police,* August 23, 1960

Craft, George. "Supplemental Report." *Michigan State Police,* July 31, 1960

Daniels, Gary. "Laboratory Report." *Michigan State Police,* April 22, 2011

Grosse, Herbert. "Supplemental Report." *Michigan State Police,* July 25, 1960

Guzin, Bruno. "Supplemental Report." *Michigan State Police,* August 5, 1960

Guzin, Bruno. "Supplemental Report." *Michigan State Police,* August 23, 1963

Hill, Edwin. "Supplemental Report." *Michigan State Police*, August 6, 1960

Hill, Edwin. "Supplemental Report." *Michigan State Police*, August 9, 1960

Hofmann, L. N. "Supplemental Report." *Michigan State Police*, August 3, 1960

Kivela, Dr. Edgar. "Report to MSP Commissioner J.A. Childs." *Michigan Department of Public Health*, August 9, 1960

Kivela, Dr. Edgar. "Toxicological Examination." *Michigan Department of Public Health*, December 20, 1960

Kivela, Dr. Edgar. "Toxicological Examination." *Michigan Department of Public Health,* October 2, 1963

Menzies, William. "Supplemental Report." *Michigan State Police*, August 4, 1960

Minzey, David. "Report to Detective Sergeant Robin Sexton." *Michigan State Police*, January 23, 2008

Nowak, Joseph. "Supplemental Report." *Michigan State Police*, July 30, 1976

Petzke, Jack. "Supplemental Report." *Michigan State Police*, June 28, 1962

Rule, Richard. "Email to [REDACTED]." January 12, 2011

Rule, Rich. "Supplemental Report." *Michigan State Police*, October 10, 2011

Seppanen, John. "Supplemental Report." *Michigan State Police*, December 14, 1967

Simmons, William. "Supplemental Report." *Michigan State Police*, September 11, 1964

Sobolewski, A. "Supplemental Report." *Michigan State Police,* August 7, 1960

Spratto, Anthony. "Supplemental Report." *Michigan State Police,* August 24, 1960

Spratto, Anthony. "Supplemental Report." *Michigan State Police*, September 4, 1960

Tanner, Roy. "Supplemental Report." *Michigan State Police*, August 4, 1960

Webster, J.H. "Autopsy Report of Frances Lacey," July 29, 1960

Whaley, Howard. "Letter to William Morris," November 17, 1960

Whaley, Howard. "Supplemental Report." *Michigan State Police*, July 28, 1960

Whaley, Howard. "Supplemental Report." *Michigan State Police,* June 4, 1962

Whaley, Howard. "Supplemental Report." *Michigan State Police*, November 22, 1961

Woodfill, W. Stewart, "Letter to the Officer in Charge," September 1, 1960

Yuill, Kenneth. "Supplemental Report." *Michigan State Police*, July 27, 1960

Letter to Mr. Frank J. Kelley, September 29, 1962

Greenwell, Wilner A., M. D., and Kirk, P. L., Journal of Criminal Law, Criminology, and Police Science, Human Hair Studies III: Refractive index of crown hair, 1941, 31:746–752

Kirk, Paul L., Journal of Criminal Law and Criminology, Human Hair Studies: General Considerations of Hair Individualization and Its Forensic Importance, Vol 31, No 4, 1940

Kirk, P. L., Journal of Criminal Law and Criminology, Human Hair Studies: 1. General considerations of hair

individualization and its forensic importance, 1940,
31:486–496

Kirk, P. L. & Gamble L. H., Journal of Criminal Law and
Criminology 31, hair studies: II. Scale counts, 1941,
627–636

FBI. "Review Article - Forensic Hair Comparison:
Background Information for Interpretation - April
2009," https://archives.fbi.gov/archives/about-us/
lab/forensic-science-communications/fsc/april2009/
review/2009_04_review02.htm

Ryan, Suzanna. "How the Lack of Serology Testing
Results in a Loss of Information," http://
ryanforensicdna.com/serology/

"Moral Re-Armament (MRA)." Encyclopedia Britannica,
https://www.britannica.com/event/Moral-Re-
Armament

For More News About Rod Sadler,
Signup For Our Newsletter:

http://wbp.bz/newsletter

Word-of-mouth is critical to an author's long-term success. If you appreciated this book please leave a review on the Amazon sales page:

http://wbp.bz/grimparadise

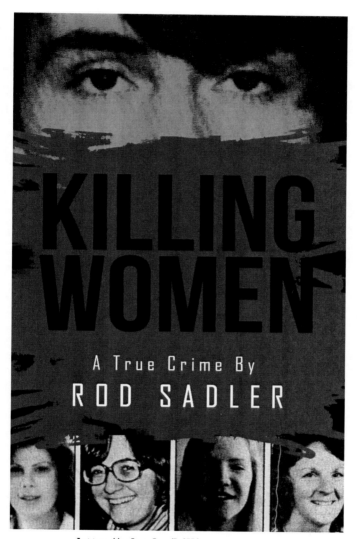

MORE TRUE CRIME FROM WILDBLUE PRESS!

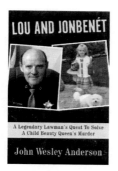
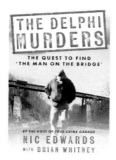